Domestic violence
Action for change

Gill Hague and Ellen Malos
with cartoons by Tamsin Wilton

Third Edition

CRAVEN COLLEGE

New Clarion Press

Issues in Social Policy

This book is dedicated to the memory of Pam Cooke (Khalil), whom we knew and who recovered from domestic violence to build a strong, new life. Pam was an inspiration to other women attempting to escape violence in the home.

On 22 August 1986, Pam was killed by her former husband.

She was just one of the many women, before and since then, who have been killed by their partners. We also wish to remember them.

Our book is part of the effort to end the violence.

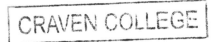

First published 1993
Reprinted 1994, 1995
Second edition 1998
Reprinted 2001
Third edition 2005

New Clarion Press
5 Church Row, Gretton
Cheltenham GL54 5HG
England

New Clarion Press is a workers' co-operative.

A catalogue record for this book is available from the British Library.

ISBN   paperback   1 873797 46 X
         hardback   1 873797 47 8

Typeset in 10/11.5 Times by Jean Wilson Typesetting, Coventry

Printed in Great Britain by The Cromwell Press, Trowbridge

Contents

Is it too much to ask?

A man can come and go and walk out of the door
If a woman sleeps around she's classed as a whore
A man is known to be a stud
A woman is treated like mud
If a woman leaves her child, she's an unfit mother
If a man leaves his child, nobody bother

Society made it this way
We want to see a change today
Now we have equal rights
But men won't accept it out of spite
When a man beats his wife, he gets away
All the woman can do is run away
The law should lock these men away
Instead these women have to pay
If the law is to take the decision
Put the men and not the women in prison!

No responsibilities and no ties
These men get away with wicked lies
The law is hard on police violence
When it comes to women they turn off their sirens
A woman has to be in her grave before action is taken
If they think they know their law, they're very well mistaken!

by two women living in a refuge

Acknowledgements

This book was made possible through the contributions of many women over many years. We would first like to thank all the women who have experienced domestic violence and their children, whom we have known and with whom we have worked. They have all freely given us their time and help throughout our work with Women's Aid, the Domestic Violence Research Group (now the Violence Against Women Research Group), University of Bristol, and the movement against domestic violence, and particularly in our writing of this book.

We are especially indebted to Nicola Harwin of the Women's Aid Federation of England for her dedicated assistance with this project which went beyond the bounds of duty, and for the many hours that she spent working with us on the original manuscript and on subsequent editions.

Jacky Barron also helped us extensively with the original writing of this book and made detailed comments on the various drafts and on this new edition. We are very grateful to her.

The book was only made possible by the assistance of our colleague, Wendy Dear, who prepared the original manuscript and assisted with the research for it. Valerie Douglas provided invaluable secretarial help for the second and third editions.

Thanks are also due to many organizations and individuals for commenting on drafts of sections of the first edition of the book and/or for helpful input and assistance about both specific points and general issues. These include: Andrea Tara-Chand, Olwen Edwards, Robyn Holder, Alison Assiter, Lorraine Radford, Maria Smith, Rachel Bentham, Mary Ann Hushlak, Margaret Boushell, Elaine Farmer, Davina James-Hanman, Gonzalo Bacigalupe, and past and present workers from Northern Ireland Women's Aid, Women's Aid in England (including, most especially, Linda Delahay – who also assisted with this edition – and previous workers, Thangam Debbonaire and Caroline McKinlay, to all of whom particular thanks are due), Scottish Women's Aid, Welsh Women's Aid, Southall Black Sisters, the original CHANGE project, and various local refuge organizations, including in the past Bristol Women's Aid.

Since the first edition was published in 1993, we have worked closely with, and learned much from, many colleagues: activists, practitioners and 'violence against women' academics. They include (among many): Marianne Hester, Liz Kelly, Audrey Mullender, Becky Morley, Umme Imam, Linda Regan, Cathy Humphreys, Shahana Rasool, Ravi Thiara, Rosemary Aris, Debbie Crisp, Betsy Stanko, Beryl Foster, Vicky Grosser, Davina James-Hanman, Atuki Turner and Mifumi in Uganda and the UK, and Helen Joseph and her team in Mumbai/Bombay. Past and present members of the Violence Against Women Research Group in Bristol (formerly the Domestic Violence Research Group) have contributed hugely to our work, and hence to this book, including – as well as Marianne Hester and Wendy Dear, already mentioned – Hilary Abrahams, Geetanjali Gangoli, Melanie McCarry, Tais Silva, Maggie Warwick, Nicole Westmarland and Emma Williamson.

We would also like particularly to thank Evanna Romain and her co-author for their poem.

On a personal level, we would like to express our sincere appreciation of the following:

For Ellen: in special remembrance of John Malos, for all his support over many years, and for my son and daughter, Robert and Anna Malos, whose childhoods were so closely intertwined with the birth of Bristol Women's Aid, 32 years ago this year, and for all the women from whose courage and sisterhood I have learned so much.

For Gill: the women from many women's groups, and from Women's Aid, who have nurtured me over the years, and my mother, Dorothy Williamson, who sadly died in 1999, Dave Merrick and my children Cassie and Keiran Hague, for help with the writing of this book and for their enduring love, patience and co-operation.

Ellen Malos and Gill Hague

Introduction to the 2005 edition

This is the third edition of *Domestic Violence: Action for Change*. The book was first published in 1993 and was conceived as a general overall reader, covering with a broad brushstroke a wide range of issues about domestic violence. As such, it has remained, over the years, one of the few general texts available. It was also meant to be written in an 'easy to read' style, although it must be said that after a while we began to call it 'easy-ish to read' instead. Nevertheless, the book has always been non-academic in format. It is not written in an academic way and there are quite deliberately no references in the text. It is meant to read smoothly, although some of the sources referred to, or which might be of use to the reader, are included in the bibliography at the end.

The book was originally written within an activist context and from an activist commitment, stemming from the women's movement of the 1970s and the resulting Women's Aid movement, which has transformed services for women experiencing domestic violence since then. From what we know of the book, it has served a purpose to inform activists and Women's Aid workers in a down-to-earth way. Apparently, it has been much used by workers in women's refuge and support services, by child support workers and by staff in domestic violence services, locally and nationally, over the 11 years since the first edition.

The book has also been of use to practitioners and policy-makers in a variety of agencies in the field and, in general, to members of the public who want to consult a fairly short and general overview of the subject. We know too that it has been a helpful text for students and academics in social work, social policy, sociology and women's studies.

We hope that the new text will still appeal to all these audiences. We have attempted to retain the activist flavour and we have continued to position ourselves within the increasingly global movement against domestic violence and other forms of violence against women. To this end, the Bristol Domestic Violence Research Group of which we were both founder members has now expanded into the Violence Against Women Research Group to reflect a broader concern about issues of gender-based violence.

Activism continues but within a different context. Both the way domestic violence is viewed and also legislative, policy and practice responses to it have been transformed since 1993. Combating domestic abuse has moved from the margins to the mainstream, which is where it now sits, although often accompanied by patchy service responses and precarious or inadequate resourcing. Nevertheless, local and central government have taken up the issue in a way that would have been unthinkable when the book was first written, and Women's Aid has become the national domestic violence charity, working as a key player with government and with strategic partnerships and policy-makers. In this third edition, we have attempted to provide an overview of this new stage in domestic violence work, to trace its development and to provide up-to-date information in a concise form. We have tried to do so without losing the activist edge.

We have also retained as much of the original material as possible. In this context, the book is perhaps able to play a special and useful role. We have retained details of the history of the last 30 years of the struggle against domestic violence to place present developments in context and to recall and record the important stages along the way. This is something that new overviews rarely do. We retain these details of past history also in order to remind readers where things have come from, and to emphasize the connection between the women's movement against domestic violence and present service and policy developments. This connection can be forgotten today as policy-makers start to evolve policies or wider strategies on domestic violence, sometimes without knowing the history of where the new commitment comes from.

This edition includes new material on the move to the mainstream. It covers the content of key legislation like the Family Law Act and the Protection from Harassment Act. Importantly, it charts the current position of the Domestic Violence, Crime and Victims Act and the (patchy) government commitments over recent years to build an integrated response to domestic violence. It also covers developments in the police service and criminal justice system regarding positive policing, positive-arrest and prosecution policies, domestic violence courts and improved evidence gathering.

The book looks at recent housing law, at developments in health and social services and the new attention to domestic violence as a child protection issue. It also reflects on the progress of perpetrators' programmes and educational initiatives in schools which have developed since the second edition was published in 1998, and on new local strategic, crime and disorder reduction and other partnerships that New Labour has established to oversee strategic development on policy issues.

This is a particularly important time for a new edition, especially in the light of the new domestic violence legislation recently passed by

Parliament and the range of initiatives coming into existence, including the new Refuges-On-Line internet referral network. Our hope is that the book will continue to play a role in providing information and back-up to these complex efforts to respond effectively to domestic violence, in ways that support and empower women victims while holding perpetrators accountable for their actions.

In 1993, we wrote about the devastating legacy of violence against women across the world and the enormous task of challenging and changing that legacy. Much has changed in the intervening years, but we hope that this new edition will continue to contribute to this worldwide endeavour.

1

What is domestic violence?

Domestic violence is one of the commonest crimes. It is present throughout society, usually hidden, but there nonetheless. In any house, on any average street, avenue or road, women regularly experience abuse and violence. Most frequently, it happens behind firmly closed doors. It is worth standing on such an average street – your street perhaps – and trying to imagine the reality of it behind those closed doors. You may not be aware that it is happening, but it is.

Many of us know someone in our close family or among our friends whom it has happened to, or we have experienced it ourselves, but we tend to think that we are different or alone, still not realizing perhaps, despite all the publicity in recent years, just how widespread and enduring domestic abuse is. It seems that it occurs in almost all cultures and countries, across all known divisions of wealth, ethnicity, caste and social class. There may never have been a time when it did not exist, and it certainly stretches back deep into history. Centuries, indeed millennia, are filled with millions of assaults, attacks, rapes, violations, psychological abuses, maimings, killings – of women by the men with whom they are intimate.

It is a profoundly disturbing and distressing picture, if we care to be aware of it. Some people choose to turn away. Some say it is inevitable, that it is just human nature and you will never change it. This book is written from an opposite conviction, a conviction that nothing is inevitable, that it is we, both men and women, who shape and build human societies and are also shaped by them. The devastating legacy of violence and abuse against women need not stay with us forever. We can try to imagine a world in which masculinity is free of violence, a world in which women's lives can be free of fear, and women and children can be safe in their own homes. The task, of course, is the making of such a world.

It seems that, throughout history, women have attempted to resist domestic violence by all sorts of means, wherever they have been able to. In the UK, there has been a social movement of women against domestic violence for many years. It was particularly evident in the nineteenth and early twentieth centuries, and became active again in the early 1970s. In the last 30 years, this movement has campaigned vigorously, its activists sustained by the vision of an end to male violence and of women growing more powerful together. Mainly as a result of its activities, we now hear about domestic violence frequently. It is talked about on radio and television, there is meant to be legal protection against it, and there are services available. This is in marked contrast to the situation before the 1970s, when there was silence about the issue, and women experiencing violence in the home had virtually no one to turn to for help.

Today, although they have been joined by others, the main co-ordinating organizations that deal with domestic violence in the UK and that represent the interests of abused women and children are the Women's Aid federations. They have established a network of local domestic violence services including refuge organizations and other related outreach, support and advocacy services across the country, and also provide extensive training, information, advice and assistance. While this is good news, the reality is that there are not enough of these services to meet the need, despite improvements in recent years. Domestic violence is still condoned by much of society and many of these improvements are small and rather piecemeal. None of them, however, would have been achieved without the determined and persistent efforts of organizations like Women's Aid and other committed women's groups and activists. It has been a hard struggle and it continues to be so.

In the last 15 years, though, as a result of this struggle, domestic violence has been in the public eye as never before. Various governments now tell us that violence in the home is a crime and that it is not to be tolerated. Statutory and voluntary agencies in many countries say that it is unacceptable and adopt policies to deal with it. International proclamations are made and conferences held. Some of the women who have been active in the struggle against domestic violence for many years might be forgiven for asking just how much has really changed, but at least the beginnings are there. We have yet to see, though, whether the public attention will last in the long term, and whether the political will exists to implement the necessary changes in increasingly comprehensive ways in the future.

At the international level, the United Nations Decade for Women led to publicity and research in many countries on the issue of violence against women. The 1985 Nairobi World Conference on Women highlighted domestic violence in its *Forward-Looking Strategies for the Advancement of Women*, to which member countries have since contributed. The United Nations adopted the historic *Declaration on the Elimination of Violence against Women* in 1993 as a specific elaboration of the more general and very important 1979 *Convention on the Elimination of All Forms of Discrimination against Women* (CEDAW), which countries all over the world have adopted and attempted (with varying degrees of commitment) to fulfil. The declaration states that domestic violence is a violation of human rights and results from the historically unequal power relationships between men and women. Another milestone was the appointment in 1994 of a UN Special Rapporteur on Violence against Women. Domestic violence was a topic at the 1995 World Conference of Women in Beijing, and features prominently in the *Platform for Action* agreed at the conference, which commits governments throughout the world to comprehensive action on the status of women. Since then, gender violence has featured in a wide variety of ('Beijing Plus') international agreements, declarations and protocols, and the Beijing Protocol Plus Ten meetings took place in early 2005.

In the UK, the Home Office is now regarded as the lead government agency on domestic violence and issued circulars in 1990 and 2000 about how the police respond to violent incidents in the home. The point was to get the police to take domestic violence more seriously, to engage in positive policing, to instigate positive-arrest and prosecution policies, and to establish domestic violence units to assist in policing violence in the home and to support abused women and children.

Police services up and down the country are now trying, with varying degrees of commitment and success, to improve their responses. And over the last ten years, they have indeed improved well beyond what activists would have predicted, although the improvements are patchy and are more associated with specialist domestic violence officers than with the force in general. The civil law and the legal remedies available have also improved greatly with the 1996 Family Law Act. Multi-agency responses have been instigated and the present government has issued a variety of proposals. At present, there is an Inter-Ministerial Group on domestic violence, and new specialist legislation on domestic violence (the Domestic Violence, Crime and Victims Act), which aims to develop a more integrated approach across agencies, has been adopted. Awareness-raising campaigns, projects for abusers and school projects on domestic violence are now on offer in some localities, and are encouraged by government. After years of campaigning, domestic violence is firmly on the public agenda. Finally we can talk about it. It is no longer a secret.

In this book, domestic violence is mainly discussed in the British context with some illustrations from developing countries, Australia, Canada and the USA. However, the Beijing Conference and a variety of other international initiatives and conferences have demonstrated clearly that campaigns and action on violence against women are developing rapidly in many parts of the world, and that ethnocentric claims that the western industrialized countries are more 'advanced' in this respect are misguided.

Definitions of domestic violence

In the British context, domestic violence is usually regarded as violence between adults who are (or have been) in an intimate or family relationship with each other – most often a sexual relationship between a woman and a man, although other family members may sometimes be involved. Research studies have estimated that at least 90 per cent of domestic violence in an adult context is perpetrated against women by men (although some estimates are somewhat lower). Over the years, there has been some publicity about the plight of men who have been abused, and it is clear that women do sometimes assault men and that violence can also occur in lesbian and gay relationships. But the overwhelming majority of domestic violence incidents consist of men abusing, intimidating and violating women whom they know intimately and often profess to love.

The general imbalance in power between men and women is revealed in a stark way by the reality of domestic violence. However, the term itself – and the use of the word 'domestic' in particular – can hide who is actually the abuser and who is being abused. It sounds general, as though it means any violence that happens in the domestic environment, even where there is no personal relationship. In consequence, many women have questioned its usefulness, along with terms like 'intimate violence' and 'spousal abuse'. The terms 'wife abuse' and 'wife-beating' are sometimes used instead, more often in North America, even for women who are not married. Some activists prefer terms like 'male violence against women in the home' or assault and abuse 'of women in their intimate relations with men'. Such phrases locate the violence much more precisely. However, they hardly slip easily from the tongue or pen. And of course domestic violence does not occur only in the home or between current sexual partners. Women can be abused by ex-partners or ex-husbands, by men with whom they have sexual relationships but no joint living arrangements, by men whom they are dating more casually, by male acquaintances and friends, by close male family members or by relatives. Some feminist activists and researchers prefer the term 'violence against women by known men' for these reasons. On a general level, 'violence against women' is a more comprehensive term than the limited 'domestic violence'. 'Gender violence' or 'gender-based violence' are often used these days too.

The term 'battered women', which focuses attention on physical violence alone, is widely used in North America, where the movement against domestic violence tends to be referred to as the 'battered women's movement'. In the UK, however, women who have experienced domestic violence have felt unhappy with the term. They have pointed out that it can make women feel that they are being judged and labelled as though they have done something wrong. The use of the general adjective 'battered' can give the impression that all women subject to violence are diminished or made pathetic by the experience, which of course is not the case. As a result, the term is no longer in general usage in the UK. It seems that some people still refer in conversation to refuges as 'battered wives' homes', but the feminist movement and agencies providing services to women use more dignified terms such as 'women experiencing domestic violence', 'abused women' or 'women survivors of domestic violence'.

In the UK, terms like this are used to differentiate domestic violence from other sorts of violence in the family, such as violence against elders and child abuse. The children of women experiencing domestic violence are very often negatively affected by witnessing or living with such violence and may be abused themselves, so that types of abuse may overlap. It is therefore important to distinguish the various forms of abuse that can occur, in order to think about them clearly.

For this reason, objections have been raised to the use of the general term 'family violence'. Usually in violent incidents, the abuser is more powerful in various ways than the abused – which is why the violence and abuse go in one direction and not the other. An expression like 'family violence' clouds this issue. It makes it sound as though everyone in the family is equally violent. Nevertheless, a large school of thought uses the term 'family violence', especially in the USA. Researchers, psychologists and social workers who do this tend to distance themselves, to some extent at least, from the social movement against domestic violence, and from feminist attempts to explain male abuse of women in the home.

Neither the term 'family violence' nor the term 'domestic violence' makes it clear that violence in the home is directed primarily against women and children. Feminists in some countries have objected to 'domestic violence' just as they have objected to 'family violence'. However, in the UK, 'domestic violence' is generally understood as shorthand for male violence against women in the home. In recent years, it has tended to be used interchangeably with 'domestic abuse' (a term which is particularly common in Scotland). These terms are limited and ambiguous about gender, but they remain in general use and are part of everyday speech. They can be used in conjunction with terms like 'woman abuse' and 'women survivors' that help to explain their meaning.

Domestic violence is now understood to extend beyond physical violence and beyond the home. Women's Aid and most women's specialist services define domestic violence as comprising a range of types of abuse, including physical, sexual, mental, emotional or psychological violence and threats. The perpetrator may be a woman's husband, boyfriend, partner, lover, cohabitee, ex-partner or ex-husband, friend, son, father, brother, uncle or other close family member. There are now moves to develop more complex, nuanced definitions that take into account all these factors, that indicate that violence in the home is rarely a one-off event, and that are explicit about the gender issue. The latter often includes a formal acknowledgement that domestic violence is most commonly experienced by women and that it is often associated with issues of gender and power.

For example, there are now attempts by Women's Aid, the Women's National Commission, Southall Black Sisters and a number of other organizations to widen the legal definition to include physical, social or psychological abuse of anyone, including a child witness, with whom a person has a 'domestic relationship'. The aim is to get the government to broaden its definition, possibly by amending the new domestic violence legislation. Possible drafts of such a new definition have included references to patterns of coercive control to which abused women may be subjected and a reference to gender differences. Current government definitions tend to be gender free (although incorporating a gender caveat), but the evidence and the lived experience of most of us point to the fact that, overwhelmingly, the recipients of the violence are female and the perpetrators are male. The government has recently extended the use of a general definition of this type which has limited reference to gender.

In general, the violence may be systematic and long term. It can, and does, occur anywhere – although the home is still the main place where it happens. The home is after all behind closed doors, away from the public eye, protected by spoken and unspoken rules about privacy, about not interfering in other people's business and about 'an Englishman's home is his castle'. And it is also the place where feelings between intimates run highest. For women and their children, the home – that warm haven, that place of comfort and security cushioned from the difficulties of the outside world – is not, and never has been, a safe place. For many women, it is a place of danger, terror and injury, and for some, a place of death.

Almost half of all women murdered in the UK are killed by their husbands or lovers, by far the largest single category of women victims. Homicide statistics consistently reveal that between 40 and 45 per cent of women victims and only about 7 per cent of male victims are killed by their intimate partners. If all killings are included, figures over several years have indicated that about 18 per cent or more have been committed by men killing their female partners, whereas women have killed their male partners in only about 2 per cent of cases. Contrary to sentiments often expressed in the popular media and to recent publicity about women who kill their husbands, the vast majority of domestic murders are by men – killing women. Between one and two women in the UK are murdered by their male partners every week.

The range of injuries that women suffer, or are threatened with, is enormous. These injuries are often accompanied by emotional and psychological abuse, and sexual violence runs through the lives of many women in this situation. All three types of abuse are often interlinked.

Thus, physical violence is just one part of domestic abuse and not necessarily the main part. In fact, some women say that other types of violence which they have experienced have been worse than the assaults. Women often experience several different kinds of violence in combination. All the evidence is that there is often a pattern to abusive behaviour by men and that the pattern may be complex.

Physical abuse

The physical violence that women experience comprises many types of assault, attack and injury. Commonly, it starts with a single slap or blow, followed by disbelief and shock on both sides and by commitments from the man that it will never be repeated. But sadly, after it has happened once, it is rare for it not to happen again. There may be long gaps with no violence, but eventually men who have acted violently once tend to do so again, and then again. Researchers from all schools of thought about domestic violence agree that it is rarely a one-off event. Incidents often start occurring more frequently as time goes on, and become gradually more severe. It is not unusual for women to endure many years of attacks without seeking or receiving any help from anybody.

Physical violence by men against women may involve anything from threatening behaviour, slaps and being pushed about, through black eyes, bruises and broken bones, to extremely serious incidents of multiple assault. It can be life threatening, resulting in internal injuries, permanent handicaps, and disabilities or death. Attempted stranglings seem to be particularly common. Women using local domestic violence services have described being burned or set fire to, being beaten, being hit against walls or with pieces of furniture, being repeatedly kicked and punched, and being stabbed or cut with knives. Some women bear the marks and scars of attack after attack. In many cases, the violence is less severe than this, but it is almost always terrifying and deeply distressing.

Women often feel violated to the core. They describe, for example, the specific humiliation and degradation of experiencing less serious forms of violence, especially if no one else seems concerned about it. Being slapped even lightly and kicked in passing, or being grabbed and pushed around, by someone whom you love and who claims to love you can be devastating experiences, even if the abuse is not severe. Small acts of violence might be repeated again and again, sometimes in an almost arbitrary way, until the women concerned begin to feel they are going mad. Such acts might be accompanied by frightening threats of further violence so that women live in distress and fear, often alone except for their partners, or with children, isolated in the home.

Some women who seek emergency accommodation from a refuge-based service manage to escape as soon as the violence begins, realizing that it may be the start of a repeating pattern. Others may have been in relationships for years and may return to their violent partners several times to give it another try, always hoping it will be better in the future, or believing their partner's protestations of remorse and promises that it will not happen again. Some women experience violence that results in hospitalization and the need for medical care. But, for others, the injuries may not show. Certain men, in fact, are very skilled at inflicting violence on their partners so that it is not visible to the outside world. Violence may happen particularly frequently during pregnancy, or in the post-separation period after a woman has tried to leave.

Sexual abuse

Women who are physically abused are very often also subjected to a range of sexual humiliations and assaults, or partners may use threats of violence in order to make women submit to coercive sex. One American research study found, for example, that a third of the women in the study who had been attacked physically had also been raped by their partners. Many women in domestic violence projects have used the idea of a continuum of male violence against women which includes sexual violence and which links day-to-day harassment to severe assault as part of the same broad spectrum.

Liz Kelly, a well-known British researcher and feminist activist, has developed this idea further in terms of sexual abuse. In her important book *Surviving Sexual Violence*, published back in 1988, she discusses the idea of a continuum of sexual violence, as a result of research in which she talked at length with women about their sexual experiences. The continuum includes the whole distressing sweep of women's experiences of sexual violence, from everyday examples of dominating sexual behaviour by men towards women, to sexual assault and rape. The ultimate form of sexual violence is the murder and sexual mutilation of girls and women by men. Short of this horrific extreme, however, Kelly and others suggest that, in general, it is not useful to think of the continuum as being graded in severity. Only women themselves can define the seriousness of a particular action as it affects them personally. Ideas of a continuum are more about the links which connect forms of sexual violence that many women experience in their lives, and that men may see as acceptable behaviour, with forms of sexual violence which are classified by society as crimes. A whole spectrum of types of harassment, degradation and coerced sexual activity is encompassed, including the use of pornography – for example, in the forced acting out of violent male sexual fantasies.

The idea of the sexual continuum – that it is focused on women's own experience of sexual violence and on their feelings about what has happened to them – is almost a revolutionary one, even in the 2000s. Many women's activists have pointed out that society does not always want to hear what women have to say about this subject, and many men have a vested interest in keeping definitions of sexual violence as narrow as possible. It is vital that women continue to speak out, to tell their stories. Naming and renaming experience of sexual violence is not a simple or easy process, however. There may be no words for the pain and the shame. Some women may block such traumatic events out of their conscious memories for many years, especially if the experiences were in childhood. We all know also that women and girls are frequently not believed when they speak. All too often they are blamed in some way for the sexual violence that they have experienced, even now in the 2000s when things are meant to have got better.

It can be particularly hard for a woman to admit that she has been sexually abused by the man she lives with, and may love, because of such woman-blaming attitudes, as well as moral disapproval, the potential for stigmatizing gossip, self-disgust and shame. All of this is amplified by the possibility of sexual voyeurism. Once certain men get to hear that a girl or a woman has been sexually assaulted, she is often viewed immediately as 'easy', as a slut, or as the justifiable butt of sexually titillating or voyeuristic joking. Although attempts have been made to stop it, there is a distressing pornographic trade in prisons, involving the circulation of details of sexual assaults on girls and women for which men have been convicted.

There is no simple division between physical and sexual violence for women being abused by their male intimates. The two are entwined. Women fleeing domestic violence describe a multitude of experiences in which the physical and sexual are combined inseparably. For example, abusive men often force women to have sex with them after violent episodes. Rape may be an integral part of a physical attack. Domestic violence activists and workers in women's domestic violence services sometimes feel that there is no end to the inventiveness of violent men when it comes to physical abuse and sexual degradation. Almost every day, they hear the unhearable, think about the unthinkable, as they attempt to comfort distraught women trying to escape from such experiences.

Psychological and emotional abuse

In all abuse, emotional and psychological issues are involved. It is very rare for women to experience physical violence that is not accompanied by emotional abuse and threats. In fact, the use of intimidating threats is one of the commonest forms of violence, often used by violent men to exert control and dominance over their partners or lovers. What is threatened can vary. It can be injury, like a beating-up or a broken arm. Very often it is murder. Though sometimes both men and women might shout, when angered, that they will kill the other, such threats are usually in no way serious. Women with a history of suffering domestic violence know, however, with fearful clarity when threats of murder are being made seriously and are real in intent. They must be listened to and their words acted on when they make such claims. Abusive men may also make threats of harm to children, imminent sexual violence (most commonly rape), financial deprivation and all manner of other degrading possibilities.

Emotional abuse takes other forms apart from verbal threats, and very often involves degradation and humiliation. Examples include being persistently insulted, or subjected continually to intimidation or verbal aggression. Mental and psychological abuse can often be financial. Women report being denied money for children's food, for example, or having their own money taken away. It can also be related to extreme possessiveness by a male partner and his fears of allowing his wife or lover to associate with other adults, particularly other men. Many women describe repeated interrogations about imagined infidelities, frequently concerning routine male visitors to the home. Abused women tell of being shut in the house all day, not being allowed to go out, having every action monitored, being stopped from having any friends.

In our time working in and with refuge-based services, women have described being kept locked in cupboards, rooms and garden sheds, being forced to stand on a chair for hours, or being made to eat continually so that they become fatter and fatter. While the last examples are extreme, analysis by domestic violence services and by researchers has confirmed that psychological abuse of widely varying types is devastatingly common, and includes being repeatedly criticized and denigrated, often in public, being stopped from working, studying or seeing friends and families, and being forced to witness children being degraded, punished or abused. Babies being dangled out of windows is an often-reported threatening act. Helping agencies are finally beginning to take this form of abuse seriously, but there is a long way to go.

The extent of the violence and how to measure it

It is notoriously difficult to estimate the full extent of domestic violence, which of course usually happens out of the public eye and behind closed doors. Concealed from view, incidents often go unreported, compounded by women's fears and shame about having experienced domestic violence, and by widely held beliefs about privacy and the myth of the happy nuclear family. Betsy Stanko is a feminist academic who has written widely about violence in women's lives and directed a large research programme on violence for the Economic and Social Research Council in the UK which finished in the early 2000s. In her work, she and others have explained how, in a world in which sexism and discrimination against women are endemic, women themselves come to understand that their own views and experiences are regarded as having less import, being of less value than men's. Also, domestic abuse happens in the family and in the home, traditionally regarded as spheres of female influence and responsibility. It can be very shaming to admit to violence within them. Women often try hard to hide, to minimize, or even to belittle, the violence they have suffered. In the USA, the FBI has stated that domestic violence is the most underreported crime, more underreported even than rape.

In addition, statistics on domestic violence, where they exist at all, tend not to distinguish types of abuse and to give no information about how severe the violence is, how often it happens or for how long it has been going on. As a result, the usefulness of such statistics is severely limited. To complicate the matter still further, it is almost impossible to extrapolate from small-scale research studies to the general population. Nevertheless many attempts to estimate the extent of domestic violence have been made.

In a ground-breaking book for its time, *Violence Against Wives*, published in 1980, the domestic violence researchers Rebecca and Russell Dobash found that more than 25 per cent of all violent crime reported to the police was domestic violence by men against women, making it the second most common violent crime. But in the same study, the Dobashes found that only about 2–3 per cent of domestic violence incidents were reported to the police in the first place. Awareness of domestic violence has increased greatly since then. More recent studies have found a much higher reporting rate (such as about 30 per cent), although they all agree that underreporting to the police remains significant. It is currently estimated that the police in the UK receive a domestic violence call every minute.

Many studies across the world, including some very rigorous and ground-breaking research such as a large Canadian study conducted in 1993 by Holly Johnson, have found that domestic violence is experienced by between one in three and one in five women globally. In the UK in 1998, Betsy Stanko and her colleagues conducted a costing study in the London Borough of Hackney, and found a figure of one in nine women attending doctors' surgeries reporting domestic violence at any one time. Women's Aid has estimated in support of other studies that, over a whole lifetime, up to one in four women may on occasion experience violence in their sexual relationships with men. For example, ten separate domestic violence prevalence studies were compared in a Council of Europe study which found that one in four women experienced domestic violence in their lives and 6 to 10 per cent in a single year. Severe, repeated and systematic violence is clearly less common, but it has been estimated to occur in at least five in a hundred marriages in the UK.

Very large-scale random studies of domestic violence are few and far between. There have been none to date in the UK, although new studies are anticipated in the next few years, and the British Crime Survey (BCS) now contains specially designed questions on the issue. Sylvia Walby and colleagues have produced a detailed self-completion questionnaire on domestic violence, sexual assault and stalking, and reported on its use in the BCS at the beginning of 2004. While self-report questionnaires of this type are not wholly reliable, the 2004 figure was that 13 per cent of women had experienced domestic abuse. Nine per cent of men had also been abused in this study. Forty-five per cent of women could recall experiencing sexual assault in their lives. About one-third of women victims overall had told no one.

Two large surveys, ten years apart, have been conducted by the well-known family violence researcher, Murray Straus, and his colleagues in the USA. Their work has dealt a comprehensive blow to any lingering idea that domestic violence is an unusual occurrence that happens only in disturbed or 'pathological' families. One in every six couples in the initial study had 'engaged in violence' in the previous year, and one in four had done so at some time in the past.

Straus' findings are contentious, however, due to his use of the Conflict Tactics Scale or CTS, which his team developed as a way of measuring incidents of violence. The scale has come in for strong criticism from other researchers and has been the subject of heated controversy for many years. Although less common in the UK, it has influenced thinking on the subject, and it is very widely used in the USA and elsewhere in evaluation research.

What the CTS does is to make it easy for research respondents to categorize the violence they have experienced or perpetrated. It lists different categories of violent acts that can be ticked off, much as in a standard questionnaire. Unfortunately, however, the scale failed in its original form to recognize differences in power between men and women or in degrees of male and female physical strength. Importantly, it did not differentiate between aggressive violence and violence used in self-defence. Nor did it distinguish between degrees of violence that could be classified similarly – say, as a 'kick' – when clearly the amount of force behind the kick and the part of the body kicked would dictate the damage and injury caused.

Some types of violence and abuse that women experience – for example, sexual violence – were left out of the original CTS. In addition, the scale suffered from the problem of obtaining truthful self-reporting. Many researchers and workers in the domestic violence field have demonstrated that men very often minimize and underreport the violence they have perpetrated, whereas women, who often feel guilty and apologetic if they have engaged in violent acts, may exaggerate or overreport their actions. Most significantly perhaps, the original CTS did not place the violence within the social situation in which it occurred. In other words, it took it out of context. The sequence of events, the process of what happened and in what order, was ignored. For example, if each partner reported a slap – which would come out equally on the scale – who was the aggressor? Was one partner defending themselves? The CTS did not give any weight to the social consequences or the effects of the violence, to how the recipient felt afterwards and what then happened. It ignored the traumatic life events that could follow and the way in which these differentially affect women and men. It is usually women not men, for example, who are forced to abandon their homes and belongings, and become homeless, as a result of domestic violence.

Using the scale, Straus and his colleagues, most notably Richard Gelles and others then at the New Hampshire Family Violence Laboratory, found that husbands were only slightly more likely to use violence against their wives than vice versa. This finding has been repeated in surveys where the CTS has been used. It has been widely disputed by women's advocates and by researchers in the field, including some who used the CTS and followed it up with in-depth interviews with the same people – and found different results. A UK medical researcher, James Nazroo, for example, arrived at the usual CTS finding of about equal numbers of violent incidents between men and women patients when using the scale. He then interviewed the study participants and found that the men's violence was much more severe, the women's violence was often laughed off by the men or casually intercepted, and the injuries incurred had almost all been sustained by the women. Indeed, 100 per cent of the most serious injuries and mental health impacts had been experienced by the women. More serious injuries for women are a feature of all studies that compare male and female intimate violence, except in some extreme cases.

The lack of detection of the severity of injury was a serious problem in the original Conflicts Tactics Scale, as Nazroo's work demonstrated. Thankfully, this has now been ameliorated to a considerable extent in the CTS2, which includes an important 'injury scale'. The scale corrects for the fact that most of the violence by women that the CTS picks up is very minor in its impact.

However, the arguments over the CTS continue to reverberate almost 30 years after the original research. Mainly they are between social scientists, with the family violence researchers on one side and researchers who could broadly be described as feminist on the other. The arguments are not just about the CTS, but tend to expand to cover how research into social issues should be done in general, and they can be fierce. The divisions are not always quite that clear-cut though, and some feminist sociologists and researchers work hard to bridge the gap, to say there is value on both sides.

It is beyond the scope of this book to analyse these academic arguments in detail. Nonetheless it is important to understand how such academic research methods can have a far-reaching effect. The influence of the CTS remains with us, not only within research circles but among social workers and service providers, and in the popular sphere as well. The world of social science, and of American social science in particular, tends to be keen on surveys and on trying to make scientific-style measurements. And the surveys done by Straus and his team using the CTS were large, and were designed to be extrapolated to the whole of the USA. Their work is extensively used as a major source of data on family violence, despite all the problems inherent in trying to impose a survey-style method of research on something like domestic violence. Although they have a role, abstract scales and surveys are not always very useful when it comes to explaining complex social problems. In the USA, further national surveys of violence against women have recently been completed, and various other scales to measure intimate violence now exist. These new violence against women scales can be of help and are being used by researchers in various countries (but particularly the USA) in order to be able to replicate studies and to provide quantitative data.

The 'battered husband syndrome'

Back in 1978, Suzanne Steinmetz, writing in the academic law journal *Victimology*, claimed the existence of a 'battered husband syndrome' on the strength of the original CTS. The media throughout North America were quick to pick up this idea and to broadcast it widely. For instance, the well-known and popular American TV programme previously hosted by Johnny Carson, the *Today Show*, claimed that 12 million American husbands were beaten by their wives. While this claim was retracted two weeks later as a faulty extrapolation of Steinmetz's figures, the idea of a battered husband syndrome persists. The scholarly and academic book *Women, Violence and Social Change*, written by the Dobashes in 1992, uses a broad-brush approach to chart the social movement of women against domestic violence in the UK and the USA. They analyse the dynamic relationship between this movement and the law, the criminal justice system and the state itself. They look at ideas about domestic violence used in therapy, and they place everything they have talked about in a theoretical and sociological context of knowledge, research and social change. All of this – and yet, on the back cover, two major questions are headlined to catch attention and sell the book. One of them is: 'Are there really as many abused husbands as abused wives?'

In the UK, the subject of battered husbands is still repeatedly raised at almost all public meetings on domestic violence. Domestic violence activists and Women's Aid staff are used to it. In the 1990s and 2000s, several television documentaries have looked at the plight of husbands who have been abused by their wives. These programmes appear to claim, as Steinmetz did in the 1970s, that the problem is nearly as common as domestic violence against women. While no one would want to minimize the plight of men in this situation (which may be aggravated by conventional notions of masculinity) or to deny them assistance and support, workers and activists throughout the domestic violence field know from everyday experience that it is simply not true that almost as many men are abused by women as vice versa. There is only one refuge for abused men, mainly for victims of same sex violence. There have been a couple of projects for men abused by women over the years which have never lasted long, and there is no widespread demand from anyone to establish one. A couple of phone lines exist in the UK which specifically respond to abused men and some general helplines will take calls from men who have suffered violence as well as from women.

Police services and other agencies are now being encouraged to monitor their referrals for domestic violence and to keep thorough data. These data demonstrate much higher levels of abuse against women than against men and, where figures are kept, many more male than female perpetrators. Consistent data are not always collected by other organizations, however, and different agencies may use different categories. Attempts are presently under way to standardize data collection across all the organizations concerned. In various local areas, for example, domestic violence data-monitoring projects have been set up across agencies, and the Home Office issued 'Development and Practice' guidance on this issue in 2004.

There is now a lot of such data and documentation around domestic violence against women, although it is still fragmented and almost all of it is about physical abuse only. From national crime surveys, police records, domestic violence projects, social services departments, hospitals, historical studies and the world of literature – all the evidence points to the continued widespread abuse of women by men. Every refuge service for women fleeing domestic violence in the UK is full almost as soon as it opens.

It is worth dwelling on this fact for a minute. Where do the women come from? Where were they before? How many more women are there waiting to come? There are now hundreds of refuge-based and support organizations in the UK. Those run by Women's Aid temporarily give shelter to many thousand women and children every year in England alone. Even so, most refuge services are constantly dealing with new referrals.

Research suggests and the testimonies of women and men who have experienced violence also confirm that, although there are a few cases where men are systematically abused by women, a large amount of violence committed by women is conducted in self-defence and is limited in its nature. Such retaliation may come only after years of intimidation and abuse. Domestic violence research in both the UK and elsewhere has found that women only rarely respond to men's attacks on them by counter-violence. Staff working in many domestic violence services, listening to story after story from women homeless due to violence by their male partners, only occasionally meet women who have engaged in counter-violence themselves.

Some studies in the USA have shown, on the other hand, that between 23 and 71 per cent of women enduring domestic violence have used violence in retaliation at least once. For example, studies by Daniel Saunders, an American researcher and male activist against woman abuse, found that a high proportion of women experiencing violence used some types of non-severe violent response, such as throwing something or 'pushing, shoving and grabbing'. The most frequent motive for this behaviour, however, was self-defence. Saunders suggests that to claim any sort of equality in rates of domestic violence between men and women is literally to add insult to injury for women who are often in fear of their lives, who would never initiate an attack, but who may strike back in self-defence. One has to ask what this stress on women's supposed violence towards men is all about. Is it because in a society still controlled by men there is an almost automatic collusion to minimize the violence, damage and injury that men do to women? Is it about blaming and victimizing still further women who are already on the receiving end of violent abuse and degradation?

The impacts on women

Many, possibly most, women are afraid of men on one level or another. On the street, women are very often afraid of violence from men they do not know, especially at night. And it is indeed true that men 'control' the streets. Walk around any city centre late in the evening to find out. In some places and at some times, the streets are literally not safe for women (or, in fact, for many men).

Much research has shown, however, that by far the most likely place for violence against women to occur is in their intimate relationships. The same is true of rape and sexual assault. For all types of violence, women are far more at risk from men in their family or with whom they have a close relationship than from male strangers. They are scarcely at risk at all from other women. In *Women, Violence and Social Change*, the Dobashes point out graphically that the onset of systematic and severe violence against women is almost exclusively associated for those individuals experiencing it with entering a permanent relationship with a man. Violence against women by their male intimates is a unique phenomenon in the world of violence.

This sort of treatment can, of course, have devastating effects on the women concerned. Most commonly, abused women describe how being exposed to violence in all its various forms can result in a loss of self-confidence and self-esteem. In western culture and in most cultures worldwide, a woman with a family still tends to be regarded as being responsible for that family's welfare and happiness, for doing the emotional 'housework', despite recent changes in some countries. So if things go wrong, it may well be assumed that it is her fault. As a result, women very often blame themselves or feel guilty if they experience violence from their partners. They might feel the classic 'if only'. If only I had been a better wife to him; if only I had been more sexually receptive; if only I had done more of what he wanted. Abused women often experience a painful mixture of guilt, blame and shame.

Domestic violence may result in physical injury and permanent physical damage, in homelessness, in loss of employment, in loss of family, friends and even children, and importantly, in depression, attempted suicide and mental illness. Abused women may experience high levels of anxiety and panic attacks, or may develop disturbed patterns of eating and sleeping, problems in concentrating and a feeling of hopelessness. Workers in domestic violence services testify, however, to the amazing resilience and spirit of many women in this situation. After only a short stay in refuge accommodation, some are able to start all over again – often literally, since women in this situation frequently have no home, no money, no family or friends close by, and no possessions.

For other women, the process is longer and harder. Some women end up seeking long-term help from the caring and mental health professions. A lot of books and articles have been written by psychiatric and social work professionals and academics, particularly in North America, about the specific psychological and behavioural problems of women who have suffered violence. Many domestic violence activists, however, tend to feel that, while some women do develop such problems as a result of violence, psychological studies that come up with general conclusions about what women in this situation feel can result in 'labelling' and stereotyping. No one who has suffered domestic violence responds exactly the same as anyone else. This means that, although services are needed to meet many different needs, there is no one set of psychological characteristics that women who have suffered violence share. To suggest that there is can imply that a woman who has suffered violence is mentally ill, and can result in 'pathologizing' the victim.

While many domestic violence workers have resisted attempts by psychologists and psychiatrists to ascribe particular behavioural and emotional symptoms to abused women, they do not pretend that no damage has been done. Increasingly, domestic violence services in the UK offer, or try to offer, formal and informal counselling services to women coming to them. Refuge organizations are called shelters or transition houses in North America, where the whole culture is more geared towards therapy, counselling and individual psychological explanations of people's problems. And this has always been reflected in the way shelters work. Some shelters in the USA run quite complicated psychiatric intervention programmes for women.

An American feminist, Lenore Walker, has developed what she calls the 'battered woman syndrome' to explain what happens when women consistently suffer violence. Her ideas have some usefulness and some abused women have been helped by them, although they have been disputed by other feminists. She suggests that women often learn over time that they can do nothing to prevent the violence, and therefore adopt a coping strategy of 'learned helplessness'. This can lead to a response of passivity and powerlessness – an extreme example of the way most women are conditioned to behave anyway. Women experiencing abuse are beaten down emotionally and physically, the theory goes, although they may eventually snap. Using the 'straw that breaks the camel's back' idea, feminist lawyers in the USA now widely use the battered woman syndrome as a defence for women who have murdered their husbands after enduring years of degradation and abuse. 'Expert witnesses' are then called in to testify that the woman has been suffering from the syndrome. Serving as an expert witness is a highly lucrative business in the USA. So far it has happened less often in the UK in relation to domestic violence, although there are now increasing numbers of cases where such expert witnesses are called.

Some domestic violence activists, however, feel that the use of the battered woman syndrome analysis can buy into judgemental ways of thinking which blame the victim by suggesting that women are guilty of causing the violence they experience. While Walker is a strong feminist and places her own work in a broader understanding of women's position in society, it has unfortunately been picked up by some social workers and other professionals who tend to explain their clients' behaviour in terms of individual failure or inadequacy – but add a supposedly woman-oriented gloss. A few women we know who have escaped from violent relationships confirm that they did indeed learn to be passive, although not necessarily helpless, to deal with the violence. But they suggest that it was only when they felt strong enough to leave the helplessness behind and to take action that they were able to get away and build new lives. Most importantly, what they needed to know was that there was somewhere to escape to and some way of financially supporting themselves and their children.

Back in 1991, an American psychological study at the University of Cincinatti confirmed, as previously suggested by various feminists in the USA, that the battered woman syndrome may be a sign, not of helplessness, but of a struggle for survival very similar to that of international hostages imprisoned by political organizations. Hostages often develop what is called the 'Stockholm syndrome', in which they may be friendly and intimate with their captors, and the suggestion is that abused women do this too. When hostages do it, however, it is widely viewed as an understandable strategy for self-preservation, not as a sign of weakness.

The impacts on children

Recognizing domestic violence as a crime, and starting to do something about it in terms of providing assistance and services, has taken long enough. Recognizing the damage done to child witnesses of domestic violence and their need for assistance and services only began in the 1990s. Children have few rights; they have very little power over what happens to them. Not many people listen to what they say and feel, or grant them any semblance of equality and respect. The Women's Aid movement tries hard to do just this, by recognizing that children are often treated unfairly by adults and are powerless in traumatic situations. It attempts to provide specialist children's support workers in all refuge-based organizations, in order to start to meet the needs of the children living there, and to provide support and services especially for them. The Women's Aid Federation of England funded and managed a research project in the 1990s investigating children's work in refuge support services, conducted by Liz Kelly, Audrey Mullender and ourselves. The study highlighted the creative, and sometimes pioneering, nature of this work, which is frequently unrecognized and overlooked by other professionals.

In fact, until recently, few other agencies have taken up the issue. Now, though, the impact on children of witnessing, experiencing or living with domestic violence against their mothers has finally become a matter of general concern. As an issue, it has 'found its time'. Two ground-breaking conferences were held in London in 1992 and, since then, there has been a stream of training programmes, conferences and new research and policy initiatives (see also Chapter 7). Audrey Mullender and Rebecca Morley produced the first British book on children and domestic violence in 1994, and research studies have since been conducted by NCH Action for Children, the NSPCC and the Economic and Social Research Council (involving a team of several universities, including our own research group).

The Women's Aid Federation in England has produced various publications on the issue. They describe how effects may include: stress-related illnesses, confused and torn loyalties, lack of trust, unnaturally good behaviour, taking on the mother role, an acceptance of abuse as 'normal', guilt, isolation, shame, anger, lack of confidence, fear of a repeat of the violence and so on. Women who have suffered violence find that their children sometimes become quiet and nervous while still at home or after leaving. Others become very active or develop disturbed or aggressive behaviour patterns. Boys in particular may respond in this way, but girls can become aggressive too, although they can sometimes be withdrawn, timid and suspicious.

Boys and girls, of course, may learn different things from domestic violence and behave in different ways as a result. However, Liz Kelly, Audrey Mullender, Rebecca Morley and others, including ourselves, have pointed out that, while the experience of domestic violence will probably affect how children develop their gender identity as either women or men, the differences between how girls and boys react are not as clear-cut as we might think. Both boys and girls may express their distress in ways that turn inward and also in ways that turn outward. Domestic violence activists and researchers suggest that we need to develop a way of understanding the impact of domestic violence on children that takes gender into account, but that allows for differences within, as well as between, the responses of girls and of boys.

Overall, the serious impacts that domestic violence has on children and young people is a matter of concern for all relevant agencies and there are some support groups and dedicated services now in existence. It is also encouraging that, despite the damage that can be caused, children may display remarkable coping strategies and resilience in the face of these difficult life circumstances, as we discuss more fully with reference to our own research in Chapter 7.

Important general work on the impacts of domestic violence on children has been conducted in North America. The contributions of Peter Jaffe in Canada have been outstanding in this respect. While his work is couched in professional, psychological language and theories perhaps more often used in a North American context, it also has relevance in the UK. In one of his books, *Children of Battered Women*, he explains some of the harsh and distressing consequences experienced by children. He describes how children of both sexes tend to blame themselves for the violence between the adults. They often try to protect and defend their mothers, and may get caught up in a conspiracy of silence about the violence, which can force them to become manipulative and ashamed. They may get depressed or hate themselves as a result. They may lose their trust and faith in adults – or even in life.

Jaffe outlines how some child survivors of domestic violence may develop at some point in their later lives symptoms very similar to those experienced by people who have gone through a major trauma – for example, a train disaster or a bombing. These symptoms have now been lumped together by doctors into post-traumatic stress disorder or syndrome. It is this disorder which some children and adults who have suffered domestic violence in childhood clearly manifest and it can be a most useful diagnosis. Like women who have experienced domestic violence, however, child witnesses respond in a wide variety of ways. It can be dangerous to elaborate specific syndromes as if the symptoms are inescapable.

It can also be dangerous or stigmatizing to suggest that propensities to receive or to perpetrate domestic violence are usually passed on between the generations. Such ideas are often expressed in 'cycle of violence' or 'inter-generational transmission' theories and we will discuss problems associated with this view more fully later. Nevertheless, older children in this situation and adults who are still being damaged by childhood experiences of domestic violence are pleased that their life experiences are finally being acknowledged, and are coming out into the open.

The children of women who have experienced violence have frequently been involved in violent incidents experienced by their mothers, and may have been hurt themselves. They may also have been physically or sexually abused independently (as we discuss further in Chapter 7). The degree of interrelatedness between domestic violence and child abuse has been studied by a variety of researchers. These studies show a varying connection between the two, both occurring together in somewhere between 30 and 60 per cent of cases. Of course, domestic violence against women is a different phenomenon from child abuse, with quite separate and distinct gender and power dynamics. It is not helpful to muddle up the two. Many men who abuse their wives or partners would never deliberately harm their children. Nevertheless, the numbers of men abusing both women and children are worryingly large and, wherever there is domestic violence, it makes sense to check for child abuse, and vice versa.

Women's Aid consistently finds that many children who have witnessed domestic violence have often also suffered physical and sexual abuse, and that many only disclose abuse once they are in the secure surroundings of a refuge and the immediate danger is removed. Over the years, they have accumulated numerous examples where the domestic abuse that women experience includes threats to abuse children, the destruction of children's toys or possessions, and even the deliberate hurting or killing of pets. Children are sometimes used as objects of manipulation and as part of the abuse by violent men. Most distressingly, some experience, or even witness, the death of their mother at the hands of their father. For example, one three-year-old recently was alone with the body of his dead mother, apparently constantly cuddling and trying to comfort her, for three days before discovery.

Which women and which men?

Perhaps the next question to ask is: which women experience domestic violence? The answer seems to be: potentially, all women. There have been various unsuccessful attempts to classify the sort of women who would be likely victims. Some of these are contradictory in a way that would be almost laughable if the issue were not such a serious one. For example, women are too passive and behave like victims, and are therefore subject to violence. Women are too aggressive and self-confident, and are therefore subject to violence. Women are too indecisive, too forceful, too masculine, too submissive. They do not stand up for themselves enough; they stand up for themselves too much. They are too independent and do not look after their menfolk properly. They are too dependent, coddling men and not giving them a chance to breathe. Many of these explanations – especially in the past – have fallen into the woman-hating or 'blame the victim' schools of thought.

Social class has been, and continues to be, an issue for researchers and activists working against domestic violence. Some research has been done, especially in the USA, which shows a concentration of domestic violence in low-income, blue-collar families. Other researchers contend that, while hardship can certainly sometimes aggravate abuse, suggestions that domestic violence is concentrated among working-class men and women should be treated with both scepticism and caution. Middle-class women are less likely to report it to the authorities, and more likely to pursue private solutions than to approach public agencies like social services. Research has shown that middle-class men are less likely to come to the attention of the police, and that social and public agencies in general are less likely to intervene in middle-class lives. Most importantly, perhaps, as far as such research is concerned, both middle-class men and women are far less likely than working-class men and women to get 'researched' by researchers!

Much of what we have all learned in recent years about domestic violence comes from refuge-based services, which have always been used by more working-class than middle-class women. Due to social and political inequalities, working-class women are more likely to have nowhere else to go, and to lack the money to buy themselves some other way out. Nevertheless, some middle-class women do use refuge accommodation. Other services for women experiencing domestic violence run by Women's Aid – for example, advice, outreach and information support services – are quite commonly used by middle-class women.

In recent years, there have been various public accounts of violence in affluent families or involving public figures. As a result, images of domestic violence as the preserve of the working class and the poor have been thoroughly dented. However, there is still a 'common-sense' view in

UK society that violence against women occurs only in the homes of working-class people, mainly in the inner cities, and is associated with poverty and, particularly, with alcoholism. This sort of view has a long history. It harks back to attitudes towards the Victorian poor, forced to live in miserable and overcrowded conditions, crammed into the rapidly growing cities after the Industrial Revolution. In the UK in the 1990s and 2000s, cutbacks in welfare state services (under the Labour government elected in May 1997 as well as under the previous Conservative one) have been a feature of social policy, and it is of course true that there can be harmful effects within some low income families. Poor housing, high unemployment, bad working conditions and lack of facilities take their toll. And in some subcultures, social conditioning of young men to be 'macho' and violent can combine with poor opportunities for life fulfilment to cause violence, some of which can be expressed against women. The recent BCS study by Sylvia Walby and colleagues found that domestic abuse was more than three times as likely to be reported by women in families on incomes of less than £10,000 a year than by those with incomes of more than £20,000. But we do know that domestic violence occurs very widely outside low-income communities and run-down council estates.

Some studies have shown large amounts of violence in affluent areas. In a study in Yorkshire carried out by Jalna Hanmer and Sheila Saunders, social class and housing type made no difference to the levels of violence experienced by women in their sample. Additionally, some research studies have indicated that abuse committed by middle-class men may be more covert, less easily visible and more psychological in nature. Put simply, what they are saying is that middle-class men know how not to leave bruises and injuries that are easily visible to outsiders.

This sort of idea was evident in the 'designer violence' of the Hollywood film *Sleeping with the Enemy*, starring Julia Roberts. In this film, a rich and fabulously beautiful young woman, whose life as far as anyone could tell was perfect, was in fact experiencing frequent and severe violence from her menacing husband. But nobody would have guessed. Celebrity domestic violence also attracts much attention. Few can forget the domestic abuse and murder case involving Nicole and O. J. Simpson.

Activists in the movement against domestic violence in several countries over the last 30 years have consistently made it clear that domestic violence, though varying, occurs across all classes and communities. Many books, documents and reports stress this point repeatedly. The result is that we all have to face up to the reality of domestic violence, whatever our class, cultural or racial background. However, some middle-class people, and perhaps middle-class professionals in particular, like to imagine that it only happens 'out there' to other people.

During one week in 2001, for example, two instances of women being killed by their partners were reported nationally. In the first instance, the couple had lived in a green, leafy residential suburb. People interviewed by the media about the killing expressed amazement that such a thing could happen 'in that area'. In the second case, the woman was a local teacher. The newspaper and television reports consistently elaborated upon this particular detail. The very fact that these instances made the headlines at all when so many women are killed annually by their husbands speaks for itself. We do not want to believe that domestic violence happens everywhere, so there is shock value for the media in exposing such cases.

A particularly well-publicized example occurred back in 1987 when a tragic case of child abuse and murder in New York, brought to court in 1988–9, grabbed the attention of the media on an international scale. Although a long time ago now, the case remains famous. It involved a woman, Hedda Nussbaum, who, after years of horrifying abuse and control by her violent, crazed partner, Joel Steinberg, could not prevent him from murdering their adopted daughter, Lisa. Steinberg had abused Lisa for some years prior to her murder. Acres of newsprint and thousands of words have been produced about this case. The murder trial was watched live on television by millions of Americans.

While the case was widely discussed, women in particular argued among themselves about it. Some castigated Nussbaum for failing to protect her daughter, and for using drugs as commanded by Steinberg. Others excused her, due to the debilitating effects of the enormous amount of abuse and violence (including psychological abuse) that she had endured. Famous feminists in the USA lined up on both sides. But, as many of them pointed out, there are many other tragic and horrifying cases of child murder in New York City. The reason why this one hit the headlines, not only in New York, not only in the USA, but in many countries worldwide, was simple. Nussbaum and Steinberg were well-off, respectable and middle class. She was a book editor. He was a lawyer.

In the UK, there is a set of ideas about what a family should be which approximates to a sort of middle-class ideal, and which is usually supported by government policies, whichever party is in power. From 1979 to 1997, however, the British Conservative governments of Margaret Thatcher and John Major took a particularly strong 'pro-family' line, similar to, although not as extreme as, the 'pro-family' stance of US Republican administrations. The government of Tony Blair has also declared itself in favour of the traditional family. Thus, dominant ideas about the family in western countries tend to give credence to only one particular family form, namely the small nuclear family consisting of a man, a woman and two or three children, usually living a fairly affluent lifestyle. A look at the advertisements on TV will reveal many examples of this sort of family. Such a picture can be very misleading, and there are all sorts of other ways of organizing families and sexual relationships. To attempt to impose this 'norm' of family life on people of varying backgrounds, races, cultures and sexualities fails to reflect real life and can be prejudiced and discriminatory. Unfortunately, it is exactly what has always happened, and continues to happen today.

Lesbians, for example, tend to be made invisible by this society, despite some improvements in recent years. They are underrepresented or not represented at all in almost all research, including much that is conducted by feminists, but some lesbians do, of course, experience violence in personal relationships. Domestic violence provision is open to all women, but specialist services for lesbians fleeing abuse are virtually non-existent. Women in this situation may face discrimination and sometimes outright hostility if they openly seek help following violence from either a male or female partner. Lesbians who have been abused by a male ex-partner or partner may get little sympathy. Instead they are quite likely to face voyeuristic or punitive attitudes, along the lines of 'she asked for that' or 'she deserves all she gets'. Young lesbians suffering abuse and living at home may experience particular difficulties, and may not know where on earth to turn for help. And a woman who is a lesbian faces a difficult situation if she has children. Seeking help to stop the violence may bring unwanted attention from the authorities. Things have got better recently, but there could still be threats to her mothering on the grounds of sexuality.

Violence between women partners does occur. However, it is a different issue from domestic violence by men against women, and needs to be thought about and understood in different ways. Women activists are currently discussing and evolving new understandings about this painful matter, research studies are being conducted on it and specific helping agencies and helplines are beginning to be set up. The Broken Rainbow LGBT Domestic Violence Service, for example, has held a pioneering conference and provides ground-breaking services to lesbian, gay, bisexual and transgender communities.

In different cultures and countries, and among the many diverse peoples of the world, relationships, communities and styles of living vary vastly. Domestic violence by men against women may take different cultural forms and mean different things in these various communities. We know that intimate abuse occurs among people of almost all racial, ethnic and cultural heritages and shows itself in the very different ways in which violence is manifested and in different patterns of behaviour and family structure. In the recent shadow report to the UK government's latest response to the CEDAW committee of the UN, Purna Sen, Liz Kelly and Cathy Humphreys discuss what they call different cultural forms of violence. The differences from culture to culture are very real but it is possible that the actual extent of the violence may be broadly similar.

Nevertheless certain myths persist. For example, some people believe that Asian women are more likely than white women to be badly treated and subjected to violence due to cultural patterns of family life. Others argue that African-Caribbean men are more violent than white men, particularly in relationships with white women. These racist ideas are not supported by research, but they have been around for a long time, going back deep into Britain's colonial and imperial history.

Discrimination against minority ethnic communities and discrimination against women can intersect in specific ways as people play out their personal lives, and this can have complex implications in some cases of domestic violence. Cultural traditions and customary practices may also play a part. Black researchers and commentators assert that there is a need for committed anti-racist research into such issues, as they affect the different ways in which domestic violence is manifested. Amina Mama in *The Hidden Struggle*, a pioneering book on black women and domestic violence, suggests that for black women domestic violence needs to be redefined. She points out that existing research has been contradictory and often tainted with racist sentiments, concentrating almost exclusively on whether black and minority families are more or less violent than white.

Despite some positive changes over recent years, racism still imbues British society. It expresses itself in the attitudes and behaviour of white people and white communities, but it is more than that. Sometimes called structural or institutional racism, it is embedded, like discrimination against women, in the very way in which society goes about organizing itself. One example is the racist nature of the immigration laws and the way that they are applied in different ways to white and to black immigrants. Another is discriminatory employment practices, which can occur in an institutional way even in organizations in which all the individuals involved claim that they are anti-racist.

For black women fleeing violence, the existence of such pervasive, although sometimes hidden, racism complicates all the options. They may find that their accounts are not believed. If they are abused by a black man, they may wish to protect both him and their community from potentially racist police intervention or surveillance – and so be reluctant to seek help. Women whose immigration status is dependent on their husbands' position may face particular difficulties, including lack of eligibility for state benefits and the risk of deportation if they leave their marriages. Immigrant women may also have no recourse to public funds, which makes leaving home due to violence very hazardous. A 2003 research study by the South Asian women's networking organization, Imkaan, found that an insecure immigrant status was one of the greatest confounding factors that confront Asian women escaping domestic violence. In addition, women who do not speak English or who are unfamiliar with the country may feel condemned to remain with their abusive husbands, due to the lack of supportive services or of language interpretation. The issues are many and complicated, and will be returned to throughout this book.

Young women may experience particular difficulties if they are subjected to violence. However, these difficulties are often overlooked, as highlighted recently by the Lilith Project in the UK, which held a conference on the issue, aptly named Forgotten Violence: Young Women and Abuse. Older women fleeing abuse may also face specific difficulties. They may experience problems in being acknowledged as victims of violence, in having their needs taken seriously, and in contacting services that respond sympathetically and show some knowledge and understanding of their situation. Women with disabilities who experience violence are often in an especially traumatic and tragic position. If their disabilities are quite severe, they may be particularly isolated, confined to the home and unable to gain access to information, support and help. This situation is magnified greatly if their abuser is also their carer. It may then be almost impossible for them to escape the violence. In addition, it is rarely acknowledged, even today, that domestic violence is a problem that women with disabilities are likely to experience, so they may have additional barriers of disbelief and unhelpful attitudes to surmount.

Women can also be disabled by the violence that they have experienced. Survivors of violence whom we have met have been blinded or deafened, or have lost the use of limbs. Among the women we talked to for a recent study, one woman had lost an eye and another could no longer stand up, except for a few minutes, due to extensive damage to her legs. Physical violence was often combined with mental or sexual violence or both, and with threats towards both the woman and her children. Some women described repeated injuries, the same bone smashed and re-smashed, brain haemorrhages, hospitalizations, attempted murder. Other women told of distressing mental cruelty, verging on torture. A few women gave accounts of children killed as babies or sustaining distressing mental handicaps as a result of violence experienced during pregnancy or after birth.

Such deeply disturbing accounts occur again and again throughout the domestic violence literature. They are heard often by workers in domestic violence services, by social workers and by the police. Everyone who works with women who have suffered domestic violence and their children hopes that the dreadful stories will stop, that women will stop needing to come forward for help, that the atrocities will come to an end. But they never do.

2

Women's and refuge-based services and the movement against domestic violence

> The great mobilization of women began with a vision, supported by action. The vision was of a world transformed.
>
> Rebecca and Russell Dobash, *Women, Violence and Social Change*

What are refuge-based domestic violence services and how are they organized?

Ever since the 'mobilization of women' in the late 1960s and early 1970s of which Rebecca and Russell Dobash speak, Women's Aid has been the key agency in the UK for women who have experienced physical, emotional and sexual violence, and for their children. Women's Aid domestic violence services provide emergency and temporary accommodation, advice, information, support and a range of other services for abused women and children. Most run refuge projects and related outreach and after-care services, and some also run separate advice centres, support groups and other special projects. The interlocking services they provide form a nationwide network, and include both general refuge and support services for all women and some specialist projects for Asian, African, African-Caribbean and other black women, for women from some other ethnic minority communities, and for certain women with special needs. However, there are not nearly enough domestic violence services of any kind, especially the latter. In general, the national domestic violence network and the associated services for abused women and their children remain inadequately funded and resourced – a problem that we shall return to throughout this book.

Women's Aid advice, refuge, advocacy and support services are co-ordinated by four autonomous but closely associated federations: Welsh Women's Aid, Scottish Women's Aid, Northern Ireland Women's

Aid and the Women's Aid Federation of England (now known generally as Women's Aid). There are now hundreds of Women's Aid organizations throughout the UK, many of which run more than one refuge project, and which together give shelter to thousands of women and children annually. Many thousands more women contact the Women's Aid federations and their member refuge groups annually for support, advice and help. Women's Aid works to end domestic violence against women and their children, which means that the federations take a much wider role than purely local domestic violence service co-ordination and provision.

The majority of domestic violence organizations running refuge services are in England due to its large size and population. The mission of the Women's Aid Federation of England is to advocate for abused women and children by working to:

- offer support and a place of safety to abused women and children
- empower women affected by domestic violence
- recognize and meet the needs of children affected by domestic violence
- promote policy and practices to prevent domestic violence
- raise awareness of its extent and impact

Women's Aid co-ordinates a national network in England of 340 local services, which support over 500 refuge projects, helplines and outreach services, including many specialist projects for black and ethnic minority women. Women's Aid in England, the national domestic violence charity, celebrated its thirtieth birthday in 2004 with a series of activities, starting with an event at 11 Downing Street and involving a range of personalities and key political figures. It now supports more than 40,000 women and children in refuge-based accommodation and provides other complex and diverse support services to a further 100,000 per year. Welsh Women's Aid consists of 33 organizations with 40 refuge projects, all offering 24-hour helplines. There is one refuge service in Wales specifically for black and ethnic minority women and 13 advice centres. Scottish Women's Aid is a network of 39 local services and there are two refuge projects in Scotland providing services specifically for black and minority ethnic women. It is worth noting that, in common with the other federations, Scottish Women's Aid can only help a small proportion of the women and children needing accommodation. For example, in 2003, Scottish Women's Aid provided support to about 65,300 women, but could only actually accommodate about 1,550 women and 2,000 children out of a total referred of nearly 13,000. Northern Ireland Women's Aid co-ordinates 11 local services, currently providing over 400 bed spaces in 14 refuge projects, with 19 'move on' houses. Each year, about 12,000 women seek help and about 1,000 women and 1,500 children are given emergency temporary accommodation.

All of the federations are committed to developing further effective services to meet the needs of abused women and their children, including refuge-based, after-care, floating support and outreach projects, as well as providing a wide range of resources for service providers, policy-makers and the general public, including domestic violence training initiatives and public awareness campaigns. There are various refuge providers and women's projects that work closely with the federations, but which are not full members, although Women's Aid plays a key role in disseminating information, publicity and training resources throughout the wider network of services involved in domestic violence work.

All of the Women's Aid federations have a national office employing national staff. They offer information, resources, advice and support to local domestic violence services, to statutory and voluntary agencies, and to the public. Overall, they co-ordinate and support Women's Aid domestic violence services, and produce directories and guides of refuge-based and outreach services, newsletters, good practice advice, codes of practice, briefing papers and many other publications. They also provide an extensive range of posters and leaflets on domestic violence, resource materials, professional refuge and outreach development services, and national publicity on domestic violence issues. The national federations conduct advocacy and campaigning. For example, Women's Aid in England has recently conducted a wide-ranging campaign on domestic violence and health. Key campaigns in the past include 'Families without Fear' in 1998 and 'A Future without Fear' to improve co-ordinated government policy on domestic violence. The federations also provide extensive training services and training programmes, and engage in multi-agency liaison, providing a strategic focus for partnership working.

Women's Aid in England, for instance, lobbies for relevant policy and legislative changes, provides information, research and public education, and delivers training and consultancy. The federation has a powerful influence on government, consulting with, and advising, government bodies. It chairs the Women's National Commission Violence against Women Sub-Committee and both services and works closely with the All-Party Parliamentary Group on Domestic Violence and a variety of ministers and MPs. Recent consultation work conducted includes responses to the 'Every Child Matters' green paper, the government papers on restorative justice and on parental separation, the Law Commission consultative paper on partial defences to murder, and 'Safety and Justice', the government's domestic violence consultation paper, which preceded the Domestic Violence, Crime and Victims Act. Women's Aid campaigned for amendments to the preceding bill and took a leading role in the process, along with other women's organizations, as we describe later.

It also conducts research projects (for example, on domestic violence and mental health) and has carried out an innovative consultation with domestic violence survivors over the Internet, named 'WomenSpeak'. A recent Women's Aid initiative has been the production and publication of a quarterly domestic violence journal, *Safe*, which provides up-to-date information on policy changes and the latest research. National commitments also include servicing and policy work on behalf of the children of abused women and on housing issues. Women's Aid runs the 24-hour Women's Aid National Helpline, now operated jointly with Refuge, and has received some government funding for this and for setting up an online referral system (although the funding does not cover all the running expenses). In 2004, the Helpline received 251,000 calls but, due to inadequate funding, could respond to only 74,000 of them. The other federations also run helplines, usually for limited times each day, but Scottish Women's Aid has run a 24-hour helpline for a finite period, and Northern Ireland has had a helpline for many years. A Women and Girls network helpline also now exists, although not run by Women's Aid.

Thus, Women's Aid, in partnership with the UK-wide network of local domestic violence services, has had a vital role over the last 30 years in ensuring that the interests of abused women and children are effectively represented, and in working to change the inadequacies of legal, welfare and housing provision. After this long struggle, the federations are now being recognized as key experts by national and local government and are able to play a significant role in domestic violence policy-making across the board in the interests of women and children experiencing domestic violence.

How do refuge-based domestic violence services work in practice?

The domestic violence services provided by Women's Aid and associated organizations aim to provide support, advocacy and safe houses for women and children escaping domestic violence. Women's Aid services include a wide variety of support initiatives, often conducted jointly with other organizations and extending far beyond refuge provision on its own. For example, there is now a key role for women's services and domestic violence specialist provision in developing and providing inter-agency support and awareness-raising projects. Importantly, this role extends beyond service provision into the policy and strategic planning realm. Women's Aid and domestic violence services take an increasing role in multi-agency initiatives and partnership approaches to domestic violence on the strategic level across localities.

Local domestic violence services, including refuge services, exist in most towns and cities throughout the UK and in some country areas as well. Their addresses and telephone numbers are kept confidential in order to protect the women and children living in them. However, social workers and the police know where they are, and many have special public contact numbers. Various agencies including social and health services and the police refer women to Women's Aid services – although women can also refer themselves in many cases. No Women's Aid refuge service will turn a woman away without help and without assisting her and any children she has with her to find somewhere safe to go. Women are also referred from one service to another, since they very often have to move around the country, and the 'UK Refuges On Line' referral system has now been set up using the Internet.

In order to be safe, women and children may have to move far away from home and they may also have to move on to another refuge service if an abusive partner discovers where they are, and starts to harass them. Violent men often try hard to find their wives or partners, and may be extremely abusive if they do. There are various disturbing examples of women being attacked and even murdered in refuges on discovery by their partners, and there is research evidence that the most dangerous period for an abused woman is often just after she leaves home. Thus domestic violence services and the refuge network work together to facilitate women and children being able to move on rapidly if they need to, and provide 24-hour contact between services when required. The national telephone helpline plays a vital role as a contact and referral point for abused women, many of whom wish to talk or seek advice or help while remaining anonymous.

In a refuge service, a woman will normally have to share a room with her children. The houses are usually full, but not dangerously overcrowded. They tend to be self-catering and the women and children are often responsible for keeping them clean. Women and children can stay for anything from one night to several months, although some Women's Aid services have a time limit for residence. Some groups operate move-on or second-stage accommodation where it is possible to live somewhat more independently and privately than may be possible in the first-stage refuge.

Most Women's Aid services are managed by voluntary management committees, which in the 1970s and 1980s were called support groups. Management members, including representatives from relevant agencies and housing associations, often put in many hours of unpaid work and commitment to manage the organization and to assist it to function smoothly and effectively. Domestic violence services may draw on the supply of trained volunteer workers, but also employ a range of professional workers. Most employ support staff, for example, who offer support and assistance to women living in the refuge or using the services offered. These workers engage in advocacy work on behalf of abused women and children with other agencies and provide information as to what options each woman has open to her. They assist women to claim benefits, apply for housing and pursue legal remedies. They also provide advice and information, and often operate a telephone helpline as well. In addition, they offer skilled emotional support. Women using domestic violence services have frequently been physically and psychologically traumatized and have left behind not only their male partners, but also their communities, families, friends and possessions. They are often in the most severe crisis of their lives and may be extremely distressed. Support staff, together with other women living in the refuge or using related services, usually offer as much support as they can, and are expert at dealing with the painful experience of domestic violence.

Many Women's Aid services also employ specialist child support workers to offer children support and assistance, to provide childcare activities and facilities for creative play, and to represent children's interests. Children's workers conduct advocacy work on behalf of children experiencing domestic abuse with social services, schools and other agencies, and are committed to 'getting alongside' children in a meaningful way. The move to a refuge service can be particularly confusing and distressing. The children are likely to have lost, not only their homes, fathers, families and relatives, but also their schools, possibly their pets and toys, and, almost certainly, all their friends, whom they may never see again. Child support workers can help to give them a sense of security and can provide emotional, practical and in-depth support.

The Women's Aid Federation of England provides training for children's workers and has produced information packs and a resource manual called *Safe and Sound* on working with children in refuges, together with a *Children's Welcome Pack* for children coming into a refuge who are aged between 4 and 10 years. In 2004, it ran a 'Listening to Children' campaign in which children who had experienced domestic abuse sent postcards to ministers and MPs saying what they needed from, and thought about, domestic violence services and policy. The powerful messages given by the children were a valuable addition to their advocacy work. In 2005, Women's Aid started an innovative website especially for children experiencing domestic violence.

Increasingly in the 2000s, domestic violence services and other women's organizations and multi-agency partnerships (for example, the Cheshire Domestic Abuse Partnership) run dedicated outreach projects to provide support to women who have suffered violence but who remain living in the community. Outreach services also do community development and education work. And some groups have developed specialist outreach projects to work with black and minority ethnic women. Briefing Notes published by the Home Office in 2000 (written by Cathy Humphreys and Liz Kelly) included advice on the necessity of outreach and its key role in increasing the safety of women and children. They were followed up, in 2002, by a study, *Routes to Safety*, also by Cathy Humphreys, but together with Ravi Thiara, and funded and produced by Women's Aid in England, which emphasized the vital role of outreach and support services. Advocacy services are also now being widely promoted.

Where possible, refuge-based services also employ follow-up, after-care or resettlement workers to offer support to women and children who have left the service and found their own accommodation, or have been rehoused by the council or housing association. Leaving the communal environment of the refuge to live in a flat or house in an unknown community can be very difficult for a woman and her children. They may be facing life as a single-parent family for the first time, and may be lonely and isolated, trying to make friends and establish themselves. They are often in a completely different and unfamiliar part of the country from their home area, where they may know no one apart from the women and workers from the refuge. Children have to start new schools or playgroups, possibly for the third or fourth time if they have had to move from one refuge to another. Resettlement or follow-up workers can assist women and children with these difficult adjustments, and can provide information and act as advocates on their behalf. In some areas, they have been able to help with setting up support groups of abused women who have moved on from temporary accommodation and ended up living quite close together.

The history of refuges and women's domestic violence services

Domestic violence service provision now extends far beyond refuge provision and encompasses a wide range of service and policy interventions and projects. In the past, though, these services concentrated on setting up refuges themselves and so this section specifically concerns refuge provision in this context before services expanded and diversified.

Services and refuge organizations for women and children escaping violence have existed in the UK for only a relatively short time. However, women have attempted to put an end to domestic violence in different places, at different times and in varying ways, and it seems that women in various countries throughout the world have sometimes established safe houses for each other in previous historical periods. A very small number of safe houses for abused women and children to use as places of hiding were set up in the nineteenth century in Britain and North America, for example, and both liberal and feminist campaigners worked on the issue.

In Britain, as in most societies, women had few rights and freedoms in the past. There has been a long tradition of men chastising and punishing their wives and daughters in order to control their behaviour. In fact, chastisement of a wife has been seen historically not only as a husband's right and privilege, but as his duty. Many people know and use the common expression 'rule of thumb' in their everyday conversation. What they may not realize is that one possible origin of the expression derives from the right of a man to beat his wife with a stick, providing it was no thicker than his thumb. Over the last two centuries, this right and duty has been slowly eroded due to the efforts of campaigners, both feminist and philanthropist, and through a slow turning of moral and public opinion. In Britain, the law allowing the chastisement of wives was repealed in 1829. But it is doubtful how much difference this change made at the time.

The history of wife-beating has been well documented by Rebecca and Russell Dobash in their ground-breaking 1980 book, *Violence Against Wives*. They point out that it has traditionally been difficult to carry out the letter of the law where domestic matters are concerned. There has been a longstanding principle of law enforcement, dating from as long ago as Roman times, which says that law-enforcers should not interfere in domestic disputes. The effectiveness of legal sanctions against wife assault has always been eroded or sabotaged by the power and control that men had – and still have – over their wives or partners.

The twentieth century brought considerable improvements in women's rights and in public attitudes. However, women continued to be beaten, abused, sexually violated and subjected to a seemingly unending range of maltreatment and violence. With the evolution of a moral climate less accepting of wife-beating (although reflecting a social system reluctant to do much about it), the abuse gradually became more hidden. People did not talk openly about it. And it was often the woman rather than the man who was gossiped about behind hands and disgraced if the truth came out. Those who remember the 1940s and 1950s can recall the moral censure, the embarrassment, the shame and the almost total silence about domestic violence – perhaps more marked among the middle class, but firmly there across classes and social boundaries nevertheless. A small 1996 book, *The Silenced Pain*, described a research study on domestic violence in the UK between 1945 and 1970. The women interviewed were reluctant to talk, often having endured very many years of domestic violence, with no help from anyone. As they reached the end of their lives, these women remained deeply saddened and silent about the damaging effects of the violence they had experienced in the 1950s and 1960s when they just had to keep quiet and put up with it, with few possibilities of escape.

Until the most recent wave of the women's movement in the late 1960s and early 1970s, women suffering domestic violence had no one to turn to. They had nowhere to escape to, no one to talk to, no one to help them, except perhaps each other. Women have always found support and drawn strength from other women. But there were no refuge organizations, no support and advice services, no housing alternatives, no counselling centres, no good practice guidelines, no publicity outlets or media coverage, not much in the way of legal remedies, and very little help from the police, who have traditionally regarded a man's home as indisputably his castle. Divorce was uncommon and frowned upon; women in violent marriages quite simply had no way out.

Public attitudes began to change in the 1960s, and towards the end of the decade the Women's Liberation movement started. From it stemmed the movement against domestic violence and the development of Women's Aid, leading to the provision of women's services, campaigns and attention from other agencies. The connection is a quite straightforward one, though it is sometimes overlooked or forgotten today. A wide range of services, projects and initiatives now exist throughout the UK. They are inadequately funded and their distribution is still patchy – but they are there. Almost all of these services derive in one way or another from the well-spring of the women's movement.

Women's Liberation in the 1960s and 1970s was characterized by political activity, demonstrations and active campaigns, and by a new radical analysis of the position of women in society, linking personal and political issues. It attempted to build a new politics for a new future for women. Its basic building block was the small consciousness-raising group in which women (mainly white in the first stages, and often, but by no means solely, middle-class) met together to share their lives and experiences and to build a grass-roots political analysis of male domination and female subordination.

Groups and campaigns started up in many towns and cities, some connected in the UK to the longstanding socialist movement, and often with acknowledged or unconscious links to national liberation struggles in the Third World and to the New Left movements in North America and continental Europe – the Black Liberation movement, the anti-Vietnam War struggle, the worldwide student rebellions and the oppositional 'counter-culture' of the time. These were heady days which transformed the lives of many who were part of them.

By the early 1970s, the consciousness-raising and the rapidly mushrooming analysis and understanding of women's oppression had started to encompass the subject of male violence in the home. It began when women who had suffered violence started coming to the new women's centres requesting help and the women working in them did not know what to suggest. Meetings and political actions began to be held about the issue, involving women who had experienced violence and others who had not. Out of these meetings came the idea of setting up safe houses or refuges to which women who had suffered violence could escape, and from which they could perhaps begin to construct new lives, free of violence.

The idea was more or less a new one. Apart from the few precedents that we have noted and about which little is known, it had rarely been done before. However, we do know that, whenever refuge services for women are established in societies dominated by men, it seems to be a challenge to the status quo, and this was also the case in the UK in the 1970s. The initiative confronted in a concrete and undeniable way men's rights and power within the family, the heart and bedrock of society. Women were taking action to leave violent marriages and partnerships, often without warning, to live with groups of other women in safe houses run by women. In a small but significant way, the very fabric of sexual politics was being challenged.

The first refuge of the period was set up by a women's group known as Chiswick Women's Aid, whose spokesperson was Erin Pizzey. Public consciousness was moved in a profound way by the media publicity and hype surrounding Chiswick – so much so that even today, 30 years later, references to the original Chiswick Women's Aid refuge sometimes occur in media coverage of domestic violence. In fact, however, refuge organizations were more or less simultaneously being fought for and established up and down the country, and some may have opened before Chiswick. It was not long before Erin Pizzey, whom the Dobashes have called 'the visible moral entrepreneur launching the issue', had quarrelled with the rest of the Women's Aid movement over her views as to the cause of the violence, which she developed along the lines that some women are 'violence-prone', and her antipathy to collective and co-operative ways of working. Chiswick Women's Aid split away from the rest of Women's Aid to go it alone – a situation that remains to this day, although its successor, Chiswick Family Rescue, relaunched in 1993 as Refuge, has repudiated Pizzey's more women-blaming perspectives on male abuse and has attempted to build wide-ranging services with the support of, among others, the late Diana, Princess of Wales and the prime minister's wife, Cherie Blair. These days, however, Women's Aid and Refuge (which is a member of the Women's Aid Federation in England) attempt to collaborate and to work jointly together on specific projects.

It is hard now, in a decade comparatively lacking in political action, to visualize the speed of almost daily change that characterized the Women's Aid movement and the wider Women's Liberation movement of the early 1970s. Women put much energy, work and commitment into trying to get refuge services set up, often pitting themselves against local resistance and opposition. More than 40 refuge organizations had come into being by 1974, with new ones being set up all the time.

As well as providing safe and secure accommodation for women and children escaping violence in the home, the new Women's Aid groups campaigned about and publicized the issue of domestic violence. In 1973–4, they established two refuge federations, the National Women's

Aid Federation (NWAF) for England, Wales and Northern Ireland, and Scottish Women's Aid for Scotland. (It was in fact at one of the very first conferences of NWAF that the split with Chiswick Women's Aid was dramatically finalized.) By 1975, more than 80 groups were part of NWAF alone. The federations co-ordinated local groups and mounted national campaigns around domestic violence. In 1978, to encourage regional autonomy further, NWAF divided into three separate federations, Northern Ireland Women's Aid, Welsh Women's Aid and the Women's Aid Federation of England (now known simply as Women's Aid).

Throughout the UK as a whole, local groups worked tirelessly on a volunteer basis, setting up more and more domestic violence services for women and children, usually with no funding at all. Many used short-life properties to establish refuges with very little in the way of facilities. As a result, conditions were often poor. All of the houses were continually overwhelmed with women and children needing refuge space. The extent of the need was painfully clear. The new projects filled up as fast as they opened, but everyone involved knew that this was merely the tip of the iceberg of domestic violence. In 1975, a government Select Committee on Violence in Marriage (set up due to the surge of interest in and publicity about the subject) recommended that refuges should be established throughout the country to provide an initial target of one family place per 10,000 of the population. This remains the aim today, even though it is widely recognized as itself an inadequate target. Thirty years later, we have only managed to reach a position of providing one half of those places. Although refuge provision is not the only support available now and related services have multiplied, the tip of the iceberg remains just that.

From the first national conferences until the present time, the Women's Aid movement has had to struggle with dilemmas and contradictions. A major issue from the beginning was how much an organization could be simultaneously both a political campaigning body and a provider of services to abused women. There is plenty of left-wing literature saying it cannot be done, as well as right-wing opinion saying it should not be attempted. Providing services almost automatically entails a degree of negotiation with the establishment, in order among other things to secure funding. This is likely to be unacceptable to many of those in a campaigning movement who are dedicated to opposition, resistance and political action. In the Women's Aid movement of the 1970s, the debate crystallized around how to provide sensitive, independent services to meet the needs of women and children, while obtaining much-needed funding through central and local government bodies. The federations attracted some grant-aid more or less from their inception, and by the end of the decade many Women's Aid groups had some sort of funding, although this was, without exception, inadequate and precarious.

Throughout the late 1970s and early 1980s, the Women's Aid movement continued to develop services for women and children. More and more groups obtained properties and funding from official government bodies and programmes. Some examples were the (long since replaced) Urban Programme, local authority housing and social services committees, and housing association special projects and joint funding schemes. All the Women's Aid federations campaigned hard (in conjunction with other women's organizations) on behalf of women and children escaping domestic violence. Some of this campaigning energy was directed towards the legislature. Women's Aid was instrumental in the drafting of various pieces of legislation, such as the Domestic Violence and Matrimonial Proceedings Act 1976, the Domestic Violence and Magistrates' Courts Act 1978, and the Housing (Homeless Persons) Act 1977, now much modified by new laws as discussed later.

The Women's Aid federations have continued this work in the 1990s and 2000s, representing and co-ordinating the growing network of domestic violence services, and lobbying and campaigning for legal and policy measures and for comprehensive provision to meet the needs of abused women and children. None of the federations has centralized management structures that directly control local groups. Affiliated organizations agree to accept certain conditions and principles but remain autonomous. The federations all have regional structures of different kinds and hold annual member conferences. In 1995, Women's Aid in England restructured its organization, changing from regional representation to targeted and nationally based women's electoral colleges, and setting up a management Women's Aid Council. National advocacy work, training, consultancy, lobbying and service provision are co-ordinated by the national staff in all the federations, together with national working groups. Women's Aid has now moved from a collective to a hierarchical structure with a director and a variety of policy, administrative, publicity, fund-raising, child support and housing posts.

Women's Aid as a whole continues to function as an independent advocacy agency and service provider outside the statutory social services. In this deliberate pursuit of political autonomy, it has been more successful than women's domestic violence movements in some other countries. Some shelters in North America, for example, have become closely associated with conventional social service agencies, and this has tended to result in workers becoming completely 'professionalized' and in a loss, in some but not all cases, of grass-roots feminist practice and principles. In some countries, refuge or shelter projects, where they exist at all, are run by official government agencies or under the auspices of religious groupings. In the UK, however, the domestic violence movement retains a specifically feminist identity as a national network of women committed to self-determination and relatively independent of both religion and the state. Although not, of course, without its fair share of problems and internal disagreement, this movement can in some ways act as a challenge for women in various countries where no independent women-run services exist. And it can learn from countries where policies against domestic violence and services for abused women and children are better developed.

Beliefs, principles and policies

In general, Women's Aid services are based on the principles of the value of mutual support, empowerment and the central importance of the perspectives and views of abused women and children. The work and standards of domestic violence services affiliated to the four federations are bound by policy statements and codes of good practice. Overall, the Women's Aid approach is: to believe women and children and to make their safety a priority; to support and empower women to take control of their own lives; to recognize and care for the needs of children affected by violence; to challenge the disadvantage and social exclusion caused by such violence; and to reflect diversity and promote equal opportunities and anti-discriminatory practices. As well as its wider role working at the strategic level with government and providing national training and publicity resources, Women's Aid has two unique functions in terms specifically of prevention work with women and children:

- to give abused women and children a voice in policy and practice
- to support, resource, inform and train domestic violence refuge and outreach staff to support abused women and children survivors in order to rebuild their lives

The values and principles of Women's Aid underlie all the work of the domestic violence network and of many other services provided for women experiencing domestic violence and their children. All of these services recognize that domestic violence is a violation of women and children's human rights, that it is related to power and control in relationships and that it is rooted in the historic status of women. They also recognize that women and children have a right to live free from violence and that society has a duty to defend this right. Self-help, self-determination and empowerment are the underlying important principles. They have always formed the foundation stones of what the Women's Aid movement stands for. What, however, do they mean?

Self-help for women means what it says – women helping themselves and other women to establish independent services to combat male violence. Empowerment has become a popular word in the last few years. It came mainly from the political left wing originally, but now the political right wing is using it as well. The notion has also been adopted by some establishment agencies. It is currently heard quite a lot in social work circles: for example, in relation to social work service users. Good social work practice is now seen to consist of empowering people – although presumably such empowerment only goes so far, since social workers also have to act as social controllers, as in many cases of child protection. One of the aims of empowerment, however, is that those who are empowered might choose to become resistant to the status quo, or might even try to challenge those who have power. The women's movement has been developing the idea for years as a way of resisting male control and power over women, and also as a means to oppose other sorts of discrimination on the grounds, for example, of race and ethnicity or social class.

Empowerment for abused women means becoming more powerful on a personal and psychological level in order to develop the strength and emotional resources to break away from or to change violent relationships, if they choose to. Importantly, it also means having the economic and other resources to do so, which is why the provision of adequate financial support through the benefits system and access to permanent housing options is so important for abused women and children. Empowerment also means women being able to help each other in a collaborative way in refuges and support groups to deal with violent relationships and to embark on violence-free lives. One of the basic tenets of refuge-based and support services has always been that women can assist each other to grow strong.

Like empowerment, self-determination is a term that has usually found its home in left-wing and feminist social movements, but which is often used these days by the political right as well. As a result it can lose its political edge. National liberation movements in colonized or occupied countries and people living under oppressive conditions commonly use the concept as a principle of organization. At its most basic level, it means that people should be able to determine their own lives and their own futures. For women who have been in abusive relationships with men, self-determination means taking control back from the abuser, and gaining self-esteem, self-confidence and the financial, material and emotional resources to control their own lives, rather than living under the influence or control of a violent man.

Over the last 30 years, the domestic violence network has developed various ways of putting empowerment, self-help and self-determination into action, of working out some practical 'how-tos', rather than allowing these principles to remain in the realm of lofty rhetoric. First and foremost, refuge-based and support services are empowering by their very existence. Women facing violence in their homes find it strengthening just knowing that there is somewhere to escape to, that there is somewhere where they will be given help and support. It can never be emphasized enough just how much the provision of refuge services has transformed the lives of abused women and their children. Having options means having a bit more power and control, and having a choice rather than being trapped. It means knowing that you are not alone. Women's Aid operates an 'open door' policy, which means that no woman or child needing refuge or support will be turned away without assistance. Women's Aid services tend not to require women to offer proof of the violence and abuse that they have experienced. A woman's word is usually enough.

Within a domestic violence service or a women's support group, the main way in which empowerment works is through the help and sustenance that both women and children can draw from each other, by offering mutual help and support and by sharing similar experiences. Finding out that other women and children have been through the same thing, that you are accepted and respected despite everything that has happened – that everyone is in the same boat and there is even the possibility of rowing that boat somewhere – these seemingly simple realizations are crucial. Women using domestic violence support or refuge services may share life together on a daily basis and frequently also share the anger and pain that they may be experiencing, which at best can assist them to become stronger both individually and collectively. Anyone who has lived or worked in a domestic violence refuge service can attest to this. Of course, it does not happen that way all the time. Women using domestic violence services, like anyone else, can behave badly towards each other and there can be rows and disputes in refuges, often caused by the lack of privacy. But it happens often enough to confirm the belief that women sharing together at their time of greatest crisis can be empowered by the experience.

A women-only organization

Women's Aid is an organization of women working with women for women. Women in general, and women who have suffered violence at the hands of men in particular, may be intimidated by the presence of men. And many women attest to how men can often try to take over, to dominate in mixed situations, to speak on women's behalf – often without even realizing it. For abused women, it can be particularly recuperative to leave these problems behind. Most important of all, women who are homeless due to male violence need to feel safe and secure. They may need to know that they are far removed from male aggression in order to have the space to start to take control of their own lives, to begin the process of recovery. Women living in refuge organizations who have previously been facing domestic violence isolated and alone often say how wonderful it is to find out that there are other women who will help them, that women can stand firm together. For these various reasons, it is empowering in itself that there are no men involved in Women's Aid groups affiliated to the federations.

At the beginning of the Women's Aid movement, some refuge organizations employed committed anti-sexist men as childcare workers to act as models (particularly perhaps for the boys) of how men can be gentle, non-violent and involved in looking after children. But in the late 1970s, the decision was made to become a women only organization and to affirm the ability of women together to oppose male violence. The 'no men rule' has been and continues to be a strategy of empowerment. Women attending gatherings of women who have suffered domestic violence are often profoundly moved by the strength of women together. However, some general domestic violence services have men on their management committees or employ male workers, and a few refuge-based or support organizations for black women feel that, because of the effects of racism, they need to work in conjunction with black men.

Autonomy and equality

While accepting common principles, each Women's Aid service is an independent and autonomous organization. Many domestic violence organizations are committed to developing participative management structures and, in the past, most aimed to work as overall collectives. This is a tall order in a society dominated by hierarchies, but it is an empowering way to work. Previously the members of staff frequently worked together in an equal, co-operative team, although these days the majority of groups employ project managers, directors or co-ordinators, and workers may have specialized roles and responsibilities. Nevertheless, staff usually try to work as equally as possible with each other and with women using the services provided.

One of the main policies of the Women's Aid network is to strive to pursue equal opportunities for all. Equality of opportunity in employment and service provision became a popular subject in the late 1980s and early 1990s, and many employers now claim that they are equal opportunity employers – a large percentage of local authorities, for example. While this claim is often accompanied by little concrete action, Women's Aid, on the other hand, is actively committed to equal opportunities and to combating oppression and exploitation of all types. This means that the federations and the individual member groups within them strive not to discriminate against any woman on the grounds of class, race, disability, age or sexuality. Refuge-based and outreach services are expected to develop equal opportunities policies and monitoring processes to cover the employment of workers, the recruitment of volunteers, the operation of the management committee, and the services offered to residents and to other women seeking advice.

In addition, Women's Aid attempts to work in a way that is anti-discriminatory. Domestic violence services often take an active role in combating prejudice and injustice. The federations expect member organizations to initiate regular discussion about equal opportunities issues and to provide appropriate training and services for both women residents and workers – for example, anti-racism and disability awareness training. These are hard matters to take on, however, and involve struggle and debate within many refuge-based and Women's Aid organizations.

In common with the rest of the early women's movement, Women's Aid was slow to take up issues of racism initially, although never as slow as is sometimes now made out. Many women's groups took a strong anti-racist line from the beginning. Nevertheless, black women were little integrated at the time. Even now, some domestic violence services are only just beginning to consider racism. Partly as a result of these failures, a few black and minority ethnic women's groups have made the strategic decision to organize separate provision. However, Women's Aid as a whole now operates anti-racist policies, and many refuge and support services previously dominated by white women have taken positive action on racism and have profoundly challenged their own previous practices.

Both inside and outside Women's Aid, black and minority ethnic women have set up dedicated projects and refuge services. Many of these are specifically for South Asian women (including young women), and are organized into a loose-knit Asian women's refuge network. These refuge projects are run and managed by Asian women, and provide safe accommodation, free of racism, specifically designed to meet the needs of women of South Asian heritage who have suffered domestic violence and of their children. An innovative national Asian women's organization, Imkaan, now provides training, support and research to assist the Asian women's domestic violence service network nationally, working with important black and minority ethnic women's organizations such as Southall Black Sisters, Newham Asian Women's Project and Brent Asian Women's Resource Centre, all of which also liaise closely with Women's Aid.

Throughout the UK, various other refuge services now exist either for black women in general or for black women from specific communities (for example, African or African-Caribbean projects), for women from other minority ethnic heritages, including Jewish, Turkish and Latin American women, and for some religious groupings, such as Muslim women. But there is not enough of any on them. Various refuge studies found in the past that, at least in London and probably throughout the country, services for black women were significantly underresourced compared with others. This appeared to be a direct example of institutionalized racism in the provision of funding. It remains the case today, even though some progressively minded housing associations and other bodies have made attempts to address this shortfall.

The Hidden Struggle, Amina Mama's influential book on violence against black women in the home (published in 1989 and 1996), explains how the egalitarian nature of women's refuge services frequently means that one of the main ways in which racism is displayed is at the level of interpersonal conflict. Although clear anti-racist policies (which include the provision of anti-racism training) now exist in refuge-based and outreach organizations, it may sometimes be the case that white workers are insufficiently committed and are ineffectual in challenging racism among both white residents and themselves. This failure can undermine the safety and security of black residents. Mama suggested that the Women's Aid federations must continue to develop effective ways of challenging racism, of providing on-going anti-racism training for all white residents and workers, of extending and monitoring their anti-racist policies, and of translating the policies into effective action – which is what Women's Aid is consistently trying to do. Good practice in this area has been gradually growing over the years.

In the past, black women have not been alone in mounting challenges and confrontations about questions of discrimination. Lesbians, working-class women and to a lesser extent women with disabilities have also challenged the domestic violence service network to improve its practice. These challenges have led to the adoption of some relevant policies by Women's Aid – for example, on heterosexism and anti-lesbianism. 'Heterosexism' refers to the way in which heterosexuality is upheld throughout society as the only true and real sexuality. Consequently, lesbians and gay men often experience disadvantage, exclusion, harassment and prejudice, even today, as part and parcel of the social structure. Refuge-based services are expected to confront anti-lesbian and heterosexist attitudes and actions both within their refuges and their group, and in society as a whole when they can. Women's Aid has produced training materials on lesbian issues and research into lesbian domestic violence is in process.

Access to refuge services remains inadequate for women with disabilities, due partly to the general problem of low funding throughout the sector, and sometimes to a lack of commitment to the issue. The situation is now improving substantially in line with the Disability Discrimination Act, as more refuge organizations take up the matter and some obtain purpose- built, fully accessible accommodation. Welsh Women's Aid, for example, has a policy of developing at least one family space in a refuge per county which is fully accessible for women with disabilities or physical injury. Women's Aid in England has also taken specific initiatives, and individual refuge organizations have developed policies, services, support networks and publicity information on disability. Women's Aid has conducted research on disabled women's needs, as have various local authorities and women's projects.

They also conducted a recent survey on services for women with mental health special needs who experience domestic violence. There are few domestic violence services which can always accept women in this situation (although they will always refer on), since they often have neither the staffing provision nor necessarily the appropriate skills. Due to the lack of overall mental health provision, women experiencing mental health difficulties quite often get referred inappropriately to general refuge providers without any information being given about their additional needs. This is also the case for women with substance misuse, drug or alcohol problems, whom domestic violence organizations are not normally equipped to assist. A recent project, named the Stella Project, has developed a 'toolkit' for working with both victims and perpetrators in this situation, and conferences and discussions on the issue began to be held in the early 2000s.

The Women's Aid federations, and perhaps Welsh Women's Aid in particular, attempt to highlight the difficult position faced by women experiencing domestic violence in rural areas. Women often live in isolated communities where everyone knows each other. In such a situation, escape can be virtually impossible. The distances involved in rural communities and the lack of public transport and of information and support services mean that rural women are in a particularly vulnerable position. The strategy of Welsh Women's Aid and of the other Women's Aid federations is to attempt to improve service provision, to help to organize transport, and to make information available in isolated communities. Women from rural areas, interviewed by ourselves for a recent study, have talked about how empowering they found it when they gained access to such information, after years of thinking that there was no way out, and when they were assisted to make use of the services available in other areas. Some rural areas have now developed specialist support outreach projects, so it is worth checking out what provision is available.

Class issues can reveal themselves starkly in refuge accommodation where most of the women may be working class, and some of the staff and voluntary management members may be from middle-class backgrounds. Women's Aid has always been committed to breaking down class barriers, although this endeavour has sometimes led to conflict and difficulty. In practical ways, though, Women's Aid services have routinely attempted to challenge discrimination on the grounds of differing educational experiences and class backgrounds.

Employment strategies and working practices

The Women's Aid network has always held that it is women who have suffered violence who are the experts on the experience, rather than professionally qualified social workers or therapists. In developing policy, therefore, the views of abused women are sought as a matter of principle. In the past, women who live in refuge accommodation have had the opportunity to be full members of the group, along with workers and management committee members. However, this has now changed in many groups because of the increasing complexity of funding and monitoring arrangements. While ex-residents may well contribute to decision-making (often after a 'breathing period' of six months or so), current residents are now normally excluded.

Women who have lived in refuge services or who have experienced domestic violence have been encouraged in the past to apply for refuge jobs. Many Women's Aid groups have considered relevant life experience to be of great value in choosing workers, while also valuing specific skills, qualifications and training. But again, this commitment has lessened in recent years with the deliberate employment of more highly qualified staff. A recent research study in the Economic and Social Research Council's Violence Research Programme, led by the Violence Against Women Research Group at Bristol and conducted jointly with the Centre for the Study of Safety and Wellbeing at the University of Warwick, looked at how much the views of domestic violence survivors and of women using refuge services were heard by service providers and by Women's Aid groups. While the latter remain the agencies that consult the most, there was still a telling decrease in the extent to which refuge residents could make decisions and influence the organization as a whole, a retraction from policies that were previously more or less universal throughout the domestic violence movement.

In recent years, domestic violence services have become far more professional with the development of detailed financial accountability to funders, training programmes for workers, performance monitoring, best practice strategies and more efficient management methods. Codes of good practice and the development of detailed policies, for example on child protection, have been developed and the federations can provide advice on these policy and practice issues.

Empowering employment strategies for women who have experienced violence do still exist, though, and there has been the development of support and training opportunities for survivors of violence in some localities. These include, for example, national vocational qualifications (NVQs) in domestic violence work and formally accredited training to qualify participants to work in practice with women and children experiencing abuse. In addition, some women without educational qualifications or job experience who have escaped violence and become Women's Aid workers have then undertaken vocational training or degree courses, or developed successful new careers.

The working practices of project staff also reflect the overall commitment to self-determination and empowerment. Women seeking shelter, support and advice from Women's Aid are encouraged to make their own decisions, to take control of their own lives, and to determine their own futures, whether this involves starting a new life elsewhere or returning home. On a practical level, workers attempt to ensure that women and children have access to the best possible services and resources. On an emotional level, women have a chance to talk about their experiences and their feelings, and to be taken seriously, sometimes for the first time in their lives. Recent research with Women's Aid in England, conducted by Hilary Abrahams and named *A Long Hard Road To Go By*, is soon to be published and shows how important this support is. Women's Aid services consciously oppose the view that male violence towards women is the fault of the woman experiencing the violence, or that blame can be equally shared between the man and the woman. Such notions are empowering and strengthening for the women concerned. Two violence survivors living in refuge accommodation whom we interviewed put it this way:

> The advantage of getting support from the workers and living with other women is that you give each other strength. You know, why it all went on, you talk about all the experiences you've been through. And you find that it wasn't you, it wasn't you. That it was the men who had the problems really. That it wasn't the women.

> I'm really grateful because I can be who I want to be here. All the workers and the volunteers are really supportive. They do a lot for you and they build you up. They encourage you to make your own decisions and decide what you want to do. There is no pressure on you. You learn to be strong here . . . You need support and you need to know that it's not your fault. While you're here, you get strong.

Women's domestic violence services usually have a policy of trying at all times to treat abused women and children non-judgementally and with respect, and of making sure that other agencies do the same. They counter the myths about domestic violence, and publicize the issue as much as they can, despite, often, extremely limited resources and woman-power. Domestic violence refuge-based and service staff deliberately 'interrupt' views expressed by other agencies which may pathologize women who have suffered violence, or which are blaming, judgemental or patronizing. Nevertheless, staff can sometimes be over-protective of 'their' women or succumb to over-work and stress due to the painful nature of the work.

The stated commitment of Women's Aid to combat discrimination against children, as well as against women, means that services believe in self-determination and empowerment for children as well as for women. In the Women's Aid view, children are not in general given much control over their own lives. They are frequently ignored, patronized, lied to, betrayed and 'spoken on behalf of'. As a conscious commitment, Women's Aid services try to combat this sort of general discrimination. It is expected that children using refuge accommodation will be treated with respect and equality, and the federations operate a comprehensive 'no smacking policy' with training available and support offered on non-violent alternatives. Child support workers also offer support to mothers on issues that affect their children, and are committed to caring for the children's emotional, developmental and educational needs. They engage in anti-discriminatory work, encouraging anti-racism among children and working with boys and girls in different ways to meet their different needs and to counter the effects of sexism. Many groups hold special children's meetings.

There is now a wide network of domestic violence services providing a variety of advocacy, outreach and support projects and partnerships between agencies in the community, as we have noted, within which the need for specific outreach for women and children from minority ethnic and other communities has been strongly identified. Such wider outreach services can play a vital role in enabling a woman to deal with the situation of abuse and violence that she is facing. Support groups, drop-in centres, follow-up support for women who have left refuges, and community projects for women survivors of violence and their children can also be empowering.

Finally, building international co-operation, and supporting other political struggles on both the international and the national stage, can assist self-determination. International conferences are frequent these days, so that activists and practitioners from different countries can meet together to work on issues related to violence against women. Recently, international conferences have been held by Women's Aid and by local authorities on positive policing and criminal justice responses, on domestic violence courts, multi-agency approaches in other countries, and so on. Women's Aid in England is currently engaged in a collaboration with similar projects in Russia, international research in Europe funded by the European Daphne initiative has been conducted, and many international partnerships now exist (some funded through the British Council). Our own research group, for example, is working with partners in China, India and several African countries.

Inadequate resources

While Women's Aid, the network of services which it co-ordinates, and the activist movement against domestic violence do their best to provide responsive and empowering services for abused women and their children, the whole enterprise has always been hampered by inadequate funding and poor resources. The Women's Aid federations would like to see a commitment from the British government to the specialist, systematic financing of the diverse domestic violence services that are needed and to the improvement of standards across the board. This would include the provision of funding not only for refuge services, but also for the linked advocacy, support and children's services that are essential to meet the needs of women who have suffered violence and their children.

The new Supporting People programme, which came into effect in 2003, was broadly welcomed by Women's Aid and provides basic funding for refuge-based support work. Gratifyingly, it also funds floating support and outreach. However, children's workers are not included, meaning that this already under-funded part of the service is now even more under-funded. So domestic violence services have to raise separate moneys for this purpose, resulting in twice the work. Such bureaucratic demands are made worse because the procedures for applying for Supporting People funding have been very complex so far. They have taken an enormous amount of worker time in the last few years which could otherwise have been spent supporting women and children. The UK government recently announced a fund of £18.8 million for refuge provision, which was a welcome drop in the ocean. However, it is limited to capital funding. An improved national funding strategy for domestic violence services as a whole to take on these issues would be welcome. This would need to include further specialist refuge and outreach provision and other services for black and other ethnic minority women.

While Supporting People has improved the situation, refuge and other services for women and children (particularly those responding to rape) disappear regularly as funding applications fail or grants are cut. Workers are still often underpaid and chronically overworked. Many regularly work greatly in excess of their official working hours. Some refuge accommodation is now purpose-built or adapted, but some remains in under-equipped housing.

All of this could be avoided by proper resourcing that takes into account the specific problems associated with domestic violence work, and by the political will to do something really comprehensive about it. Government is currently putting in place some more comprehensive new strategies, programmes and legislative changes (see Chapters 5 and 8), and policy and practice changes are taking place in many agencies, such as the police and various local authorities, to improve responses to women and their children who suffer abuse. However, without the provision of sufficient, good-standard local domestic violence services, including refuge-based accommodation and linked support, after-care, children's and outreach provision provided by dedicated and specialized women's services, these changes will run aground.

At present, all specialist domestic violence accommodation services have many times more women wanting to move in than they can accommodate. Some cannot assist more than half the women, most with dependent children, who are referred to them in desperate need of emergency accommodation. Despite current improvements and a stated government commitment, in a male-dominated world, the traumas experienced by women and children fleeing male violence still seem to have low priority.

3
Why does domestic violence happen? Attitudes and explanations

Attitudes towards domestic violence and explanations of why it happens are critical in deciding what kind of support women will get from family, friends and neighbours, and from state and voluntary agencies. This chapter is not designed to explain complex and sophisticated theoretical stances; rather it is concerned with how explanations of domestic violence relate to the way in which different agencies approach it.

Traditional attitudes

In the past, the overriding attitude to domestic violence was the belief that it is a private affair between husband and wife, and that nobody should interfere unless it is happening constantly and causing serious and visible injury to the woman or, more importantly, injury to the children. This attitude went along with reactions that tended to excuse the violence and blame the woman. Traditionally, if people were concerned at all about the man's violent behaviour, they would often put it down to drink. In the past, this was the most common explanation favoured by professionals – as found, for example, in a study called *Marital Violence* by Margaret Borkowski, Mervyn Murch and Val Walker in the early 1980s. Yet from the same time period, the Scottish study by the Dobashes for their 1980 book *Violence Against Wives* found that alcohol was a factor in only 25 per cent of the relationships studied, and was important in only a very few cases. However, such an explanation meant that there was no need to ask any further questions about why the violence happened. People might then ask, 'Why doesn't she leave?' or 'Why does she put up with it?', or else they would see treating the alcohol dependency of the man as the key issue. These days, of course, the more dominant belief is that, while alcohol undoubtedly aggravates situations of domestic violence sometimes very severely, it cannot be seen as the cause of the violence in the first place.

Often in the past, the explanations that the man gave for his violence would be accepted. He might say he was jealous because he thought the woman was paying attention to other men. His other 'reasons' could include: 'She spent too much time outside the home, with her family or her friends.' 'She was a bad housekeeper.' 'She spent too much of my money.' 'She was too independent.' 'She answered back.' 'She nagged me.' 'She wouldn't have sex with me.' 'She didn't control the children properly.' Professionals might add that she tried to be too 'controlling' or, the complete opposite, that she was too timid and invited aggression because of her passivity. Since women often feel that the violence is their fault, such attitudes tended to intensify the guilt that they already experienced.

A group of women writing an account of their own experiences as survivors of domestic violence, *Breaking Through*, listed a number of these explanations and commented: 'Explanations that blame the woman go on and on. Sometimes they are the excuses given by the man for his behaviour, sometimes they are explanations given by perfectly "well meaning" people – doctors, social workers, friends, family.' These explanations are part of what women are up against when they are trying to survive domestic violence or to escape it. So we need to look at why it is that domestic violence has traditionally been either taken for granted or blamed on women.

One of the most important reasons is that, as we saw in Chapter 1, men were historically given the right in law to discipline their wives, children and servants. So physical punishment of a wife was acceptable provided that it was not 'excessive'. In their book *Women and the Law*, Susan Atkins and Brenda Hoggett gave a history of what they call 'the breadwinner's legal authority', which makes it clear that these attitudes persisted in the courts into the 1980s, as they still do to a lesser extent today.

Violent men *still* believe in their right to control their wives and partners, and so probably do many, although, hopefully, a diminishing proportion of men who are not themselves violent. Such attitudes on the part of violent men have remained remarkably similar over time. A systematic survey carried out in Islington by researchers from Middlesex University reported in 1994 that only 37 per cent of men did not see violence against their partners as an option, and 19 per cent of men admitted that they had struck their partners; and little seems to have changed since then. Men are also traditionally 'excused' for violence including murder if they are 'provoked', one of the most common reasons for 'understandable' violence being that they know, or suspect, that their wives or partners are unfaithful. This tradition remains very strong both in the courts and among men themselves. In the Islington survey, for example, 50 per cent of those men who admitted physically attacking their wife or partner gave infidelity as the reason. Women in the Dobashes' earlier Scottish study, on the other hand, described the major occasions of violence as arising from unreasonable possessiveness and jealousy; or anger, for example because household tasks were not performed to the man's liking.

Such attitudes have been confirmed by studies since, including in-depth interviews on men's attitudes to violence, on a London housing estate in 1995, published by the Home Office. Jeff Hearn's 1998 study of violent men highlights both possessiveness and an inability to tolerate any kind of 'winding up' or affront to their pride by their partner. Thus their violence is seen by the men as a loss of control over themselves because of a challenge to their control over their partner's behaviour. The Glasgow Zero Tolerance survey of attitudes of young people, very recent research on young peoples attitudes by Melanie McCarry (2004 and 2005) and a study by Lynne Harne of violent men as fathers (2004 and 2005) all suggest similar views.

Explanations of domestic violence in terms of the privacy of the home and the right of a man to be in control of his household, providing he does not go too far, often lie behind the more formal and theoretical accounts that sometimes concentrate on attempting to explain 'excessive' violence. Such accounts may also look to individual deviancy and pathology in men, and to women's errant behaviour, as reasons why men 'lose control'.

In the recent past, traditionalist explanations like those mentioned above tended to hold sway in the UK, not least in the courts and in the police force. And in many countries of the world, marriage remains almost universal with wives typically expected to obey their husbands. There are, however, a number of alternative types of explanation, some of which overlap and emphasize different key ways of analysing or describing violence against women by their partners.

Individual pathological models of explanation

This kind of explanation is based on the idea that the individual using violence suffers from a pathological condition which leads to deviance from a non-violent norm. In practice, it might only be quite extreme forms of violence or repeated violence that would be included in this kind of diagnosis. A certain kind of 'low-level' aggression might be seen as 'normal', at least in some families. Pathological deviance, however, might be thought to be based on either psychiatric illness or faults of temperament in one or both partners. Often it has been regarded as a sign of inadequacy, of an inarticulate person who has not learned to assert himself in non-violent ways.

When violence within families began to be perceived as a major problem in the early 1970s, it was in the context of medical evidence of the physical abuse of children in the United States. Initial explanations of violence within families at that time arose from concern about child abuse and focused on 'abusive families'. Women, as mothers, were viewed as colluding in the abuse of their children and also colluding in, or provoking, violence against themselves. The early research into 'family violence' more widely again mainly in the United States where most of the large scale studies have been carried out, was often based on this kind of assumption.

Such ideas are still current in psychiatry and psychology. They also persist in certain kinds of therapeutic social work, where individualistic explanations shade over into theories of group pathology in which those who experience the violence are themselves often seen as helping to cause it. Certain kinds of psychotherapy, too, involve the idea that violence arises from 'issues' which the individuals concerned have not 'worked through' in their relationship. In recent years, some researchers and practitioners with such views have been moving towards other types of explanation as they have asked more sophisticated questions.

Cycles of violence

The 'cycle of violence' theory, also known as the 'inter-generational transmission of violence', suggests that there is a direct transmission of violence down the generations by learned behaviour, creating a cycle in which the violence continuously reproduces itself. This theory has a variant in which it is argued that the behaviour is learned by children who either witness or experience violence within an individual family. There is also a 'subcultural model' in which the use of violence is learned as part of a wider way of life, either in neighbourhoods in criminal subcultures or gangs, or in certain professions such as the police and the army.

There is certainly some evidence that violence can be learned or passed on in this way, but these theories cannot explain why many individuals who observe such behaviour or live in such environments are not violent, or why many people are violent who do not live in this kind of family or social setting. Nor can they explain why, according to a rather indiscriminate lumping together of different kinds of learned behaviour, it ends up that boys both observing and experiencing violence should become perpetrators of violence whereas girls apparently learn to choose violent partners and 'enjoy', or passively put up with, violent assault.

The theory rests ultimately on unacknowledged assumptions about the 'natural' aggressiveness of boys and men, and the passivity of girls and women. This kind of explanation also loses force if violence, and violence against women in particular, is both very common and often accepted in the whole society, as suggested by Elizabeth Wilson in 1983 and in much of the recent literature on violence against women:

> If you are one of only 500 abused women in a population of 50 million, then you have certainly been more than unlucky and there may perhaps be something very peculiar about your husband, or unusual about your circumstances, or about you On the other hand, if you are one of 5 million abused women out of 50 million, then that suggests something very different – that there is something wrong not with a few individual men, or women, or marriages, but with the *situation* in which *many* women and children regularly get assaulted – that situation being home and the family.

Yet, as we will see in later chapters, the cycle of violence is still a very popular kind of explanation. One possible reason for its popularity is that it seems to suggest that those men who attack their wives or partners, and those women who experience violence, are not 'people like us' – but rather belong to a special deviant group of 'violent families', who are completely different from the rest of us. Even if the violence happens more often than we would like to think and is much worse than we ever imagined, it has been explained. And, using the theory, it can be dealt with, perhaps by removing children from the violent family or violent subculture – and thus 'breaking the cycle'.

As to the adults, it might be too late to change the ingrained pattern. Perhaps all you can do is to recognize the fact, or perhaps you can help the women and children to get away. Perhaps you prosecute the man, or break the cycle by re-educating the parents or the perpetrator (in more optimistic variants of the theory which think it is actually possible to change what happens). Ultimately, though, if you believe that this is why domestic violence takes place, all you can probably hope to do is to minimize the transmission of violence, because it is all a result of some unalterable situation in the violent past.

While it is important to recognize that the 'inter-generational transmission of violence' does occur in a number of individual cases, it is also important to stress that basing an entire theory on it to explain domestic violence just does not hold water. Indeed, according to Dr Neil Frude of the University of Wales, research has shown that 80 per cent of abused children do not become abusers and that it is therefore important to avoid any suggestion that abused children are destined to abuse their own children or partners.

Biological explanations

Biological explanations offer a set of causal theories about domestic violence which are based on sciences such as biochemistry or genetics, and which are regarded as scientific, although there appears to be little systematic research to establish whether they are firmly based, as they apply to men's violence against their partners. For example, the propensity of the male hormone, testosterone, to increase aggression can be claimed as a cause of men's personal violence, and it is certainly true that, if you inject women with testosterone, they do become rather more aggressive. This is sometimes known by critics as the 'cows and bulls' argument

Medicobiological explanations often incorporate notions of addiction to violence. This can take a conventional psychiatric form, which rests on a description of symptomatic 'types' of personality. An example of this was that developed by Jasper Gayford back in 1976 from interviews with a small number of women in Chiswick refuge. Other explanations of addiction rest on ideas of chemical imbalances of adrenalin or cortisone, for example, or other hormonal disturbances. These usually involve the application to domestic violence of medical research on the relationship between chemical substances and aggression, mood changes, deviant behaviour and mental illness. They are often based on very small samples, of women rather than men, and are not necessarily carried out by trained scientific observers.

Sociobiological explanations are rather different. They have much in common with the traditional viewpoints described at the beginning of the chapter. The dominance of men over women is seen as a biosocial necessity dating from the evolutionary past or from genetic imperatives. In this view, there is an evolutionary need for men to be dominant, and (in some versions) modern society ignores this at its peril. These sorts of explanation often base themselves on comparisons with selected non-human species, particularly the primate apes, but ignore research on other species or anthropological studies of hunter-gatherer societies that do not confirm their views. For example, works like those of Desmond Morris in *The Naked Ape* and of the aptly named Lionel Tiger and Robin Fox propose that modern man is a frustrated version of 'man the hunter', blocked by modern social organization and egalitarian ideas of relations between the sexes from a productive evolutionary path. This school of thought is called 'the Tarzanists' by Elaine Morgan in her book *The Descent of Woman*, which puts forward an alternative evolutionary model. Sarah Blaffer-Hrdy, herself a sociobiologist, questions the sociobiological view from an interactive investigation of the evidence in her book *Mother Nature*.

In the view of some sociobiologists, dominance by 'man' and submission by 'woman' is good for all our futures. Fortunately, there is little evidence that these ideas hold sway in any of the agencies called in to help women experiencing domestic violence, at the official level at least, though they can give comfort to violent men and those who would support men's claim to dominance in the family.

Social-structural explanations

This is another kind of explanation of 'family violence'. It bases itself on the stress caused by lack of access to money, housing, education and other opportunities, common to both men and women in the family. In this view, violence flows from socioeconomic conditions, such as low wages, bad housing, isolation and unfavourable and frustrating work conditions for the man; lack of job opportunities for adolescent school leavers; and lack of facilities such as children's day care, adequate transport, a pleasant environment and play space and recreational facilities, for the mother and children.

This kind of explanation usually assumes that violence occurs mainly in working-class and poor families. There is a 'middle-class' version in terms of financial pressures and stressful careers, but more commonly in this view the greater resources of middle-class families or, in some cases, the ability of middle-class men to maintain dominance without resorting to physical violence are thought to explain what is believed to be the relative lack of violence in these families.

However, it is likely that violence in middle-class families can more easily remain hidden from neighbours and public agencies like the police and social services. A variety of studies have found that the more significant class differential was not in whether violence occurred but in the kind of agencies consulted, the middle class being more likely to use lawyers and the divorce courts than the police, social services or women's refuge services. Although it does seem very likely that the pressures of poverty might increase the occurrence of violence or make it worse, this type of analysis fails adequately to account for the predominant one-way direction of serious violence from men towards women or the fact that it occurs in all social classes.

Moralist explanations: the breakdown of the family

Violence in the family can be explained in terms of a number of different historical perspectives. One, based on the historical disabilities of women before the law, has already been mentioned. It is an important component of feminist explanations of domestic violence and will be discussed again briefly below. But there is another explanation, arising in the writings of Ferdinand Mount, Norman Stone, Roger Scruton and others, which has been very influential in government circles in the past. It is based on the idea of a current crisis in the family caused by a decline in morality and family values in the twentieth century and, more particularly, since the Second World War.

This kind of explanation fails to account for evidence both of widespread cohabitation outside marriage, and of widespread violence towards wives and female partners in the 'golden past', notably in the Victorian era. Legislation giving women greater civil rights was passed in the second half of the nineteenth century because women at that time, though lacking the parliamentary vote, were able to convince Parliament that some husbands were abusing their powers to control the property and income of their wives, and were often violent towards them. The first legal separation was allowed to women in the Matrimonial Causes Amendment Act 1878, if their husbands were convicted of aggravated assault against them; and the Married Women's Property Acts were passed to allow women control over their property and their earnings after marriage. Previously the husband had a right to control his wife's property and earnings even if they were legally separated.

As in other cases, moralist explanations can overlap to some extent, albeit with differences of emphasis. So there are traditional, democratic and radical models to explain family violence based on moral failings and the breakdown of the family. Some rest on the failure of the 'nuclear' family consisting of the couple and their children, and see the traditional extended form of family, or a communal model, as superior. Others argue that the nuclear family is potentially better. What they all tend to have in common is the notion of an ideal family form to which we should all aspire. Often this is thought to have existed in the past and to have been capable of satisfying the needs of all family members without conflict.

Such a view emphasizes the interrelationships and bonds that hold the family together, and the harmonious divisions of responsibility (or 'roles') along gender and age lines within it. The family is thought of as a symbiotic whole in which each member functions for the good of the others and on behalf of the 'good society'. But it is important to remember that what some see as both natural and right, or as mere differences in the functional 'roles' of people within the family, others see as inequalities of power. In addition, these ideas about family forms often refer only to western societies and to white family forms. They have little to say about the variety of ways in which relationships between people are organized in different societies, cultural contexts and ethnic communities.

Feminist explanations

Feminist explanations of domestic violence, like those of the sociobiologists, focus on the central importance of male dominance, but they see that as precisely the problem to be overcome, rather than as an ideal to be restored. In the feminist view, domestic violence arises out of men's power over women in the family. This male power has been built into family life historically, through laws which assume that men have the right to authority over both women and children within families, where this does not conflict with public policy and the interests of the state. Rebecca and Russell Dobash in *Violence Against Wives*, for example, describe the inferior historical position of women in British and North American society and in marriage, which arose from laws and customs that excluded women from public life and placed them under the authority of their husband or their father within the private sphere of the family.

As Susan Schechter has pointed out in *Women and Male Violence*, this does not necessarily mean that feminists are 'dismissing psychology or ignoring violent individuals'. Rather:

> They are stressing the need for a psychology that analyses wife beating in its proper contexts, accounts for power differentials, and asks why women have been brutalized. Rather than label battering as pathology or a family systems failure, it is more conceptually accurate to assume that violence against women, like that directed towards children, is behaviour approved of and sanctioned in many parts of the culture. Extreme cases in which women are mutilated by psychotic men are only one end of a continuum of violent behaviour the more moderate forms of which are viewed as normal. Many in this culture approve of hitting women.

Many feminists would use the kind of explanation that stresses the need to examine the historical position of women in particular societies and the way in which it was, and still is, embodied in law and custom. However, some forms of feminist explanation, basing themselves on the male-dominated nature of most known forms of society, come close to arguing that inherent biological differences between men and women are at the core of male violence and female non-violence.

More recently, others have argued that there can be no such definite categories as 'men' and 'women', or 'patriarchy', but that we live among conflicting or intersecting sets of inequalities, pluralities and differences in power, in which all positions are to some extent contestable so that there can be no overriding 'truth'. Some postmodern or poststructuralist feminists argue for more subtle, complex and interactive forms of theory or, like Suruchi Thapar-Bjorkert and Sonia Reverter-Banon, re-emphasize the overall political nature of the struggle against patriarchal social formations instead of what they see as over-reliance on state and agency action. Others, such as Liz Trinder, in their rejection of 'standpoint feminism' seem to come close to rejecting any possibility of understanding social phenomena except in terms of 'local, specific constructed realities' which are not more or less true than one another but simply more or less informed and/or sophisticated. The object of research, in this view, is to focus on 'language, or discourse itself' as the object of study. Hence the 'subject' of the research and the 'object' appear to be the same and it is rather hard to imagine what the consequences might be for research that informs action.

Most feminist accounts, however, draw attention to the social and economic position of women, whatever their class, ethnicity or country, although it is clearly necessary to look at the differences that do exist and develop responses to specific situations. Standpoint feminists such as Sandra Harding claim that looking at the world from the viewpoint of women in all their diversity and difference leads to a wide variety of specifically 'feminist standpoints', all of which differ from the dominant, patriarchal view in any society. In this context, most feminists point to the way in which the responsibility that society assigns to women for looking after children often places them in a position of enforced financial dependency on their partners or ex-partners, a situation that was reinforced in the UK by the 1991 Child Support Act. It is also used as an excuse for paying women low wages or minimal state income support. Some feminists would also want to argue that class and racial oppression, and social stresses such as unemployment, bad housing and poverty, are likely to increase violence and make it harder to escape. Yet they would point out that this does not explain why it is that it is predominantly men who become violent in these circumstances, or why so much of the violence is directed towards women whom the men would profess to love.

Black feminists in particular (such as Amina Mama in *The Hidden Struggle*, Parita Trivedi in 'Many voices, one chant' and Hannana Siddiqui, in 'Black women's activism: coming of age?') emphasize the need to develop perspectives that take into account the specific histories of black and minority ethnic communities. They point especially to differences that the experience of racism and colonization make to the situation of black and minority ethnic people, both women and men, in the UK, to say nothing of recognizing the need for analyses that are sensitive to racism worldwide. In criticizing writers who talk simply of a 'public/private divide', authors like Mama demonstrate that under slavery, and in colonial regimes, state agencies have shown themselves far from reluctant to intervene very directly to regulate or destroy the personal lives of black families in certain circumstances, while black women are still not protected from domestic violence. They would argue that this remains true in the UK today. In a different context this also holds true for poorer working-class white families. This analysis suggests that the problem is not so much one of overcoming a general reluctance to intervene in family life, as one of ensuring that what agencies do is sensitive to the needs of the women concerned and is not based on repressive models of control.

Despite differences, however, what unites almost all forms of feminist explanation is the belief that domestic violence arises from the power and control that men exercise over women, and from the unequal position of women in society. With differences of emphasis, most feminists argue that there is a need to develop strategies to enable women to challenge that abuse of power, and the power itself, both individually and collectively. Part of this strategy rests on challenging the views of state agencies and their reluctance to provide appropriate backing for women experiencing domestic violence.

Agency responses

Traditionally and historically, it has been difficult for women to get help from state and other agencies when facing domestic violence. There are a number of reasons for this and many of them arise from traditional assumptions about women's place in society and the home, and the continuing inequality of women before the law. One important influence is the fact that the violence takes place in the home – a private domain and one in which men are still often seen as the 'breadwinners' and heads of household. This feeds the view that women are people with lesser rights in general within society.

In criminal justice agencies, these influences can be related to observable differences in attitude to offences and offenders across a number of dimensions, which can be useful as an index for testing the reactions of society, and of other social agencies. Reactions are affected by who the aggressor or offender is and who the 'victim' is; by where the offence takes place; and by the degree of violence or the seriousness of the damage or loss. All these are independent variables, which can intersect in various ways. So, for example, violence against someone who is of a higher social status, or violence in a public place, is likely to be treated more seriously. In contrast, violence by a person of higher social status, in a private place, especially his own home, against a social inferior or someone over whom he has authority – for example, his children or his wife (or daughter-in-law) – has often been taken less seriously. The attitude of state agencies, therefore, may relate back to the fact that traditionally the husband/father had the right and obligation to discipline, within reason, those under his control, and that such matters were not normally the concern of the public authorities.

In this kind of view, the role of the wife and mother was to care for the head of household: her husband and their children, under his general authority (or that of others in authority in the family), so that the family thrived as a healthy part of the social organism. She, therefore, essentially lived for and through other people and gained her fulfilment through their happiness. Since it was assumed that this was the normal and natural state of affairs, the focus was often on the woman's failures if things went wrong.

In the last few years – because of the work of women's groups, of Women's Aid domestic violence services and the national Women's Aid federations, and of feminist activists, researchers and writers – many professionals, including those in state agencies and government bodies, have come to accept, to some degree at least, the argument that domestic violence is an abuse of the power of men over women in the family. Only feminists, including some who work in state agencies, are seriously questioning the legitimacy of the power relationship itself. The following chapters will look at the ways in which the responses of statutory and other agencies to domestic violence have been changing, beginning with the police and the legal system.

4
Policing domestic violence: prosecuting, preventing and reducing crime

In theory, assault is a crime wherever it happens and whoever does it. There should be no difference whether it is committed in the home or outside, by a husband or by a stranger. In practice, it has made a great deal of difference. In the past, the law and the police were of little help to women who had been attacked by their husbands or partners – or by former husbands or partners – especially within their own homes.

Despite changes in these attitudes, most crime prevention advice highlights the danger from burglary (e.g. Neighbourhood Watch) or from being attacked by strangers in public places. Yet, despite the very real and frightening vulnerability of women to attacks in public, especially at night, it is men, particularly young men, who are most in danger in the street from other men. Women (and children) are more at risk in their own homes and from the men who are closest to them than they are from strangers. However, it is only comparatively recently that domestic violence (like sexual violence more generally) has been recognized, incorporated into strategies to protect women and given intermittent public prominence by awareness campaigns.

The police and hospital casualty departments are the only agencies available 24 hours a day, and the police have a particular responsibility to keep the peace and to prevent crime, although since the introduction of the Crime and Disorder Act 1998 this duty is shared with both local authorities and primary care trusts (PCTs) as 'responsible authorities' with a legal duty to prevent crime. As discussed below, police responses have changed significantly from their former stance of ignoring or playing down the seriousness of domestic violence, but the evidence suggests that calling the police is still often seen as a last resort after repeated violent attacks.

A survey conducted by Jayne Mooney in Islington, published back in 1994, showed that, while one in ten of the women in the survey had experienced an attack from her partner in the past year, only 22 per cent of these had contacted the police at some time for help. In general, women had only ever reported 28 per cent of the assaults they had experienced. The survey confirmed earlier research. These results were also of particular importance because Islington was one of the areas that pioneered a new approach to policing domestic violence in the UK after the mid-1980s, setting up one of the first Domestic Violence Units, and then a civilian Domestic Violence Intervention Team (Domestic Violence Matters) initially with special funding from the Home Office (see Chapter 5). Later research, such as the British Crime Surveys (BCS), confirms this general picture. Successive BCS figures report slow increases in reporting until the mid-1990s, followed by a decline at a somewhat greater rate than that of other violent crimes. However, Sylvia Walby and Jonathan Allen in their 2004 analysis of a self-completion questionnaire on domestic violence, sexual assault and stalking, which was part of the 2001 BCS, found that the police were informed of less than one in four of the incidents of domestic violence disclosed in their survey. In 2002, on the other hand, the research by Cathy Humphreys and Ravi Thiara, in *Routes to Safety*, found that 80 per cent of the 200 women respondents in their study had turned to the police, possibly indicating the severity and frequency of the abuse they had experienced.

Background to the change in police practice

From the early 1970s women began to highlight the problem of sexual and physical attacks both in the street and in the home, and the failure of the police to help them when they reported these assaults. Women's Aid activists, among others, have for many years been involved in attempts to develop a more sympathetic and helpful attitude among police when called to incidents of domestic violence. One aspect of this has been the push over more than 20 years to have domestic violence, as well as other forms of violence against women, taken seriously as 'real crime', 'real violence'.

Concerns about police responses spread far beyond the feminist movement in the late 1970s and the 1980s. First the Select Committee on Violence in Marriage in 1975, and later the Women's National Commission in 1985, broadly endorsed the viewpoint of grass-roots women's campaigns. It was also backed up by research in the period, such as that of Jan Pahl and Susan Edwards in London and various locations in the south of England, of Jalna Hanmer and Sheila Saunders in West Yorkshire, and of Rebecca and Russell Dobash and Fran Wasoff in Scotland.

This concern about the policing of crimes of violence against women was first acted on at governmental level in the 1980s, mainly in relation to rape and attacks against women in public, especially following the notorious documentary shown in the early 1980s about Thames Valley Police bullying a woman who reported a rape, and the horrifying murders of women in Leeds by Peter Sutcliffe. The fact that statistics showed that many women were murdered by their husbands in their own homes did not have the same impact.

At about the same time, questions of policing in general also became a focus of attention in some local authority areas. In the early 1980s there was a series of local government initiatives examining police practice from the Greater London Council and some other councils, mainly in London. These involved Women's Units, Civil Rights Committees, and Police and Community Safety Units, which began monitoring police activities because of a concern about bad police–community relations, oppressive policing and poor service to black people and women. The work of such organizations also fed into a growing concern in some police forces and the Home Office itself about public criticism of police practices, and of their failure to deal adequately and fairly with women and with black and minority ethnic communities.

The need for changes in police practice on domestic violence was accepted in Parliament in November 1986, following a circular from the Home Office and the report of a Metropolitan Police Working Party in the same year. A substantial Home Office circular was issued in 1990 to give guidance to chief officers of police throughout the UK. This has been revised and strengthened by Circular 19/2000, which emphasizes arrest and evidence gathering to strengthen the case for prosecution. The Crown Prosecution Service also issued new and comprehensive guidance on prosecuting cases of domestic violence in 2001. Details of these moves and their results are given later in this chapter.

There was much to be changed. Women calling the police for help often found them unsympathetic and unhelpful. There was considerable evidence that serious assaults were treated as minor, or even disregarded altogether. Independent research into police practice carried out by Susan Edwards, Alan Bourlet and Ian Blair in the early 1980s suggested that this was systematic practice amounting to policy in the areas studied. Local studies like that by Jill Radford in Wandsworth, others in Manchester and Camden, the Islington crime survey in 1986 and many small-scale surveys of women in refuges confirmed both the prevalence of violence against women and the lack of an adequate response if it was reported.

Police officers generally felt that domestic disputes were private matters and were uneasy when dealing with them. In the early research on police practice, male police officers, who make up the vast majority, expressed their strong dislike of dealing with 'domestics'. These offences were widely regarded as not 'real' crime or proper police work by both beat officers and their superiors up to chief officer level. For example, the

London Strategic Policy Unit's Police Monitoring and Research Group reported that Commissioner Newman of the Metropolitan Police suggested in 1983 that domestic disputes should be hived off to social services.

Until comparatively recently too, domestic violence has been invisible in crime statistics. Often no record was kept of requests for help. Where an assault was recorded, it might have been simply entered in the incident book as a minor assault even if it was more serious or, if recorded as a criminal offence initially, it was often not proceeded with and 'no crimed' (i.e. not entered in returns for inclusion in the official Home Office crime statistics). Many police officers called to intervene would see the attack as largely the woman's fault. They frequently accepted the husband's version of events or made their own moral judgements about the woman. Women's Aid refuge workers were often told that 'women had only themselves to blame' because they were bad housewives or had provoked the man in some way.

Police rarely intervened to arrest the man and protect the woman. At best, they would perhaps advise the woman to take out an injunction or a private prosecution for assault, even when the attack had caused her injury. Studies of police records have shown that this minimizing of domestic violence happened even where women were visibly injured. Assaults that should have been classified as causing actual bodily harm (ABH) or grievous bodily harm (GBH) might be described as common assault and the woman told that she herself would have to prosecute in the magistrates' court or apply for civil protection orders. Although in fact they had the same powers under the Offences Against the Person Act 1861 in domestic violence as in any other assault, the police would often say that they had no power to arrest the man. In some cases they maintained that they could not arrest him unless they or someone else had witnessed the offence. Even where the attack was so serious that the man was arrested, normally either no charge was laid or it would be withdrawn before proceeding to prosecution. Since in so many cases no crime report was ever filled out, repeated serious offences would not necessarily leave any trace in the records.

Where the police were called to deal with an attack on a woman in her own home, she often found that it was treated as her husband's home only. Moreover, women using refuge services have given accounts of being assaulted in public places by their husbands or partners, and the assault still being treated as a private matter. Police were much more willing to press charges if they themselves had been insulted or attacked, or if the man was 'known' to the police or suspected of other criminal activity.

Black women in particular have faced the problem that police either might not act or else might overreact, possibly because of racist perceptions of black people. Amina Mama in *The Hidden Struggle* gives accounts of women who were themselves assaulted by the police or threatened with arrest when police were called to the scene of domestic violence. In some circumstances, following the 1983 Immigration Act, calling the police has resulted in the deportation of women or their husbands if they were immigrants. Black women in Camden and Islington, responding to surveys in the 1980s and 1990s, said that they were especially reluctant to contact the police for these reasons. (Despite modifications this still applies to those unable to show documentary proof of violence. Southall Black Sisters, Imkaan and others have long campaigned to end discrimination against women who are recent immigrants and sponsored two unsuccessful amendments to the Domestic Violence, Crime and Victims Act on the subject.)

Criticisms of police practice on domestic violence have centred mainly on failure to act: failure to log calls for assistance; failure to respond quickly; failure to take the assault seriously, to arrest or charge the attacker, or even to remove him from the home; failure to consider prosecution, or to record the assault as a crime; or a subsequent downgrading of an attack to 'no crime' even following charges, if a prosecution was not being proceeded with. Police also failed to give women advice and support in the majority of cases where they were not going to press charges, and showed little knowledge of what support was available in the community. Nor did they usually have an accurate idea of the nature and scope of the protection orders available in civil courts. If there were an injunction with powers of arrest in force, they would often not act on it. Occasionally, however, they might remove the man from the house or offer to take the woman and children to a refuge or another safe place. Often no separate interviews would be carried out with the woman and her attacker to try to discover what had happened. Moreover, it was rare for a woman to be interviewed by a woman officer – and because there are still relatively few women in police forces, this is still likely to be the case.

Police reluctance to prosecute has been justified by the unreliability of women and their tendency to withdraw charges or to refuse to act as witnesses. The studies of police practice show that the police often gave women no support in reaching a decision in the first place and little help in proceeding when they were willing for the police to prosecute. Where the woman has wanted to press charges, the police have sometimes themselves suggested that she should not proceed, or have not charged the man immediately in order to allow a 'cooling off' period – which is a time of great uncertainty and danger for the woman. Despite recent changes in policing, problems remain in supporting women through the prosecution process. This will be looked at further later in this chapter.

Little recognition has been given to the fact that, except in the most serious cases, or where they leave their homes, women will often have to go on living with their attacker while waiting for the case to come to court, during the proceedings and even afterwards if he is not given a custodial sentence. In *Breaking Through*, written by women experiencing violence, the writers wonder whether policemen have ever had to share a house with someone they are in the process of prosecuting for assault!

Many studies documented a lack of sympathy or backing for women, a lack of understanding of a woman's frequently justified fears of making the violence worse by taking action, or of her concern at the effects of prosecution. In many cases women may want the attacks to stop and the attacker to be removed, temporarily or permanently, but they may not wish to send him to gaol, perhaps out of love or fear of retaliation, or because they and their children might then face the public stigma of having him declared a criminal. Even though attitudes have changed, there seems to be little understanding that the man's imprisonment or even the imposition of a fine means that the whole family might suffer financial hardship, especially where there are children and the woman is financially dependent on her partner.

One of the barriers to change in police practice has been the traditionalist masculine culture of the police. As an overwhelmingly male organization, they have developed what has been described by the Policy Studies Institute as 'an occupational culture of their own'. This culture has not often been welcoming to women, as surveys showing the prevalence of sexual harassment and sexual assault against women police officers have demonstrated. The existence of such attitudes increased the possibility that police officers would side with the man more easily in domestic violence incidents and believe his story. However, this tendency to excuse the man did not always occur when he was black, or was not someone the police officer could have a fellow feeling for. Such attitudes began to change after all police authorities implemented Home Office Circular 60/1990 as described below. Increased co-operation between the police and other agencies such as Women's Aid, which can include their participation in police training, has had an impact, although it does not reach all officers even in the areas where it is provided.

The belief that it is sometimes reasonable or excusable for a man to discipline his wife, or to use violence when provoked, has not disappeared and is not confined to the police. The approach of the police reflects many conventional social attitudes that are not easily changed, but which need a response at a variety of levels. These include work in schools and public awareness campaigns such as 'Zero Tolerance', which are discussed later.

Recommendations and guidelines for improved practice

By the mid-1980s, as a result of women speaking about their negative experiences of police responses, the activities of Women's Aid and other organizations, and the development of research and monitoring of police practice, the need for change was becoming clear. A number of detailed recommendations were developed, such as those listed in the comprehensive report of the London Strategic Policy Unit's (LSPU) Police Monitoring and Research Group in 1986. The group had worked with Women's Aid and refuge organizations and the London Women and Policing Network in drawing up their proposals. At about the same time, similar proposals were put forward by the Women's National Commission, which appear to have had considerable influence on government thinking and legislation, such as Part IV of the Family Law Act 1996 and the Protection from Harassment Act 1997.

As a result of these and similar recommendations, a start was made after the mid-1980s in developing better police practice, first by individual action in a few police forces – Bedfordshire, West Yorkshire and Tottenham in London being notable examples. This was followed, as noted earlier, by an influential policy directive from the Home Office in 1986 and by a Metropolitan Police report in 1987. These recommendations were picked up in the advice given to chief officers of police forces by the Home Office in 1990 and amplified in 2000, as described below.

As we have seen, a major problem was police reluctance to act against domestic violence using their powers under the Offences against the Person Act 1861. In 1986 they were reminded of these powers by the Home Office and advised also to make use of their powers to make an arrest under the Police and Criminal Evidence Act 1984, where there was a reasonable suspicion that a crime of domestic violence was about to be committed.

The 1986 circular accepted a number of the recommendations contained in the LSPU report and the Women's National Commission report of 1985, including a request to chief officers to review training and record- keeping arrangements, and instructions to officers, on arrest, that they should provide women with information, take them to a refuge, if necessary, and liaise with local support groups, including Women's Aid. The circular was an important step forward, stating clearly that 'there must be an overriding concern to ensure the safety of victims of domestic violence and to reduce the risk of further violence both to the spouse and to any children who may be present'. However, it did not appear to accept criticism of current police practice or regard change as a matter of national policy. Rather it was left to the discretion of chief officers to decide 'the extent to which the recommendations of the Women's National Commission may appropriately be implemented in their area'. The initiative was, therefore, passed back to chief officers and local police forces.

At this time, the Metropolitan Police already had the report of their working party, which had carried out a review of policy and practice on domestic violence between 1984 and 1986. This report examined international evidence, including an important and much used research report by Sherman and Berk on mandatory pro-arrest policies in Minneapolis in the USA and the experience of pro-arrest policies combined with multi-agency support services in Duluth, Minnesota, and in London, Ontario in Canada. Sherman and Berk had found that mandatory arrest policies worked in reducing domestic violence whereas some other researchers have found that mandatory arrest policies could increase women's reluctance to call the police in the first place. This discrepancy resulted in considerable attention being paid in the 1980s and 1990s to research into criminal justice in many countries, but particularly in the United States. The issue, which was examined in a study for the Home Office by Rebecca Morley and Audrey Mullender in 1994, has now been resolved in the American context. The final outcome shows pro-arrest policies (though not necessarily mandatory arrest) to be more successful than not, and there is a general acceptance in many countries that pro-arrest, pro-prosecution policies, especially when combined in a co-ordinated criminal justice and community response, are one of the main ways forward in what is now called 'positive policing' of domestic violence.

The Metropolitan Police have followed these debates internationally although there were some problems with the original 1987 report. Its recommendations became very well known because they were made public in a House of Commons debate, although the report itself was never published in full. It apparently endorsed many of the criticisms that had been voiced by the Women's National Commission, by the various police monitoring reports and by voluntary organizations including Women's Aid.

The report was followed up with a Strategy Statement and new and very influential Metropolitan Police Force Orders in 1987. As well as the changes in practice and recording procedures described earlier there was a commitment to the introduction of training which would work on changing entrenched attitudes. The guiding instruction was that 'an assault which occurs in the home is as much a criminal act as one which may occur in the street'. The definition of violence was to be expanded to include 'threats or attempts to cause physical harm to another family or household member'. Officers were told to respond more positively by giving 'enhanced support, care and concern to victims of crime, including the victims of domestic violence'. A beginning was made, too, in developing a multi-agency approach to providing support and information, with more effective liaison between police and supporting agencies. A number of police stations in the Metropolitan Police area and elsewhere developed specialized Domestic Violence Units, which were often staffed by women officers, on the model of those that had been set up earlier to improve the treatment of women reporting offences of rape and sexual assault.

These developments were further encouraged by the issuing in 1990 of new Home Office guidelines in Circular 60/90. This circular, which marked a major national policy change on policing domestic violence, followed the publication of a comprehensive review of the literature on domestic violence by Lorna Smith in 1989, which gave serious consideration to the view that domestic violence had deep historical roots and was grounded in the inequality of power between men and women in marriage and in society at large. The 1990 circular adopted a much wider perspective on domestic violence, and a much less piecemeal approach than earlier circulars, though it had little to say on other forms of violence against women. It commended the adoption of explicit force policies on domestic violence, and approved the establishment 'where practicable and cost effective' of special units to deal with it. It also made a clear statement of the approach to be taken and the expectation of a national response to the advice that it contained:

> The Home Secretary regards a violent assault, or brutal and threatening behaviour over a period of time by a person with whom the victim lives, as no less serious than an attack by a stranger . . . [The] purpose of this circular, which has been agreed with the Association of Chief Police Officers, is to offer guidance to the police on their response to the problems of domestic violence and to encourage the development and publicizing of force policy statements and strategies to deal with it.

The police were urged to ensure that they make a speedy and effective response to calls to incidents of domestic violence. Officers were reminded that domestic violence is a crime and that it was their primary duty 'to protect the victim and any children from further abuse and then to consider what action should be taken against the offender'. The immediate protection could include 'referring or taking her to a shelter' as well as liaising with other statutory or voluntary agencies that could supply longer-term help and support. Agencies mentioned included 'doctors; health, social services and housing authorities; voluntary bodies such as victim support groups and refuges for battered women; and citizens' advice bureaux, and legal advice centres'. Surprisingly, there was no explicit reference to Women's Aid as a key source of long-term support, nor to referring women to local offices of the Department of Social Security, which might well be crucial to their ability to survive financially.

Chief officers were reminded of the interest of the CPS and the courts in police policies on domestic violence, and were advised to discuss evidential and other matters with their local Chief Crown Prosecutor before finalizing their policy, to ensure consistency of aims and approach. They were also urged to consider setting up Domestic Violence Units with specially trained officers 'where it is practicable and cost effective to do so', or at least to ensure that all officers have up-to-date knowledge of suitable referral points in other agencies. The 1990 circular specified the central features that should be included in force policy statements: the overriding duty to protect victims and children; the need to treat domestic violence at least as seriously as other forms of violence; and the use and value of powers of arrest. It also emphasized the dangers of seeking conciliation between assailant and victim, and the importance of comprehensive record keeping to allow the effectiveness of the policy to be monitored.

The circular spelled out in detail the process of responding to an incident from first contact. It stressed the need to check records of previous incidents and any injunctions in force, and the importance of keeping these records. It gave a detailed description of possible action at the scene of the incident, reminding officers that physical signs of violence may not be initially obvious. There was also a reminder that it is desirable for a woman officer to be present, and that a woman should be interviewed separately and should never be asked in the presence of the assailant whether she would be prepared to give evidence against him. The circular also stressed that removal of the woman and any children to a place of safety should be the immediate priority.

Officers were told to consider using the power of arrest and detention, both because of the indication from experience in other countries of its possible deterrent effect and because of its importance as a means of showing the woman that 'she is entitled to, and will receive, society's protection and support'. They were also reminded of the importance of establishing whether there were witnesses, in view of the difficulties of bringing a prosecution in cases of domestic violence.

Further detailed advice on action after the incident included a warning against making a decision not to initiate a prosecution because of a belief that the woman may not be prepared to give evidence in court. The advice was that the same factors should be considered as those relevant in attacks by strangers, and that women may gain in confidence with proper support and recognize that prosecution is in their own interests. There was also advice to consider the use of police bail if there was a need for further inquiries in making a decision about prosecution.

Detail was given on the information needed by the Crown Prosecution Service, on the need for support and written information for the woman prior to trial, and on questions to be considered if she wished to withdraw, including the possibility that she might be compelled to give evidence. There was a reminder that action could be taken against the man if the woman was being intimidated into withdrawing. Where the man did receive a sentence, chief officers were advised that the woman should be informed of his release from custody. Finally, they were advised that all officers likely to be involved in incidents of domestic violence should receive training in their powers under the law and in understanding force policies and procedures, particularly as they involved working with other agencies. Overall, the circular encouraged the adoption of a pro-arrest, pro-prosecution response. Women's Aid services, the Greater London Domestic Violence Project and others have been involved in police training on these issues for more than a decade now and more recently Circular 19/2000 has reiterated and strengthened this advice, relating it to new powers under more recent legislation. This further impetus towards change has been strengthened by the recent development of a long-awaited national training package by the Association of Chief Police Officers.

How much has police practice changed?

Writing in 1989, Susan Edwards stated that many police forces in England and Wales were reviewing their policies in dealing with domestic violence, but that policing priorities differed in each of the 43 police forces. In his study published in the same year, Alan Bourlet found that only nine had any specific policy. In the early 1990s, however, there was a gathering momentum in drawing up force policies, providing information booklets for women seeking police help and developing liaison with other agencies and organizations, including Women's Aid refuges. There was a rather slower response in terms of other changes, such as appointing specialized domestic violence officers and setting up Domestic Violence Units. This general picture was documented both by a survey of refuges carried out by Women's Aid in England, and incorporated in its evidence to the House of Commons Home Affairs Committee in 1993, and by the research of Sharon Grace on police forces for the Home Office between 1992 and 1994.

The Women's Aid survey suggested a continuum of change since the 1980s as well as a new, if initially limited, stimulus from the 1990 Home Office circular. Of the 102 refuges responding to the survey, 67 said that the policy of their police force on domestic violence had changed within the last five years and 59 said there had been a change in practice. But in only 11 areas had the change resulted in quicker responses, giving domestic violence higher priority and/or the introduction of a pro-arrest policy.

Although there was a significant increase in the number of Domestic Violence Units or domestic violence liaison officers following the circular, a number of police forces did not set up a specific DVU. Some forces had more general Family Protection Units, and in others domestic violence work was grouped with work on non-domestic rape and child abuse; or with racial harassment, homophobic attacks on lesbians and gay men, and elder abuse. More recently, there has been a general shift to Community

Safety Units (CSUs), especially in London, or Anti-Harassment Units, combining action on domestic violence with racial and sexual harassment, and homophobic crime. Alternatively, some police services have set up Vulnerable Persons Units. There is a need for clarity in grouping such different kinds of abuse together and for careful monitoring of the service provided, and much depends on how the services are staffed and resourced, and how they coordinate with other services

Earlier Women's Aid experience with Sexual Abuse and Family Protection Units suggested that priority was often given to rape or, more commonly, child abuse at the expense of the support of women experiencing domestic violence. However, this does not appear to be true generally of CSUs, where they exist. Since their inception, the percentage of their work that is domestic violence related has been over 80 per cent and it is climbing – it currently stands at about 87 per cent in the Metropolitan area. Moreover, DVUs often used to usually have only two staff whereas CSUs typically have 10–15 staff. One key difference between CSUs and DVUs is that the former are often investigative units and may have less emphasis on the 'victim support' role; however, they may have an informal role in monitoring responses by front-line officers.

There may be other difficulties for both DVUs and CSUs. Domestic Violence Units must be bound by the policing priorities of the force they belong to, and may face conflict with other areas of police work. They can come under pressure to ignore cases that do not fit the criminal justice model, neglecting issues of crime prevention and reduction. However, as Sharon Grace's research indicated, they can also act as a support for the woman through the prosecution process, explain the law and the court system, inform her what is happening in the investigation, and act as a reassuring presence in the hearing itself. When supplemented by independent advocacy from Women's Aid or other community advocacy services, they can provide more far-reaching support with the criminal or civil justice system, or with housing problems – including protection in women's own homes – and with children's services, which may be needed whether or not they are involved in court proceedings.

Apart from one-to-one inter-agency co-operation with Women's Aid or other agencies, a number of models for co-operation between different statutory and voluntary services, including independent advocacy, have existed for some time. For example, the Domestic Violence Matters Project (DVM) in Islington based independent advocates in a police station; Croydon, in Surrey, set up a 'one-stop shop' in the 1990s for women experiencing domestic violence and victims of other kinds of abuse. More recently, a number of different pilot models of multi-agency support projects on violence against women were set up through the Home Office Crime Reduction Programme.

Officers in DVUs and CSUs can be a point of liaison with the community, Women's Aid and other services, and can develop a high level of expertise and effectiveness in the right circumstances. In other situations, they can be relatively isolated and their ideas may not necessarily feed through into policy or into general police practice. Nevertheless, they can and do act as a catalyst within the police and may keep up pressure for training and policy and practice discussions with other police officers. It is important that DVUs, CSUs and referrals to refuge organizations and to advocacy and other services are not regarded as excuses for inaction by patrol officers and other uniformed officers called to deal with this kind of assault, on the grounds that it is the responsibility of specialist domestic violence officers or others. Nor can they be seen as a substitute for general police training and awareness on issues involving domestic violence.

The research of Sharon Grace showed that domestic violence officers, DVUs and CSUs were generally highly regarded by Crown Prosecutors and other agencies involved in multi-agency work, for their detailed knowledge and their support and understanding of women experiencing domestic violence. Our own study of multi-agency initiatives, discussed in more detail in Chapter 8, also showed the important impact of domestic violence officers and units, and the respect that they had earned. Initially activists in the refuge movement were ambivalent about DVUs and CSUs, but they are now much more likely to view them with appreciation.

In fact, women's activists and support projects regard police DVUs and CSUs far more positively in the 2000s than they ever thought they would. Survivors also very much value the specific support offered by DVUs, as chronicled in the 2002 *Routes to Safety* study. However, the study's authors, Humphreys and Thiara, found that the police (particularly outside the DVUs and CSUs, but inside them too) were more likely to respond positively to women whom they saw as deserving and who behaved well and presented a conventional view of an abused, 'put upon' woman. Victims who behaved less well or were awkward tended to be regarded as 'bad' victims and were assisted less. Old habits die hard.

Of the 160 women interviewed who had used the police, only 36 per cent had found them helpful; 33 per cent had found them fairly helpful and 31 per cent really unhelpful. The women's experiences were very uneven and the positives were strongly associated with the specialist officers rather than the general uniformed staff. The women interviewed valued and strongly advocated an immediate police response, accurate information and advice, a respectful and professional attitude, proactive and effective action in relation to the perpetrator, systematic and thorough evidence gathering and consistency across social divisions of 'race', class, sexuality and disability.

More recently, our study in the ESRC Violence Research Programme analysed survivors' views of the effectiveness of agency responses with

112 women. The police were judged to have improved their response in about 54 per cent of cases overall, but when only specialist domestic violence liaison officers and units were included this jumped to 96 per cent. The women had almost unanimously found that these units and officers had been helpful, often beyond the bounds of duty. However, it should be noted that, in many police services, these units are the very ones being cut back or further amalgamated.

Assessing the impact of the changes

As yet there has been no comprehensive research to monitor the overall impact of changes in police practice. The evidence we have suggests that these have been far reaching, though far from complete, and still subject to variations in response from individual officers, as well as from different police stations and areas within authorities. All forces have now adopted domestic violence policies based on Circular 60/90, and strengthened by Circular 19/2000. In most areas DVUs or CSUs have been set up or domestic violence liaison officers appointed to try to ensure more active intervention as well as a more supportive approach. More recently, in some areas women have been provided with alarms, mobile phones and other safety devices, even including specially strengthened safety rooms. These are sometimes called 'target hardening measures'. Many police forces have also been active in fostering multi-agency domestic violence initiatives (see Chapter 8), and a number of pilot projects have been funded through Safer Cities or the recent Crime Reduction Programme Violence Against Women Initiative. Several of these projects have been successful in obtaining continuing funding from other sources for at least some of the services they are providing.

There has been a significant increase over time in the number of women reporting to the police and an improvement in the response women receive when they do report an incident of domestic violence, even when this does not meet the strict definition of a crime. This may include a comprehensive 'cocoon' protection service, as in the Yorkshire 'Killingbeck' project where police operate a graded response depending on seriousness. There has also been an increase in the use of arrest and detention for a short time to ensure the woman's safety, and in the use of bail conditions that prevent an arrested man either from being immediately released or from being able to return to commit further abuse.

The Police and Criminal Evidence Act 1984 gave the police the power to arrest on reasonable suspicion that an offence may have been committed, or may be about to be committed, which then may not necessarily lead to prosecution. This increase in police powers to arrest on suspicion gave rise to widespread concern about possible abuse of police power under the Act and its implications for civil liberties. (Such concerns have since been repeated in relation to the Crime and Disorder legislation of the late 1990s and early 2000s and other new criminal justice measures.) Considerations like these are not entirely absent in situations of domestic violence, especially for people from minority ethnic communities and anyone who might be a focus of police suspicion for other reasons. But it is probable that in most incidents of domestic violence the power of preventive arrest has acted mainly to overcome the general reluctance to intervene in such cases in the first instance. This does not necessarily feed through to a corresponding increase in the prosecution rate, or in the rate of convictions.

The research of Antonia Cretney and Gwynn Davis, published in 1996, suggested that the more active role of the police was resulting in a higher rate of cases going forward to prosecution, but that 30 per cent were dropped because the woman withdrew from the case. Not surprisingly, the rate was higher when the couple were still living together. The researchers found that the management of cases at this stage, the liaison between courts and police and the support given to women was far from satisfactory, particularly where there was a likelihood of intimidation and where the women did not have independent legal advice. More recent research, by Jalna Hanmer and others in the Killingbeck project in West Yorkshire, has suggested that a more structured and consistent approach by the police can lead to significant improvement in the rate of prosecution. The Killingbeck study also found that a strong police response worked better where outreach and advocacy support was provided simultaneously to the victims. The police offered a staged response, increasing in seriousness in a phased and standardized way with the severity or number of attacks. Thus positive policing, including pro-arrest policies, specialist units, target hardening and support for victims have all improved the policing response.

When it comes to successful prosecution, however, the situation seems little changed. While the Police and Criminal Evidence Act gave increased powers to arrest and detain, prosecutions for assault still had to be processed under the previously existing law and rules of evidence. The main change was in the possibility of compelling the woman to give evidence. The alternative, as the 1990 Home Office circular suggests, is using the woman's original statement to the police as evidence under section 23 of the Criminal Justice Act 1988, possibly along with the evidence of police officers and any other witnesses.

Compelling a woman to give evidence when she may be under threat of retaliation remains a difficult and controversial subject. While compulsion could relieve a woman of some of the guilt or apprehension that she might feel in participating in the prosecution of her husband, it has also been suggested – for example, in the Cretney and Davis research – that the Crown Prosecution Service was extremely reluctant to proceed in this situation. It is also true that the change in the law makes no difference where the couple are not married. In these situations the woman has always been a compellable witness and yet the prosecution rate has remained low.

Disquiet about the possible impact of compulsion on women was increased by the case of Michelle Renshaw, who was committed to prison for contempt of court at Leeds Crown Court in 1989 when she refused to testify against her partner, accused of wounding her, because she feared for her safety. This case and others like it since have suggested a danger that compulsion might be used according to the perceived needs of the criminal justice system rather than for the good of the women concerned. However, most commentators, including Cretney and Davis, accurately predicted that the compellability provision would rarely be used.

More recently, greater attention has been paid to the alternative approach of using the woman's original statement and other forms of evidence if the woman is reluctant to testify, although there are dangers if no attention is paid to what may be legitimate fears of intimidation and other consequences of prosecution for the woman and the family. These approaches, sometimes called enhanced or effective evidence gathering, can include the collection of photographic evidence to increase the likelihood of successful prosecution, or may involve more mundane methods, such as gathering witness statements or using police or medical evidence. There is evidence from Home Office and other studies that using cameras to produce photographs to support prosecution can result in improved justice outcomes. Photographic evidence can also be particularly effective in bail hearings. However, the availability of cameras and film can be a problem. In a recent study in which we were involved, there was only one camera per police station, so that the officers had to go and get it for domestic violence cases, and even though the equipment was dedicated for this work only, other officers were often using it for something else. However, with sufficient resources, camera evidence can be very effective.

Such initiatives need to be followed through by the CPS and the courts. Susan Edwards and others, such as Jackie Barron, and Marianne Hester and her colleagues, have pointed out the huge rate of attrition in domestic violence prosecutions. Few cases are prosecuted and even fewer lead to convictions. Many are still dropped on grounds of insufficient evidence, and charges are still downgraded, both trivializing the nature of the crime and further risking the safety of the woman if the sentence is non-custodial, which is the most common outcome. In their study in the north-east in 2003, Marianne Hester, Nicole Westmarland and colleagues found that in 869 incidents reported to the police, there were 222 arrests, 60 prosecutions and 31 convictions – just 4.3 per cent of the original incidents. There were just four (brief) custodial sentences – a staggeringly small 0.5 per cent.

This picture is borne out by the report of the HMIC and CPS Inspectorate in 2003. It is also corroborated by the 2004 report on the 2001 British Crime Survey Self Completion Questionnaire, which shows that in the worst cases of domestic violence in the study, as far as the women were aware, the police had arrested the perpetrators in only 21 per cent of cases and had 'spoken to him' in 42 per cent of cases. The man had been 'sent to court' in only 10 per cent of cases. In 29 per cent of the cases the police had not found or arrested him, and nor had he appeared in court. Despite this, among the minority of women in the study who used the police service, 68 per cent said they were fairly or very satisfied while 31 per cent were a bit or very dissatisfied. By contrast, Bossy and Coleman in the internet consultation in 2000 (to which we refer later) found that 90 per cent of the women in the study who had used the criminal justice system said that they did not receive an adequate response overall. Not only did the police not take them seriously, but the courts did not protect them.

It was partly because of dissatisfaction with the operation of the existing criminal legislation that the more active police officers welcomed the Protection from Harassment Act 1997. They favoured its more inclusive scope, the possibility of its use in both civil and criminal proceedings and its focus on an overall course of abusive actions rather than on the single incident as in other legislation (see Chapter 5). Additionally, as a result of such high rates of attrition as those documented above, the Home Office, the police and the CPS have been concerned in the 2000s to improve the conviction rate and to reduce domestic violence. One strand of this has been a particularly strong emphasis (not yet very successful in most areas) to try to reduce repeat victimization of women victims. Various new initiatives have been put into place, some funded through the Home Office and others not.

The Cardiff Women's Safety Unit, for example, works with the police to provide a central access point for victims, to improve protocols and intervention standards used by agencies and to provide a network of support, advocacy, target hardening, evidence collecting etc., including supporting women individually through the justice system. The Women's Safety Unit has reduced the number of repeat victims by 36 per cent and the number of women refusing to make a complaint by 18 per cent. It has established improved court procedures, which allow cases to be processed in half the normal time. Other Crime Reduction Projects in Bradford, Camden, Cheshire and Northampton also worked directly with the police and the criminal justice system, using a number of different service models, and the overall evaluation of these projects is being prepared at the time of writing.

The Metropolitan Police (the Met) introduced a range of new initiatives in the 2000s through their Community Safety Units, including risk assessments, checklists and other approaches. The Met has now developed a complex proactive strategy, named 'Enough is Enough'. A small selection of the measures that have been introduced include a comprehensive advertising campaign aimed at women, a domestic violence protocol with standards to be met at each stage of the justice process, extensive evidence-gathering systems and a bimonthly meeting to take forward dementia violence strategies across London. A powerful new advertising campaign aimed at violent men was launched at Arsenal football stadium in 2003. Posters have been displayed in previously unused sites, such as men's toilets, pubs, restaurants and the sports sections of London newspapers.

Several London boroughs now base civilian support workers in police stations. Third-party and self-reporting sites including same-sex domestic violence sites have been set up, and the police in London are now particularly developing services within South Asian communities. The Met conducted a 'day of raids' on domestic violence in September 2003 to demonstrate a snapshot of domestic violence in the capital. One hundred and fifteen arrests were made on this day to illustrate the Met's work, in which 500 specialist officers across London handle over 7,650 domestic violence incidents each month. The Association of Chief Police Officers has also issued a comprehensive strategy on domestic violence. However, the results of such initiatives remain problematic due to inconsistent implementation, and although it is helpful that the Domestic Violence, Crime and Victims Act makes common assault an arrestable offence, there is still a long way to go in obtaining consistent, supportive police and criminal justice system responses.

Prosecution is not always possible because many acts of domestic violence are not physical assaults; nor is it always desirable, and it is important to recognize that there has been an improvement in the more general protective role of the police: giving the woman information about Women's Aid or other support services, referring or transporting her to a refuge, or helping her to collect clothes from home after leaving. It is also possible, of course, that it is still easier to get effective support if women leave and are backed up by Women's Aid or some other agency when they seek police help. Various Women's Aid surveys as well as other research make it clear that the participating refuge services have played a significant role by supporting women in seeking police help with a number of important matters, including trying to get their children back or bringing complaints or charges against their partner. They are also very likely to have been in contact with the police when necessary to assist the women in making a complaint about the police response, or about racist or discriminatory treatment of women from minority ethnic communities.

Why have these changes taken place?

The hard work of Women's Aid and other women's organizations in the UK, and the research and monitoring work described earlier, have had an important impact on changes in police practice, but other factors must also be considered. A change took place at the level of central government guidance between 1986, when the Home Office circular was at pains to emphasize the discretionary powers of chief officers of police over operational matters, and the 1990 circular, which expected a clear response. A major factor may have been the influential action taken by the Metropolitan Police and the publicity it received.

Other influences were international. The British government was a signatory to the United Nations Convention on the Elimination of All Forms of Discrimination Against Women (CEDAW), which was later strengthened by the Declaration on the Elimination of Violence Against Women, and further emphasized in the statements from the Beijing Conference in 1995. By 1990, the government was overdue in reporting on action it had taken to implement CEDAW. It is possible that the Home Office circulars and later government action – for example, the funding of development projects under various initiatives and their evaluation – resulted partly from the need to show progress on this subject. Other international bodies, such as the Council of Europe, the European Commission and the European Parliament, were also active, and possibly influenced the climate of opinion within government towards a more interventionist position.

This might also help to explain the central position occupied by questions of policing and criminal justice responses in British government actions, particularly before the 1995 inter-agency circular. A number of the countries that had played a leading international role in action against domestic violence had highlighted action in the field of policing and pro-arrest policies in both the civil and criminal justice system. Although policing has been regarded as an important issue by UK activists and researchers, it was seen within a context that included not only the provision of refuge accommodation for temporary safety, but also the involvement of local housing authorities in the provision of safe permanent housing for women made homeless by domestic violence. This was an emphasis not present in many countries because the UK was unusual in the extent of its publicly owned housing, much of which has now been sold or is under pressure from public expenditure restrictions (see Chapter 6).

It may be, therefore, that the awakening interest of the former Conservative government in policing domestic violence, in crime prevention measures such as Safer Cities Projects and in inter-agency initiatives linking statutory and voluntary agencies, arose partly from a reluctance to recognize women's need to have access to alternative housing and other services in the community. Although the emphasis of the current New Labour government has changed, for example in recognizing the contribution to be made by advocacy and by health services, and appreciating the situation of children living with domestic violence, the promised overall strategy for action on domestic violence and violence against women in the UK has not yet materialized (although more has happened in Scotland and Wales). The main approach, as the Domestic Violence, Crime and Victims Act shows, is still to rely mainly on a more effective use of the justice system. This is not to say that arrest, detention and prosecution, backed up by civil protection orders, may not be important. It may ensure the woman's safety in the short and intermediate term, and give a clear signal that society regards domestic violence as both unacceptable behaviour and a crime that is as serious as assault of any other kind. However, it is not sufficient in itself.

The UK can also learn from other countries with similar legal systems. Legislative changes, policing practice and liaison with voluntary agencies in such countries as Australia, Canada and the USA have much to teach. But, until recently at least, it was also the case that these countries had much to learn from the UK, both from the Women's Aid movement and from the possibility for women to be safely rehoused in public sector and social rented housing, and to benefit from other social welfare provisions. The Domestic Violence, Crime and Victims Act, if strengthened by the suggested amendments put forward by a number of women's organizations and others active in the field, would have been an important first step in placing the United Kingdom once more in the forefront of action on domestic violence. However, none of the key amendments was passed.

Fears remain, therefore, among domestic violence workers that, despite an emphasis on multi-agency action since the mid-1990s and the stated need for a wide-ranging comprehensive and co-ordinated response, the current preferences of British governments are still being reflected in an emphasis on policing and prosecution with a lesser emphasis on the use of civil remedies in the courts. However, the latter are not always easily available to women who need them because the legal aid programme has become less accessible.

It is feared that policing and legal remedies may be viewed as an alternative to more holistic and vigorous government action. A comprehensive policy would mean funding much more adequate emergency, temporary and permanent housing for women escaping from domestic violence. It would involve more extensive public awareness and outreach services in the community, including services for children; and the provision of other important public welfare measures, such as reasonable income support. It would also involve more support for women who are currently still barred under the immigration laws from receiving public support. All of these involve significant public expenditure of a type not currently regarded as popular.

Even accepting the importance of the policy changes on policing, arrest and prosecution through the justice system, and even leaving other questions on one side, much less attention has been directed, so far, at the courts and the judiciary. There is scope for these to draw up their own practice guidelines, to develop their own training programmes, and to become involved in multi-agency initiatives at a national level as some have done locally. The Crown Prosecution Service recently developed comprehensive guidelines as the probation service did some years ago in consultation with Women's Aid in England. A new CPS policy, further amended and revised, was adopted in 2005. Other parts of the justice system, especially magistrates and judges, seem to have been less open to change, although the government has been developing improved training for the judiciary in some areas as recommended in 'Safety and Justice' (2003).

There have been policy improvements on some circuits (for example, in the north-east), and West London magistrates' court is leading a two-pronged approach, supporting victims while addressing perpetrator behaviour through an 18-month perpetrators' programme, as part of a wider co-ordinated response, and through a specialist domestic violence court. The Hammersmith and Fulham Standing Together project is also monitoring the justice response by tracking cases through the system (as is done in the much admired project in Duluth, Minnesota) and training workers across the criminal justice system and in the judiciary itself. (Both the Duluth Domestic Abuse Intervention Project and Standing Together are discussed in later chapters.) However, the criminal justice system as a whole may benefit from clear government encouragement to consider their overall practices in a multi-service perspective. This has improved with the new multi-agency partnerships and strategies on crime and disorder reduction, but these do not always prioritize domestic violence. Without consistent good practice in both the Crown Prosecution Service and the courts, serious assaults may still be treated lightly or excused.

Prosecution is certainly not the whole answer, and it is not always what is needed in every case. The real possibility of prosecution and conviction under criminal law must be part of an overall process in which domestic violence is taken seriously. In fact, prosecution will only work effectively if it is just one part of such a multifaceted community and agency response. The most important recommendation of all is the one summed up in the evidence given to the House of Commons Home Affairs Committee by the Women's Aid Federation of England as long ago as 1992: 'The safety and well-being of the woman and her children should always be the first priority.' This priority has been echoed by government documents: 'Living without Fear' in 1999, 'Safety and Justice' in 2003 and the 2004 Domestic Violence, Crime and Victims Act. It remains to be seen whether, as a society, we have the will to put it into practice.

5

Legal remedies and the court system

Just as policing practice has improved, so also has legal protection. The legal remedies available to women who experience domestic violence in both the criminal and the civil courts have increased significantly over the last 25–30 years, largely as a result of strong campaigning by Women's Aid and other women's organizations and services. Prosecution and court practice has not always kept pace with changes in the law, but over time improved policies and guidance on practice have been developed by agencies such as the probation service and the Crown Prosecution Service, which introduced comprehensive new guidelines in 2001, updated in 2004/5 with a revised code and further guidance, to be accompanied by a comprehensive national training programme. In addition, the 2004 Domestic Violence, Crime and Victims Act further strengthens the prosecution process and integrates the available criminal and civil remedies.

The situation was very different when the network of women's refuges grew up in the early 1970s. Then, the lack of protection for women experiencing domestic violence became very apparent. Although remedies against assault existed in both the criminal and the civil law, they were often not easy to use or not adequately enforced. As we have seen, at that time the police commonly failed to use the remedies that existed to protect women from assault under the criminal law. It was possible to obtain protection as part of an action for damages or in divorce proceedings, but only where the woman was married to her attacker, and where she had decided that she wanted the marriage to end.

Domestic violence and the civil law

Many women who came to refuge organizations did not want to use the criminal law. Often, they had left home as a last resort, sometimes in order to give themselves a breathing space, and perhaps to bring home to their partner the effect that his violence was having on their relationship and the family. Yet often the only way they could escape from repeated violence was by staying away and finding a safe, permanent place to live, since there was no easy way of getting protection against continuing assault, or of getting their violent partner removed from the house.

The Women's Aid movement, therefore, began to campaign for changes in the civil law so that women could apply for the protection available under matrimonial law, but on grounds of domestic violence alone and without the action having to be linked to any other legal proceedings. The intention was to give women some degree of choice in deciding whether or not they wanted to try to preserve their relationship. Changes in the law to give a woman the right to apply for a court order for protection from domestic violence, including both assault and harassment, were also recommended by the Select Committee on Violence in Marriage, in 1975.

Largely because of these developments, the Domestic Violence and Matrimonial Proceedings Act 1976, which applied to action in the county courts, was introduced as a private member's bill, though with government support, by Jo Richardson MP. It was followed by the Domestic Proceedings and Magistrates' Courts Act 1978 and by further changes to the law on occupation of the matrimonial home during and after divorce, in 1983. (Because of its different legal system, different though similar provisions applied in Scotland.) These laws introduced important new possibilities for women to seek legal remedies against domestic violence. They gave some women protection, in the short term at least, and a chance to think about what long-term steps to take. In practice, though, they proved to have limitations.

What follows is a brief description of the 1970s legislation and subsequent changes. There is a more detailed account of the original civil legislation on domestic violence in *Not Worth the Paper?* by Jackie Barron, which reported in 1990 on the limitations of the law in practice. The nature of the legislation and its application was also examined in two Law Commission reports, published in 1989 and 1992. These provisions are described in some detail here because of their important legal innovations, although they have now been replaced by Part IV of the Family Law Act 1996.

The Domestic Violence and Matrimonial Proceedings Act 1976 (or DVA) made important changes to existing law. One of its most far-reaching innovations was that it could be used if the couple were 'living in the same household as husband and wife' at the time of the incident of abuse or assault, whether or not they were legally married. It was also very important that applications for protection did not have to be linked to any other proceedings, such as divorce or damages.

The DVA provided for two types of order (or injunction). The first, a non-molestation order, was aimed at preventing further abuse or harassment and providing emergency protection for the applicant or any child living in the household. The second, an exclusion order, or ouster, would exclude the violent partner from the home (or part of it) for a specified period, or prevent him from returning if he had left. He could also be ordered to keep away from certain areas, such as those surrounding the home, or particular places, such as the children's school or the woman's workplace. Both types of injunction could, in some circumstances, initially be obtained without the man being present in court (*ex parte*), and an order could be backed up with police power to arrest the man if he disregarded it.

This was the first time that married and unmarried women were treated as equals in legislation affecting their shared home or their relationship. It was regarded as contentious by some judges and lawyers, and was challenged in the courts. (As we will see, this equality before the law has been modified by Part IV of the Family Law Act 1996.) The power of arrest was also contentious, even though it could be used only in cases where it had been demonstrated that a defendant had caused actual bodily harm to the applicant or to a child in the household, and if the judge was satisfied that the violence was likely to be repeated.

A power of arrest can be particularly important as a protective measure for women and children experiencing violence. It means that the police can arrest without a warrant if they have cause to believe that an injunction has been broken, even if no other arrestable offence, such as further violence, has occurred. An injunction without a power of arrest only allows the police to arrest for offences under criminal or common law. A power of arrest also means that, if arrested, the man must then be brought back to court within 24 hours for the case to be heard. Without this, the woman, or her solicitor, must apply to the court for a committal for contempt of court. A court summons then has to be served on the man, who is often able to avoid being served and may disappear, evading the summons and the court appearance indefinitely.

There were many problems with the enforcement of this law, not least because judges were reluctant to attach powers of arrest or to interfere with the property rights of the men concerned. The DVA, as described later in this chapter, was modified by case law following appeals, and by practice directions from the President of the Family Division of the High Court.

The second Act passed to deal specifically with domestic violence was the Domestic Proceedings and Magistrates' Courts Act 1978 (DPMCA). Magistrates' courts have traditionally been regarded as cheaper and more accessible, especially to working-class women, than the county courts or high courts. The purpose of the DPMCA, though more limited, was to bring matrimonial and family law in the magistrates' courts into line with that in the county courts. The DPMCA permitted magistrates to grant 'personal protection orders' and 'exclusion' or 'ouster' orders that were very similar to the injunctions of the county courts. Powers of arrest could also be attached to these orders, but the law was restricted by the fact that applicants to the magistrates' courts had to be legally married to their attacker, and magistrates were empowered to make personal protection orders only against physical violence and not against other forms of molestation or harassment. This changed when the two laws were amalgamated in Part IV of the Family Law Act 1996, which will be discussed further below.

The Matrimonial Homes Act 1983 (MHA), the third piece of legislation that provided for civil injunctions against domestic violence, applied only if a couple were married, as with the legislation in the magistrates' courts. The powers of the county court or the High Court under the MHA were not primarily intended to offer emergency protection, but were aimed at the more long-term resolution of disputes over the occupation of the matrimonial home following divorce. The court had the power to prohibit, suspend or restrict the right of either spouse to occupy the family home, or to require either to permit the other to exercise that right. These orders could have the same force as exclusion orders.

After the House of Lords' judgment in the Richards case in 1984, if a married woman was applying to exclude her husband from the home, the judge had to apply the criteria laid down in the MHA when deciding whether or not to grant the order, even if the application was made under the DVA. This meant that criteria that were intended to apply to temporary procedures on the way to a permanent property settlement between married partners were also used in deciding whether or not a woman and her children could be protected in the family home in the short term. The judgment had a very restrictive impact on the use of ouster and exclusion orders.

By raising the question of the conduct of both partners, this judgment threw the emphasis on to considering the seriousness of the violence rather than the need of the women and children for safety. After the Richards case, according to the Law Commission's Working Party Report in 1989, there appear to have been no reported cases in which a man was ousted unless there had been physical violence. Susan Atkins and Brenda Hoggett have pointed out in their book on women and the law that the multiplication of the issues to be considered also gave greater opportunities for the man to use delaying tactics to stall the making of an order.

The domestic violence legislation assumed that the woman and her partner were living together in the same home, but as we have seen, some domestic violence originates outside the home. The legislation could apply when former partners or former husbands continued to assault or harass women after they had stopped living together, but not when violence was directed at a woman by a man who had never shared a home with her.

After 1989, if the children needed protection from attack and the couple had never lived together, the Children Act could be used to obtain an injunction to protect both the mother and the children in proceedings for residence and contact orders in the Family Court (formerly custody and access), but not to oust someone who had a right of occupation. Injunctions could also be granted to protect children in the course of wardship proceedings.

After 1997, where violence was coming from outside the home and children were not involved, action could be taken under the Protection from Harassment Act. The domestic violence legislation did not apply when it was a close male relative – a father, son or brother – who was the attacker, whether or not these men were living in the same household as the woman; nor did it apply to same-sex couples. In these cases the only possibility in civil law was to apply for an injunction under action for damages. This will change, for same-sex couples at least, under the 2004 Domestic Violence Act.

Problems with civil protection after 1976: the 1990 Women's Aid research

To put present-day developments into context, it is worth considering in more detail the situation historically up until the mid-1990s. The 1990 study by Jackie Barron for Women's Aid considered three main questions: first, how likely were women to obtain the kind of order they asked for; second, whether orders lasted for as long as women needed; and third, how effective court orders were in protecting women from further abuse. The evidence from interviews and the court hearings attended suggested that, while almost everyone was successful in obtaining a non-molestation order or an undertaking, it could be difficult to get stronger protection. A number of women were unable to obtain exclusion orders even though they saw them as vital for their protection. Even in cases where there was a long history of violence, some judges and solicitors appeared to believe that it was perfectly safe for a woman to return home and that her partner would not molest her once she had a non-molestation order or an undertaking to keep the peace.

The reluctance of courts to grant ouster and exclusion orders seemed to arise because they were unwilling to interfere with men's property rights, especially where the couple were not married. Although the DVA was specifically intended to give the right to exclude the man from the family home where there had been physical violence, this was subject to much dispute and several appeals. The most important case was that of *Davis* v. *Johnson*, where an appeal to the House of Lords established that, even when those concerned were not married, an exclusion order could apply in cases where the man had rights in the property – for example, a joint tenancy with his partner. As the Law Commission pointed out in 1992, however, there was still uneasiness and confusion in the courts, especially where the woman did not have a clear legal right to occupy the family home. This led to a general Practice Direction that an exclusion or ouster order should not operate for longer than three months.

On several occasions in the course of the Women's Aid research, judges referred to Appeal Court rulings that exclusion and ouster orders were 'draconian'. A number of judges also said that they were unable to make an exclusion order unless the man was present to argue his side of the case, which was not actually the position in law. This reluctance could be overcome if the situation was seen as very serious – for example, if the woman was severely injured, or where serious criminal charges were being pursued. In other cases, if there had been a failure to serve notice of the hearing or if the man had failed to attend, the case was usually adjourned.

Men were sometimes given several weeks to make arrangements to move out, especially when the woman had left the home after a violent incident. Sometimes the judge might refuse an exclusion order altogether, on the grounds that the woman had a place to go, even if this was temporary accommodation, whereas the man did not. This was especially likely to happen if the woman had left the children behind and there was a dispute over custody (now residence). In one such case, the woman concerned told the researchers that the man had dropped the custody case once the exclusion order had been refused. In these cases, women who had not left previously would either have to remain in situations where they were likely to experience further threats or physical danger, or else have to move out, with or without their children, often into overcrowded temporary accommodation.

Ladies and gentlemen of the jury -- I ask you to consider how long you would be able to tolerate shoddy housework before being driven to hit out at your spouse in despair!

Courts were also reluctant to grant orders excluding the man from an area surrounding the home, on the grounds that they were difficult to enforce. In addition, judges and magistrates were very often unwilling to attach powers of arrest even in cases of very serious assault, particularly in some courts and some areas. Concern for the legal rights of the men, particularly their right not to be deprived of their home except under the most extreme circumstances, frequently involved a denial of the rights of the women to live in their home. It could lead to the woman, and possibly the children too, being forced out as a result of illegal actions on the man's part. In some cases identified in *Not Worth the Paper*, a non-molestation order alone had been sufficient to calm the situation down, or an exclusion order was enough to make things reasonably quiet while the man made arrangements to move out. Women themselves were often able to anticipate this. However, where they were afraid of further violence without the basic order being strengthened by adding a power of arrest to it, their knowledge of the man concerned was rarely taken into account.

Injunctions of all kinds were usually granted for three months. Occasionally they might be for six months, and they could be extended further on application. In divorce proceedings in the county courts, they could be granted until divorce was finalized and a property adjustment order made, or for an indefinite period. In some cases in the Women's Aid research, women did not realize that their original injunctions would expire on divorce, or that there was an expiry date at all. Divorced husbands returned to assault and harass their ex-wives in several instances, and in other cases men moved back in when the exclusion order expired. Some women did not know they could apply for an extension or another order, and lawyers did not always give adequate advice.

One of the chief problems with civil protection orders under the previous laws had been their enforcement. In the 1990 research, half of the women interviewed said that their partner had disobeyed the order or undertaking on at least one occasion. Some of these breaches were more serious than others, but even where they were serious and repeated, neither the police nor the courts seemed able to prevent them. The effectiveness of the orders seemed to rest mainly on the extent to which men were prepared to respect the court judgment. It seemed that the women's solicitors often acted as a filter, resisting action on breach of injunctions according to their own view of what a court would take seriously. Cases are quoted in which assaults following an injunction or undertaking were not taken back to court, including one in which the woman's finger was broken and her partner was constantly threatening her.

It was apparently common practice for solicitors merely to write a letter warning that further breaches would be taken to court. In some cases this might happen many times and the solicitor would not act. Women also found they got little help from the police when the injunctions were broken, even when they had been physically attacked. In one case quoted, the man came back to the house on the day the injunction was granted. When the police came, the man had hold of both the woman's arms, but the police only told him to let her go. The woman told the police she had an injunction and asked them what they were going to do. 'And they said, "Nothing. We'll just let him go . . . we haven't seen nothing happen."'

This research was carried out before the issuing of the Home Office Guidelines in 1990, but as noted in the previous chapter, there had been earlier guidelines in 1986 from the Home Office, and the Metropolitan Police Force Orders of 1987 had received national publicity. As it happens, the police force in the main research area had adopted force orders which recommended that officers take domestic violence seriously. However, women were still told by police in the area that they could act only if there were powers of arrest attached to the injunctions.

Police apparently failed to recognize that the courts were reluctant to grant a power of arrest in the first place. Then, in addition, when the courts did attach powers of arrest after there had been severe assault, the police often refused to use these powers. And courts were also unwilling to commit a man to prison for contempt even where there were frequent and serious breaches of injunctions or undertakings. The research describes a failure to act which stretches from solicitors through the police to the courts themselves – which appeared simultaneously to insist on the sanctity of court orders in words and to collude with the man's contempt for court orders in practice.

A large study for the *Dispatches* television programme in 1998 confirmed this seminal Women's Aid study and found that almost nothing had changed. It is still not clear that that these problems have been solved by the Family Law Act, Part IV, since Susan Edwards' court statistics survey in 2000 showed a wide variation in court practice. However, research for Women's Aid by Jackie Barron, published in 2002, showed that 65 per cent of refuges responding to a survey believed that the Family Law Act had improved the protection available, even though only 43 per cent were satisfied by the protection offered by occupation orders, as compared with 54 per cent satisfaction with non-molestation orders.

The Law Commission's proposals for change

The Law Commission considered the question of domestic violence and the occupation of the family home for a number of years. A report published in 1992 made recommendations for rationalizing the civil legislation on domestic violence and drew up a draft Family Homes and Domestic Violence Bill. These proposals were endorsed, in the main, by the House of Commons Home Affairs Committee in 1993. After much delay, the draft bill formed the basis of legislation put before Parliament in 1995. The Family Homes and Domestic Violence Bill proposed to introduce a unified law on the civil remedies available for protection against violence and harassment, and for regulating the occupation of the family home after a relationship breakdown.

After it was introduced into Parliament, a coalition of right-wing journalists, organizations convinced that men's rights in the family are being undermined, and disaffected government MPs combined to force the abandonment of the bill late in 1995. (If nothing else this showed that domestic violence had become a highly politicized issue.) The substance of the bill was then reintroduced in 1996 as part of the Family Law Bill, which also contained new proposals on divorce and was passed amid a flurry of amendments and much lobbying by a variety of groups. Women's Aid nationally played a very significant part in preserving most of the spirit of the original bill despite a variety of attempts to alter it radically. However, the law as passed did differ from the original proposals in a number of significant ways, particularly in distinguishing between married and unmarried couples in relation to the property rights of the parties when deciding the length of occupation orders.

The Family Law Act 1996, Part IV

The 1996 law provided, as the previous legislation did, for two types of civil remedy, a non-molestation order and an occupation order, the first being designed to prevent violence or molestation of another family member, and the second to order one partner or other 'associated persons' to leave or stay away from the family home. The occupation order regulates the occupation of the family home in either the short or the long term where the relationship has broken down. The Law Commission had recommended that a decision to make an occupation order should be based on the 'balance of need' and decided in the interests of whoever had the most need to occupy the family home, taking into account the welfare of any children, but not the conduct of either party. However, the amended Act reintroduced the question of conduct prior to a 'balance of harm' test.

The Family Law Act allows orders to be used for a much broader range of people and relationships than before. They can be made for any specified period or indefinitely for as long as they are needed – beyond the end of a relationship if necessary. The previous normal limit for exclusion and ouster orders of three months was seen as too short to allow a proper examination of housing options and to find alternative accommodation. This initial period had already been changed to six months in Scotland because it led to too many applications for extension. However, 3–6 months still appears to be the unofficial 'norm' for orders.

These orders have a very broad scope. The potential applicants include both those who are already legally entitled by ownership or tenancy to occupy the family home and those who are not, but the rights of those who are not legally entitled are more limited. For most women, including cohabitants and other 'entitled persons' who are sole or joint owners or tenants of their home, any order can be made for any specified period or indefinitely. This means that now, in England and Wales, as in Scotland previously, cohabitants with a right to occupy the family home will be treated the same as married women with property rights. But the agitation against the law made itself felt in a distinction according to marital status, in applications by former partners who are not legally entitled to occupy the family home, against a partner with property rights. An occupation order for a married or formerly married partner can be made for an initial period of up to six months and extended for further periods of six months on several occasions. A former cohabitant in the same situation can be granted an order for up to six months, but this can only be extended for one period of up to six months. The restriction applied regardless of the length of time the couple have lived together or the financial or other contributions a woman may have made to the family home. As mentioned above, these restrictions relating to unmarried status and to same-sex couples will be substantially removed when the 2004 Act comes into effect.

However, even with these restrictions, the 1996 law was a great advance. It offered protection for a much wider range of women in a much wider range of situations and for a longer period. It extended protection to abused children by amending the Children Act 1989, so that the abuser may be excluded, if another person living in the home is able and willing to care for the child and consents to the exclusion requirement. There is also provision for applications to be made by children. Part IV was accompanied by a Department of Health circular giving guidance to Social Service Departments on its use.

The Family Law Act strengthened and broadened the scope of orders in other ways. The orders are available, as before, without any other proceeding being necessary, but also in the course of any family proceedings, with or without an application being made first. Application can be made in any family court with provisions for the transfer of a case, to link it with other proceedings or to allow it to be transferred to a different court or different level of court. For example, it is possible to transfer more complex cases from a magistrates' court to a county court or the High Court.

Under the Act, a court is required to attach a power of arrest to specified provisions of an order 'unless in all the circumstances the applicant or a child would be adequately protected without such a power'. Where the respondent is not present, the court is not required to attach a power of arrest, but should do so if it is satisfied that there is a risk of significant harm. The power of the magistrates' court to remand a man in custody or on bail in the course of committal proceedings has also been extended to other courts.

The Act has a number of other strengths. The power to transfer a joint tenancy to the one name could lead to an easier exchange of tenancies, so that women afraid to stay in their former homes may need to spend less time in refuges or other temporary accommodation. There is also an opportunity to pilot the use of orders applied for by third parties, such as police, to protect abused women in conjunction with other court actions. Such actions have been used successfully with the woman's consent in the USA and Australia, as described in 1977 by Cathy Humphreys of the University of Warwick and others, but has not been implemented in the UK. Two useful explanatory booklets on the law were published by the former Lord Chancellor's Department in 1997. Nicola Harwin, the Director of the Women's Aid Federation of England, looked in more detail at the advantages and disadvantages of the Act in a chapter in *Making an Impact*, written by Marianne Hester, Chris Pearson and Nicola Harwin for the Department of Health in 2000 and updated in 2004–5.

The limited amount of research undertaken so far suggests that the 1996 law is having a positive effect, with some reservations on the length of time injunctions apply, the use of occupation orders and the degree to which powers of arrest are being attached, particularly *ex parte*, and especially to occupation orders. However, the history of the original domestic violence legislation of the 1970s suggests that changing the law in itself will not always be enough. The Women's Aid research in 2000 suggests a reluctance to use occupation orders to secure the family home for women and children, and Susan Edwards' court records survey in 2000 shows the law being applied unevenly in different court areas. Given the previous reluctance of many courts to attach powers of arrest, and a preference in some courts for the use of undertakings rather than orders, some doubts must remain as to how far the legal system has taken on board the full spirit of the legislation, and how far its impact is being muffled by the use of discretion.

Some general aspects of civil legal proceedings and orders

A woman seeking civil legal remedies will normally consult a solicitor and have legal representation in court, although she has the right to present her own case if she chooses, or if she is unable to instruct a lawyer for financial or other reasons. It is easier for a woman to present her own case in the magistrates' court because the clerk to the justices has a duty to help her and there is no need to present typed and sworn affidavits. In the past, women have often been eligible for legal aid, but this has become more difficult to obtain because of government measures to restrict the numbers eligible by using stricter means tests.

In an emergency, all injunctions may be applied for *ex parte*. If the assault is likely to happen again or if the woman has nowhere to go, this should mean that there will be a court hearing the same day, or the next day at the latest. In practice, though, the courts have been very reluctant to make *ex parte* exclusion or ouster (now 'occupation') orders, and powers of arrest have very rarely been attached *ex parte*. It still remains unclear how far practice has changed under the Family Law Act, Part IV.

In the county courts it has been a common practice to substitute an 'undertaking' for a court order. This may happen when the man or his lawyers suggest to the woman's legal representative that he is willing to 'undertake' not to assault her, and perhaps also to promise to leave the home by a particular date. None of the evidence will be heard and no judgment will be made on the truth of the allegations, so women have often been advised by lawyers to agree in order to simplify the hearing. The application would then be withdrawn or adjourned, and the man asked to sign an undertaking instead. An undertaking signed in court is, in theory, similar to a court order, and a breach of an undertaking carries the same penalties as any other breach of the court's directives. However, in practice it is not regarded as seriously, and no power of arrest can be attached because the man has signed the undertaking willingly. Women's Aid therefore recommended the abolition of the use of undertakings in cases of domestic violence by the 2004 Domestic Violence, Crime and Victims Act, but without success.

If a man leaves shortly after attacking his partner, it can be difficult to serve an injunction or a notice on him to attend the court. This can mean that further assaults occur and that the police and representatives of the court are unable to catch up with him. The inability to serve notice can delay a full hearing for several days. If the case is heard *ex parte*, any order will probably be temporary, usually for a week, and the woman will have to return to court when it expires. In the past, at least, she was also unlikely to be granted an exclusion order (now occupation order) except in extreme circumstances. Courts do have the power to rule that service is 'deemed good', if, for example, the woman is prepared to swear that she has told the man of the hearing date, but courts are reluctant to do this until several attempts have been made to hold a full hearing.

The most serious problem in this situation is that, in general, no court order is in force until it has been served. If the man has disappeared or is evading service, it is possible to serve the documents on someone else who is known to be seeing the man regularly, but solicitors often seem unaware of this possibility. Evasion of service can prevent a woman and children being able to stay in their home because of delays in hearing dates, and can allow further violence to take place without remedy, even if an *ex parte* order has been made. Such problems remain even with the strengthened and simplified proceedings of the Family Law Act.

The Protection from Harassment Act 1997

Although it is usually thought to apply to harassment by strangers, the 1977 legislation on 'stalking' is most often used to protect women who no longer live with their abuser or who have never lived with him. A survey by chief police officers, quoted by Nicola Harwin in *Making an Impact*, found that 60 per cent of the worst cases of stalking involved a close relationship. In most cases the person being harassed was a woman who would probably not have been able to use the Family Law Act.

The Protection from Harassment Act (PfHA) links civil and criminal law, and an order can be made under one or the other depending on circumstances. As well as civil law injunctions for protection from harassment (which are also available to those who are not eligible under the Family Law Act 1996) the law introduces two new criminal offences. These are criminal harassment, which can be tried only in the magistrates' court, and an offence involving fear of violence, which can be tried in either a magistrates' court or a crown court. A restraining order can be issued for either offence and the scope of restraining orders will be widened by Part 2 of the 2004 Domestic Violence, Crime and Victims Act.

Under the Protection from Harassment Act, an offence can be committed by following a course of conduct that amounts to harassment or causes fear of violence to another person, if the perpetrator 'knows, or ought to know' that it would cause a fear of violence. The advantage of this Act over other criminal law is that the incidents do not have to be all serious or of the same kind, and police can arrest without warrant if they suspect that either of these offences is being committed, without having to wait for serious physical or psychological harm to be caused. Nicola Harwin points out the importance of the law for women without children who do not live with their abusers, and of courts being able to offer protection to women against men who continue to harass and threaten them after the relationship has ended, especially since we now know that women are more likely to be killed by an abusive partner in what is now often called 'post-separation violence'.

Together the Family Law Act 1996, Part IV and the Protection from Harassment Act 1997 have the potential to offer more flexible protection than before. The use of criminal proceedings under the second could avoid the problem of costs involved in civil law action if women do not need occupation orders to exclude their abuser from their home.

As mentioned above, the Domestic Violence, Crime and Victims Act will extend the availability of restraining orders under the Protection from Harassment Act to cover all criminal proceedings relating to violent offences under the PfHA, including in cases short of conviction, if the court considers it is necessary to make an order to protect the victim. However, many women will still need to use the existing criminal law on assault despite its problems.

The criminal law

The law on assault is in theory the same for domestic violence as for violence of any other kind, and is largely contained in the Offences Against the Person Act 1861. This Act deals with all forms of assault from common assault to murder – and includes sexual assault, although this is also covered in the Sexual Offences Act 1956, the Sexual Offences (Amendment) Act 1976 and, along with physical assault, in the Protection from Harassment Act 1997. The four sections of the Offences Against the Person Act that are most likely to be relevant to domestic violence are those covering common assault, assault causing actual bodily harm (ABH), malicious wounding, and grievous bodily harm (GBH). There is also the possibility that the man may not actually attack the woman or the children personally, but may break windows or furniture, destroy her clothing or even burn down the house. These actions are also clearly subject to legal sanctions for criminal damage (although potentially limited if the property damaged is held to be owned by the man himself) or other criminal charges under laws that have long been on the statute books. Action under common law for breach of the peace is also possible. Here it is relevant that research suggests that the downgrading of assault causing bodily harm to the currently non-arrestable offence of common assault is still relatively common. It is encouraging that Part 2 of the Domestic Violence, Crime and Victims Act, when implemented, will make common assault an arrestable offence. This has the potential to offer more immediate protection even if it does not entirely remove the possibility of downgrading.

Although sexual assault and rape by partners are often involved in domestic violence, women are less likely to report these than other kinds of assault. Until a House of Lords judgment in 1991, it was regarded as impossible in law for a man to rape his wife because of the assumption that sexual intercourse within marriage could not be unlawful. An offence of sexual assault was legally possible where there had been violence, but ruling attitudes in the justice system tended to make charges unlikely unless the violence was extreme.

As we saw in Chapter 1, the murder of women by their husbands has been seen as a lesser crime than the killing of other people, or the killing by women of their violent partners. The question of justice for women who kill their husbands or partners after experiencing years of violent abuse has been brought out sharply in recent years. As we will discuss in Chapter 9, campaigns on behalf of a number of women who have killed their violent husbands or partners have taken up issues arising out of the legal definitions of provocation, diminished responsibility and self-defence. Public attention has focused mainly on the way in which the defence of provocation has been interpreted by the courts. This appears to have worked to the advantage of men who have killed their wives and who plead successfully that this has been provoked by a succession of comparatively trivial acts, the last of which has caused them to kill in a moment of 'sudden loss of self-control'. As we have seen, a resulting conviction for manslaughter can lead to a light sentence of a few years' imprisonment, or even no imprisonment at all. Yet for women the defence has often been rejected – or in certain cases not put forward by the woman's lawyer – where the provocation has consisted of repeated and extreme acts of violence, but where the woman's retaliation has been delayed. This leads to a supposition of premeditation and a conviction for murder, which carries an automatic life sentence.

In its report on domestic violence, the House of Commons All-Party Committee on Home Affairs endorsed the recommendation of a new statutory definition for the defence of provocation made by the Law Commission in its Draft Criminal Code for England and Wales in 1989. However, Southall Black Sisters, who have been closely involved in women's campaigns for justice, saw the Law Commission's proposals as a step backwards from the position that was established by Lord Taylor in his judgment in the appeal of Kiranjit Ahluwalia in 1992. This stated that the question of self-control should be examined in the light of the evidence in the case, rather than relying on the concept of 'suddenness' as a rule of law.

The Home Affairs Committee rejected changes to the current definition of 'sufficient force' in self-defence to allow for women's lesser physical strength, and also rejected the introduction of a new defence of self-preservation, which would differ from self-defence because it would not require a life-threatening act immediately to precede it. This was because the committee feared the possibility of 'revenge killings committed while defendants were fully in control of their emotions resulting in convictions only for manslaughter'. Yet, as we have seen, it is clear that very few women commit homicide of any kind, while a significant proportion of homicides are committed by men against their wives or female partners. It therefore seems very unlikely that a change in the law would lead to an outbreak of revenge killings by women. However, a careless redrafting of the law might lead to an even greater toll of deaths among women, which could be successfully defended on the grounds of provocation. Rights of Women has recommended a partial defence of 'self-preservation' on the grounds of prolonged abuse and intimidation. This and a number of other similar submissions have been made in response to the 2004 Law Commission consultation paper on partial defences to murder, and the proposed new defences suggested in it will partly address the problem. Currently, though, there is no alternative to reliance on the findings of recent appeal cases, following successful campaigns against a number of convictions, and a somewhat less punitive interpretation of existing law. Whatever changes may take place in legal definitions, there is no short cut to changing the culture and climate in which the law operates.

Enforcement of the law and the nature of the legal system

Many legal and feminist scholars and researchers have seen the organization of the law and the legal system itself as part of the reason why women who experienced domestic violence find it difficult to get justice. Susan Edwards, for example, in her 1989 study of the police concluded that the law in the widest sense 'subverts rather than facilitates protection for women'. These defects in the legal system can be seen as interacting with perceptions by those within the system that violence against wives or female partners is both distinct from, and less serious than, violence against other people.

Susan Edwards at that time saw the distinction between public and private law as part of the problem, and regarded as mistaken those feminists and others who saw civil remedies as in some ways more useful than criminal proceedings. For her the use of the civil law reinforced the public/private divide and the cultural fabric that sees men as masters within the home and 'possessed of a natural entitlement to correct, chastise and sometimes batter justifiably'. Although practice has changed in many respects, such attitudes have been evident in relation to some of the court judgements in civil law discussed above and in the vociferous opposition to the changes finally implemented in the Family Law Act 1996. They are still shown in the differential entitlement to occupation orders under the Act and what appears to be a reluctance of the courts to use them.

In the criminal justice system there can also be a reluctance to take action despite all of the policy changes since the mid-1980s. When women are willing to press charges we still see a downgrading of charges during the arrest and prosecution process and an apparent reluctance to use custodial sentences. One general problem in relation to prosecuting an assault under criminal law is in assessing whether a case is strong enough to proceed. In Chapter 4, we described the past reluctance of the police to take domestic violence cases forward, even where the woman was willing for a prosecution to take place. Now that the police are being advised by the Home Office that prosecution should be considered seriously in a wider range of such assaults, the actual decision to prosecute rests no longer with them, but with the Crown Prosecution Service (CPS). The police were advised in the Home Office circular of 1990 to consult with the CPS on the criteria to be considered in these cases before sending a case forward. However, like solicitors, they are likely to exercise their own discretion first and the Home office evaluation of the Protection from Harassment Act in 2000 showed that no police in that study did consult the CPS in advance. They may therefore attempt to anticipate the views of the CPS in relation to the strength of the evidence, the likelihood of a conviction and whether such a prosecution would be in the public interest, and this is likely to influence the nature of the cases that the police refer to the CPS.

When cases do come forward for prosecution, despite the important 2001 guidance and further 2005 policy from the CPS on positive prosecution policies, mentioned in the previous chapter, attitudes in different areas are likely to vary. Individual prosecutors will exercise discretion, although within limits set by these national guidelines, which are very detailed and contain a comprehensive checklist of matters to be considered and decisions or comments on these. Therefore the recommendation in various government publications since the 1990s that the CPS should gather regional and national figures on prosecution, and remedy existing regional disparities, continues to be very important in trying to ensure that there is consistency in prosecution policy throughout the country. Such efforts to ensure consistency will be strengthened by the pilot projects on charging and prosecution being carried out and evaluated in a number of areas, including Croydon and South Wales.

When dealing with the possibility that a woman might withdraw her complaint, Home Office circulars draw the attention of the police to the powers of the CPS, under the Magistrates' Courts Act 1980 and the Police and Criminal Evidence Act 1984, to compel a spouse or cohabitee to attend court for the purpose of giving evidence. The question of the compellability of witnesses is a very difficult matter, as we saw in Chapter 4. The most recent CPS guidelines, though referring to powers of compulsion, highlight many of the background factors that may lead to withdrawal by women, to all of the relevant legislation and types of evidence gathering that may be used to strengthen the case for prosecution even in the absence of the women's direct testimony, to alternative sentences which may be seen as more acceptable by them, to protective measures which may be used in cases of intimidation and to measures possible under the Youth Justice and Criminal Evidence Act to assist vulnerable and intimidated witnesses in giving evidence.

However, the difficult issues remain. On the one hand, policies of dropping prosecution whenever a police officer or prosecutor feels that a woman may be reluctant to proceed are not at all helpful. On the other hand, a decision to call the police for protection should not set off an unstoppable juggernaut in which a decision to arrest and detain a man in order to prevent further violence progresses inevitably to prosecution, despite the wishes of the woman. This could be especially dangerous where other evidence is not obtainable and the woman is the only witness, who might be compelled to give evidence despite threats of retaliation, or be imprisoned for contempt of court if she refuses. There are various attempts in the UK to prosecute domestic violence without requiring the woman to give evidence, and to introduce new initiatives, including victim support programmes, which could make it less intimidating for her to go through the prosecution process. A number of research studies have suggested that such policies can help, but ultimately the decision of the woman not to proceed with a complaint does normally lead to an automatic dropping of the prosecution.

The 1993 Home Affairs Committee and subsequent reports recognized the danger of the intimidation of witnesses in these cases and recommended the prosecution of men responsible. This is now available under the Protection from Harassment Act and has been extended by an amendment to that Act by section 4 of the Criminal Justice and Police Act 2001 to apply to collective harassment in which the former partner involves other people in harassment and intimidation. It is also welcome that the CPS undertakes to explain decisions directly to the women concerned, including giving reasons for downgrading charges. However, both the police, in the stages leading up to the decision to charge the man and send the details to the CPS, and the CPS itself, in deciding whether to proceed with a prosecution, should consult the woman concerned and make decisions jointly with her about when and how to proceed, especially when she is reluctant to testify.

It is heartening that the new CPS guidance states the necessity for the police and CPS 'to consult with each other and with the victim at all stages'. Although it is envisaged that the police will normally carry out such consultation, the guidelines state that under new regulations the CPS role in direct communication with witnesses will expand. Even here, there is a need to appreciate the dangers a woman may face if a prosecution proceeds on the basis of her statement under section 23 of the Criminal Justice Act 1988, even if she does not testify, and to recognize the need to provide adequate support.

The Domestic Violence, Crime and Victims Act: a new approach or a missed opportunity?

Following a White Paper, 'Justice for All', in 2002 and a consultation paper, 'Safety and Justice', in June 2003, the government drew up a new bill on domestic violence: the Domestic Violence, Crime and Victims Bill, which was passed by Parliament in November 2004, although no implementation date had been set at the time of writing. The White Paper and the consultation documents contained a wide range of proposals, and aimed to develop a comprehensive strategy on domestic violence covering prevention, protection, justice and support. However, as its name suggests, the core of the Act lies in measures to improve legal protection through the justice system. To summarise: by amendments to Part IV of the Family Law Act, breach of a non-molestation order will become a criminal offence; most of the distinctions in the Family Law Act between married and non-married couples will be repealed; cohabitees will include same-sex couples; and 'associated persons' to whom the Act applies will include non-cohabiting couples and relatives who are closely associated with the household, including cousins where relevant. New restraining orders will be introduced in the Protection from Harassment Act which can be ordered by the court on acquittal of an offence if the court thinks it necessary to protect a person from harassment, and common assault will become an arrestable offence in criminal law. Other changes to the criminal law will include a new offence of causing or abetting the death of a child or vulnerable adult. In addition, Domestic Homicide Reviews will be set up and a Code of Practice for victims, a Victim Advisory Panel and a Commissioner for Victims and Witnesses will be established.

The Domestic Violence Bill had a narrower scope than the strategic perspective developed in previous policy and consultation documents. Women's Aid, the Women's National Commission Violence Against Women Working Group, the Greater London Domestic Violence Project, Southall Black Sisters, and Imkaan and a number of other Asian women's organizations, among others, jointly sponsored a number of suggested amendments, mainly concentrating on the justice system, criminal justice, civil law, immigration law and the family courts. A briefing from Women's Aid in January 2004 contains a very useful summary of the main government proposals and the responses to them.

All of these organizations welcomed the bill, but wished to see some measures strengthened and extended, or qualified to make them more precise. The major proposals that breach of a non-molestation order should become a criminal offence, that the definition of 'co-habitants' should include same-sex couples and that the Act should apply to non-cohabiting couples were welcomed. However, suggested amendments included proposals that the breach of an occupation order should also be a criminal offence where there is a risk of harm, that undertakings to keep the peace should not be used as a substitute for a substantive order in domestic violence cases, and that protection orders should be for at least a year's duration, extendable until protection is no longer needed.

The amendment of Part IV of the Family Law Act to create a new offence of causing or allowing the death of a child or a vulnerable adult raises concerns that a woman experiencing domestic violence may be charged with this proposed offence for not taking 'reasonable steps' to protect her child, even though she may be powerless to do so. Women's Aid proposed exempting adult victims of domestic violence from this offence. The suggested exemption was linked to a proposed new legal definition of domestic violence to include issues of child protection. The proposed definition is based on the New Zealand definition, as agreed with the Women's National Commission on Violence Against Women Working Group and other associated organizations, and supported by the Lord Chancellor's Department Children Act Sub Committee in 2001.

The proposal to amend criminal legislation to make common assault an arrestable offence (i.e. allowing police to arrest for common assault without a warrant) was welcomed. But the Women's National Commission (WNC) working group further proposed that consideration be given to the Austrian law, now also in effect in Germany, Norway and Switzerland, giving police power to remove perpetrators for 10 days, extendable by an injunction application, and that police be required by law to inform domestic violence victims about advocacy and support services including women's refuge-based organizations.

The WNC working group also welcomed the proposal in the Act to extend the availability of restraining orders under the Protection from Harassment Act and to give the victim the right to make representation to the court about the terms of the order. However, the working group considered that this would be ineffective without judicial training, since, despite guidance to judges that they should issue restraining orders under the Act when they make a conviction, Home Office research published in 2000 showed that only 50 per cent did so. There have also been concerns about the accessibility of information on restraining orders and their enforceability, and a fear that these may be undermined by family court orders. The WNC group suggested that it would need to be a requirement that family court judges, in hearing applications for residence or contact in domestic violence cases, should not issue orders that contradict existing criminal or civil court orders, and this was incorporated in the Act.

A number of other important amendments were suggested by the WNC and associated organisations. These were not incorporated in the Act, but form part of a continuing programme of reform. It was suggested that family courts should have the power to issue restraining orders in contact proceedings to protect children and their non-abusive primary carer before, during and after any contact order is made. However, the usefulness of restraining orders on conviction or acquittal was seen as limited because the majority of women needing protection do not get to court or enter the criminal justice system. Better protection might be given by issuing guidance to judges reinforcing the power to refuse bail when the offender is likely to harass the victim or commit further offences against her; to strengthen enforcement of penalties for breach of bail; and to apply suitable conditions to bail, which should not be varied without notice to the victim. Women's Aid also proposed amendments, not incorporated in the Act, to give power to the courts to issue restraining orders, at the point at which the CPS charges perpetrators pending trial, which could have kept perpetrators away from the home, the surrounding area and other places frequented by the victim;

A further 15 proposed amendments include the introduction of a new legal definition of domestic violence to cover all forms of violence, recognizing the effect of domestic violence on other family members including children, and recognizing in law perpetrators who are other family members. A three-part amendment to the Children Act 1989 was proposed on contact in domestic violence related cases – to safeguard children's wishes on contact and to apply a mandatory risk assessment checklist. There is also a proposal to prohibit perpetrators' use of recovery orders to locate and remove a child from the care of a victim of domestic violence, without adequate risk assessment or the opportunity for the court to hear evidence of abuse or the views of both parties. Some of these suggested measures are being discussed with the government in connection with the draft Children (Contact) and Adoption Bill.

A number of important amendments originally proposed by Southall Black Sisters were endorsed by the other organizations. These cover the extension of the domestic violence exemption within immigration rules to all women whose status has not been confirmed and an exemption to the 'no recourse to public funds' rule so that women experiencing domestic violence and subject to immigration control can access government benefits or other government funding for housing and living expenses.

Other suggested measures would also be important in bringing a wider range of safeguards and plugging gaps in the law. On the eve of the second reading in the House of Commons, attention was drawn to the omission from the bill of any provision for an effective advocacy service. Amendments were put forward by the Greater London Authority, the Greater London Domestic Violence Project and Women's Aid, calling for a nationally funded but locally delivered advocacy system, so that women could have access to advice and support independently of, or 'before, during and long after any court process' (to quote the Women's Aid submission). They were also supported by the WNC working group and a national coalition of organizations and experts.

The relatively narrow scope of the Act as passed was disappointing to many activists and service providers despite its positive features. Because of the time taken over the consultation and drafting of the legislation, the wide-ranging nature of its proposals and the suggested amendments, the Act provided the best opportunity so far to develop the government's promised strategy on domestic violence, producing a truly comprehensive approach that would honour the commitment to 'joined-up government'. As it stands, the broader elements of multi-service support remain uneasily related to a strategy of widening and extending the existing primary reliance on policing and the justice system.

Prosecution and after

In looking at possible action in the legal system, it is important to stress that arrest will not always lead to prosecution, prosecution will not always result in conviction and conviction seldom leads to a prison sentence (as shown by the examples of attrition discussed in the last chapter). The use of 'preliminary intent' under the Criminal Justice Act however, can be seen as something that might protect women and help to overcome the complications, and the work involved for the police, if a prosecution is started and not proceeded with.

As we saw in Chapter 4, there are many reasons why abused women might not wish their partner to be prosecuted or imprisoned. There is also the problem of a lack of protection for women in the process of prosecution and following the release of a man – even one who is given a custodial sentence. The advice of the Home Office that the woman should be informed when the man is about to be released deals with only part of the problem. In our research study on domestic violence and housing, we found that the release of a husband or partner from custody could lead to a woman becoming homeless either from a well-founded fear of further violence, or because of actual attacks on her or the house following her partner's release.

In fact, it is still less likely that a man will be imprisoned in cases of domestic violence than for other kinds of assault or for property crime, and, as for any other crime, there are debates in any case about the effectiveness of imprisonment. However, even though imprisonment is not always desirable, it is very important that the offence is not trivialized by being treated more leniently than other offences of similar seriousness. Women's Aid workers and abused women themselves are often frustrated by the sentencing policy of judges in these cases. After the trauma involved for a woman in going through the prosecution process, and the filtering that operates to divert all but the most serious cases from prosecution, a fine or a suspended sentence, and the kind of remarks sometimes made by judges in the process, can give a man the impression that his attacks on his partner are being condoned by the justice system.

One welcome recent development in areas such as Leeds and Hammersmith and Fulham in West London is the piloting of specialist Domestic Violence Courts where all types of civil, criminal and family proceedings related to domestic violence cases can be heard together, with back-up from domestic violence witness support services and other community-based services. These are still at an experimental stage and it is too early to tell whether they will become more widespread, but their impact looks positive so far.

Benefits and limitations of using the legal system

There has been a continuing debate among feminists as to whether domestic violence falls most appropriately within the scope of the civil or the criminal law. On the one hand, there are those who regard the 'diversion' of domestic violence protection into civil courts as an error because it reinforces popular family ideology, and reaffirms a belief that marital violence is different from other violent crime. On the other hand, while not denying the possible deterrent effect of prosecution in itself, it is the case that custodial sentences are still rare, and that any protection given to the woman and children by bail conditions no longer operates after the hearing. There is also the problem that the woman herself is not legally represented in criminal prosecution and has no control over the process of the case or the outcome, as she does to some extent in civil actions.

In our opinion, which is shared by many others, it is important to recognize that neither civil nor criminal sanctions can offer a solution to domestic violence, or deal adequately with its consequences for those who experience it. Only a comprehensive approach involving many different services and agencies will even begin to deal with these consequences. This must include adequate, independent advice and advocacy services and emergency, temporary and permanent alternative accommodation, as well as safeguarding women and children in their own homes wherever possible.

Domestic violence and violence against women overall is not simply a legal problem, which can be eradicated by appropriate legal remedies. It is also a social and psychological problem, which can be eliminated only by fundamental changes in society and in attitudes to women and children. While legal remedies are an attempt to alleviate the symptoms of domestic violence, they can do little to tackle the causes. Yet, as the Law Commission recognized, the alleviation of symptoms is important. The same judgement applies also to the actions of other agencies, such as social services and the health services, and in the provision of housing, which will be discussed in the following chapters. If a comprehensive and coordinated attempt were made to alleviate the symptoms, it might at least make tackling the causes a little easier.

6

Finding somewhere safe to live: housing options

One of the most important needs of women leaving home due to violence is access to safe, secure permanent housing. Women's Aid and the domestic violence movement provide a network of refuge projects and other services, but the accommodation is available only on an emergency and temporary basis. Legal remedies, as laid out in the 1996 Family Law Act, can assist some women in remaining in or returning safely to their former homes, but for very many women, the protection offered is insufficient or ineffective. In any case, a large number of women who have left home because of violence do not feel safe in going back to the same property even if the man has been effectively excluded.

For very large numbers of women in this situation, then, the only way to be really safe is to make a fresh start far away from their home area and in a place that their violent partners do not know about. Women fleeing violence are usually quite clear about the dangers that they face. They may well know that, if they are found by their partners, it will all start up again, that the only safe possibility is to disappear and begin again somewhere else. Such a dramatic life-move takes great courage, but many women and children take the enormous step, often with only a suitcase or perhaps just the clothes they stand up in.

To get away from a violent relationship in this way means first and foremost having somewhere safe and permanent to escape to. Temporary accommodation in refuges becomes merely a dead end, the hope it offers a charade, if there is no permanent accommodation available afterwards. For many women in the UK, applying to be rehoused by local councils or housing associations is often their only option. However, privately rented accommodation can sometimes help, and some women are able to become owner occupiers in their own right. These options have been much favoured by recent governments and are discussed in the next section.

Private accommodation: owned or rented

Some women may be able to find private rented accommodation. This can have the advantage, if furnished, of providing furniture and facilities, which can be helpful for women who have been forced to leave all their possessions behind. It can be a particularly useful option for women without children. However, renting from a private landlord does not usually offer a good source of long-term, permanent accommodation. Private tenancies are almost always insecure. This is particularly so since the introduction of the shorthold tenancies that many private landlords currently offer, and which are often for as brief a period as six months. In addition, privately rented accommodation can be very expensive, priced outside the range of people on low incomes.

In the cheaper tenancies, conditions are sometimes poor and the accommodation is often limited to bedsits with little comfort and no security, leaving women fleeing domestic violence particularly vulnerable. Tenants' rights have been eroded over recent years, so it can be hard to get such properties improved. But even these cheaper options may cost more than women can afford, especially in the capital. Jenny Muir and Mandy Ross of the London Housing Unit produced a book in 1993 called *Housing the Poorer Sex*, which detailed how difficult it was for many women in London to make use of private rented accommodation, and the basic situation has not changed since. On average, women have lower incomes than men and therefore find it harder to gain access to housing in the private sector. The London Housing Unit found that only 19 per cent of women could afford to rent a bedsit in London without assistance from housing benefit, as compared with 57 per cent of men. It demonstrated that privately rented housing, in London at least, was only slightly more affordable than owner occupation. This has remained the case to date with rents in many cities, especially London, prohibitively high.

Rented accommodation can also be hard to find. The private rented sector remains very small in the UK compared with other western countries. In many areas, private tenancies are extremely scarce, and the competition to procure them may be fierce. In major cities, for example, such tenancies are often taken within hours of being advertised. Crucially, a very large number of private landlords refuse to take children. For these reasons, the private rented sector does not offer a satisfactory permanent solution for many women fleeing domestic violence, especially those with dependent children.

Many women who have left their homes due to violence may be in a position to buy their own accommodation, most commonly after a property settlement with their ex-partner. This option can work well for abused women and their children who have some financial resources, especially when property prices are not prohibitively high as they became in the late

1980s and are again in 2004. The legal and housing issues involved are complicated, however, and can work to a woman's disadvantage. It is essential for women in this situation to seek advice both from a good solicitor experienced in matrimonial work and, if possible, from a housing adviser in a housing advice agency. To settle property matters can take a long time and, at the end of it, the settlement may be insufficient to enable a satisfactory purchase of another property of the size required. For a woman who has fled to a safe location, divorce and property settlement can be particularly traumatic and may become almost impossible if it is not safe for either her or her representatives to have any contact with the male partner. Women in this situation may be able to disguise their location by arranging to be represented by solicitors in a different part of the country. Nevertheless, they will need somewhere safe and permanent to live during the process. Refuge-based accommodation is not suitable for the lengthy stays that may be involved.

Thus owner occupation, though a satisfactory solution for many women homeless due to violence, can also be a problematic housing option. And even where it is a possibility, the well-documented poverty trap that often awaits women who leave their partners and become single parents may preclude it. Women without children are also likely to find it difficult to become owner occupiers due to financial considerations. The London Housing Unit found that only 15 per cent of women, as compared with 49 per cent of men, earned enough to qualify for a mortgage for a one-bedroom flat in London.

While both owner occupation and private renting have a role to play in meeting the housing needs of women who have left home because of violence, many women turn to the social housing sector, which includes the property of both local councils and housing associations. Women rely on public sector housing to a greater extent than men do because they are less likely to be able to use the private market, especially if they have children or other caring responsibilities or are elderly. Getting rehoused by the local council or by a housing association may therefore be the principal viable options. It is vital that these possibilities remain open to women and children who are homeless due to domestic violence.

Local authority provision

During the twentieth century, a large and solid heritage of public sector housing was gradually built up in the UK. Every town and city, and almost every village, has – or had – a stock of council houses in it. Until recently, we have all been so familiar with this scenario that it has sometimes been a shock to find that such estates of housing owned by the local council do not exist in many other countries. While poorly built or run-down estates, with all their attendant problems, are numerous, UK council housing has provided decent and well-built accommodation for many millions of citizens at affordable rents. In the past at least, there has been so much of it that tenants have not felt as stigmatized and 'labelled' as people often have been in public or welfare housing projects in other countries.

All this, however, has been changing. Between 1979 and 1997, the Conservative government in the UK attempted by a variety of means to break up the solid stock of publicly owned housing which had previously been a benchmark of British policy. Funding and spending restrictions on local councils coupled with the introduction of right-to-buy legislation, under which many council tenants have been enabled to buy their homes at a discount, followed later by wholesale transfer of property to housing associations or companies, have resulted in a large decrease in the amount of council housing, and in under-investment and poor maintenance. Many housing authorities have lost half or more of their units – and of course it is always the best stock that is sold. The properties that people have bought are the houses with gardens, the units with three or four bedrooms, the older properties with period features that have been recently renovated at council expense. Councils are often left with a disproportionate number of smaller units, maisonettes and flats, commonly the high-rise ones that nobody wants.

Thus, the supply of council housing has been substantially diminished and the remaining stock is usually of poorer quality. Additionally, from the 1980s onwards, council building programmes were wound down almost completely under the impact of government restrictions and cutbacks in public expenditure. The result is a crisis in the availability of social housing at reasonable rents, despite government encouragement of the housing association sector to fill the gap. There is now a chronic shortage of such accommodation coupled with a growth in homelessness in many parts of the UK. Women and children who have left home because of male violence and who have no other permanent housing options can be disproportionately affected by this situation.

Legal rehousing obligations

The legislation dealing with homelessness is different in Scotland and Northern Ireland from England and Wales. In the following account, some of the details given do not always apply to Scotland and Northern Ireland.

Historically, before 1977, there was some confusion about homelessness. Under the National Assistance Act 1948, homelessness was seen as the responsibility of social services departments, but under the Housing Act 1957, it became the duty of local housing authorities to provide housing. The homeless families' accommodation that social services provided often carried a stigma. Meanwhile, homelessness was growing and there was beginning to be an awareness that people were homeless not because of their own poor conduct or personal inadequacy, but because there was insufficient housing. By the mid-1970s, women who had suffered domestic violence and the newly formed Women's Aid movement were putting pressure on the government to improve the permanent housing options available to women who were homeless because of violence. Over several years, there were moves from a variety of quarters to pass fresh legislation on homelessness.

In 1977, under a Labour government, the Housing (Homeless Persons) Act was passed. A private member's bill put forward by a Liberal MP, this was essentially a government measure, reproducing a former Department of the Environment draft bill. Its main intention was to give housing departments of local councils the principal responsibility for homelessness, and a formal duty in law to secure housing for certain categories of homeless person on both a temporary and a permanent basis.

The 1977 Act, later consolidated within Part III of the 1985 Housing Act, represented a breakthrough in terms of housing the homeless and has been much envied by homelessness advocates in other countries. Over the years, it was substantially modified by case law and was accompanied by Codes of Guidance, issued by the government and reissued from time to time, which very many housing authorities attempted to follow. However, the 1977 Act excluded several categories of people, most notably the single homeless, who have become increasingly visible on the streets of British cities in recent years. Being homeless was not sufficient. To be eligible for any help under the Act, a person had to pass various 'tests', which were assessed by staff employed by local authority housing departments.

From the mid-1980s onwards, public housing was put under such extreme pressure, due to under-investment in the social housing sector and to the chronic depletion of council housing stock, that local authorities were placed in an almost impossible situation in their attempts to operate the Act and to follow the Code of Guidance. Some councils were forced to interpret the homelessness legislation much more stringently than they wanted to, while others adopted a policy of 'minimal legal compliance' on principle. Housing officers in homelessness sections and homeless persons units often suffered high levels of stress and exhaustion, due to their large workloads and the almost impossible rationing job they were expected to do.

The Housing Act 1996

The 1996 Housing Act was a Conservative government response to the situation outlined above. It was inspired by a political commitment to private ownership, a crusade against council housing and a conviction that the 1977 Act represented some kind of fast track for the homeless to permanent housing. Faced with increased homelessness, coupled with the decrease in social housing provision brought about by their own policies, the government's response was simple: remove the legal duty permanently to rehouse statutorily homeless people.

Under the 1996 Act, as passed, the homeless had to compete with other housing applicants on a unified housing list and permanent accommodation no longer had to be secured. There was merely a duty to provide temporary accommodation for up to two years, possibly on a recurring basis. The Act strongly encouraged the use of private rented accommodation to fulfil this duty. A further distressing feature of the Act was that in many cases it removed housing responsibility for 'persons from abroad'.

When the bill was introduced, there was massive protest from housing agencies, and also from domestic violence agencies and the Women's Aid federations. Severe effects were predicted for the homeless in general, including women and children homeless due to violence. In practice, in respect of domestic violence, many local housing authorities have continued to take seriously their responsibility permanently to house abused women and children by adopting a points system for the new unified waiting list or by using other administrative devices.

Since it was passed, the 1996 Act has been substantially modified under Labour by regulations which have made it plain that any private tenancy available to a local authority should not be regarded as suitable unless available for more than two years, and, vitally, that homelessness should be given 'due weight' in the allocation of points on the waiting list for the provision of permanent accommodation. The Code of Guidance that accompanied the Act supports a generous interpretation by local authorities. However, these changes still left room for those authorities that took a less sympathetic line to pursue policies which kept people trapped in a revolving door of homelessness and temporary accommodation.

The Homelessness Act 2002

It was not until 2002 that a new Act was passed, which redeemed Labour's pledge to remove the harmful provisions of the 1996 Act, and in some respects goes well beyond the pre-1996 law. Its main provisions and those particularly affecting people who are at risk of violence are summarized in a May 2002 briefing by Linda Delahay, Women's Aid's National Housing Officer in England, while a later briefing in October 2002 considers some of the limitations to its successful implementation. Both of these useful documents are available on the Women's Aid website. Only a few of the main provisions of the Act can be described here.

Overall the Act requires local authorities to adopt a strategic approach to homelessness, and encourages joint working between housing and social services departments and any other public authority, voluntary organization or other person whose activities are capable of contributing to the achievement of key objectives. It abolishes the two-year limit on the duty of local authorities to secure suitable accommodation, replacing it with a duty to secure such accommodation until a settled home is found. It also abolishes the duty to consider whether other suitable accommodation is available before the authority secures accommodation itself, and gives new powers to secure accommodation for those who are homeless and in priority need, thus, hopefully, speeding up the process. Statutory arrangements for housing allocations are amended to allow local authorities to offer more choice to homeless people and those in priority need. The Act also makes additions to the existing priority need categories for the first time since 1977, harmonizing with the Children (Leaving Care Act) 2000 for young people, and adding a number of categories of vulnerable people, including 'a person who is vulnerable as a result of ceasing to occupy accommodation by reason of violence from another person or threats of violence from another person which are likely to be carried out'. Guidance on domestic violence points out the cumulative nature of the violence and cautions against judgements based on the 'immediate circumstances in which they left home'. It also reiterates and strengthens existing guidance against seeking proof of violence or contacting the perpetrator.

The new Homelessness Act therefore has greatly strengthened the safety net for homeless people in general and for those who experience violence in particular. However, the Women's Aid briefing of October 2002 is not optimistic about the working of the new law in some local authorities. In relation to single women experiencing domestic violence, it appears that a number of local authorities are applying the test of 'vulnerability' very stringently. The briefing concludes that, until this is tested in the courts, single women experiencing domestic violence are not likely to achieve priority for rehousing in such areas. So it seems that the era of minimal legal compliance is not yet over, but there have been many improvements.

Delivering housing services

This is the legislative backdrop against which the delivery of housing services by local councils must be understood. Under the Housing Act 1996, as before, the first test that housing authorities must apply is to ascertain whether a person is homeless or not according to the terms of the Act. Second, applicants must be in 'priority need' as discussed above. The person must also be homeless unintentionally, which means that they are not homeless through any deliberate act or omission of their own. And in general they should have a 'local connection' with the authority to which they apply, although this should not be required in situations of domestic violence.

For women who have suffered violence, there are special points to consider about the legislation. Importantly, being homeless due to domestic violence counts as 'homelessness' and not as 'intentional homelessness'. The Women's Aid movement and others active in the domestic violence and the housing fields at the time that the 1977 Act was passed lobbied hard for domestic violence to be included as a reason for homelessness. However, although it was, there have often been problems of women fleeing violence being regarded as intentionally homeless.

In addition, although successive Codes of Guidance recommended a wider interpretation, until comparatively recently women were classified as homeless because of domestic violence only if they had suffered violence from someone actually living with them. The reality is that women frequently experience domestic violence from men whom they do not live with. They may be abused by ex-partners, estranged partners or boyfriends who have their own accommodation elsewhere. In *The Hidden Struggle*, Amina Mama suggests that some black women – and in her study, women of Caribbean descent in particular – have long-term 'visiting relationships' with men who do not actually live with them. None of these women would have been eligible under the 1977 Act for rehousing following violence. A useful feature of the 1996 Act was that it made it plain that domestic violence may apply even if the violence does not take place within the home and the people concerned are not living together. Many councils welcomed this expanded definition and the new law is even more inclusive. However, there are always those councils that seek to define their duties as narrowly as possible.

In the late 1980s and early 1990s, some local councils began to introduce policies requiring women fleeing domestic violence to visit a solicitor before they could be considered homeless. The idea of these policies is that, if a woman is able to take out a legal order against her partner, she may be able to return to her former home. Women may then be told that they are intentionally homeless if they do not go back. Some local authorities take this hard line even if there is previous evidence that legal action has not worked and the woman herself is adamant that she does not want to pursue this course of action. In our 1993 study of domestic violence and housing, we accumulated substantial evidence of the devastating effects that such policies can have on the lives of women homeless because of violence.

Local connection has been another area of difficulty. Women fleeing domestic violence frequently apply for housing in local authorities far removed from their own home area. If a woman homeless due to violence does not have a local connection, the authority she applies to should disregard this factor providing that she cannot be referred to any other authority where she does have a local connection because of the threat of violence. Many authorities follow this policy, but others, particularly perhaps in London and in rural areas, may dispute cases strongly and make every effort to refer women elsewhere. In some areas, councils use a variety of methods which together have the effect of making it almost impossible for women without a local connection to be rehoused.

It should be obvious by now that local councils vary widely in how they interpret the homelessness legislation. The way in which housing departments process applications also varies widely. Some ask very few questions about the violence and conduct few or no enquiries into it. In others, homelessness interviews are quite adversarial and women are subjected to detailed questioning about the violence that they have experienced. In such authorities, the maximum possible amount of evidence may be required before a woman stands a chance of being accepted for even temporary rehousing, especially where stocks of council housing have been depleted. Women applicants are likely to be successful only if they have active support from voluntary sector and housing advice agencies, and from legal representatives working hard on their behalf. This can be exhausting for the women concerned. Many lose heart and give up on their applications. It is also a considerable drain on the limited resources of refuge services and other voluntary organizations, and on the time and energy of solicitors.

In other authorities, applications may proceed in a straightforward manner and officers may be as helpful and sympathetic as they can. However, it seems from all the relevant research that, in most authorities, some women complain of intrusive and insensitive questioning when they are being interviewed. Women fleeing violence want to be treated with dignity and respect, and to be believed. What they do not want is to be forced to go into embarrassing and distressing detail about their violent experiences. One woman fleeing violence put it this way:

> I felt in a way like I was being judged and it was all my fault, my failings, and that's how he made me feel. I came out very upset . . . you just feel stripped afterwards . . . You shouldn't have to give a detailed account of [the violence], I mean you don't want to recall it at the best of times . . . Because you feel like a failure anyway. You feel awful having to sit there and say it all. And to have to say it to a total stranger, it's really demoralizing. It makes you feel degraded. It makes you feel dirty. And it's your life. And you don't want to put it all on the table for discussion. You don't want that.

The investigations which are conducted can also be a source of anxiety and insecurity to women who have fled from violence and who are living in secret locations to avoid discovery by their violent partners. Local authorities attempt to be as careful as possible about confidentiality issues and about protecting women's safety, and the new law reiterates its importance, but most domestic violence services can report incidences where breaches have occurred.

A wide range of agencies have recommended that women who have suffered violence should be interviewed by a woman or by a specialist officer. A large number of women are very grateful if this option is offered, even if it means coming back for another appointment (providing this can be done safely). Many, however, are quite happy to be interviewed by a man. Thus, offering a choice does not necessarily place undue pressure on women officers. A considerable number of authorities now operate policies of this sort. Similarly, many authorities offer black women the option of being interviewed by a black officer, preferably a woman and of a similar racial and cultural heritage. In this context, various housing officers and workers in the field have noted that, for some black women and women from minority ethnic communities fleeing violence, interview by a male officer of the same ethnic or cultural background might be particularly inappropriate. The possible choices of officer need to be offered actively so that women are aware of their options and can make informed decisions. Even where authorities have such policies in place, there can be a problem regarding the attitudes and opinions that housing department staff hold about women who have suffered domestic violence. One woman whom we interviewed summed this up as follows:

> They never take me seriously. Because I've got a ring in my nose. They just dismiss me, don't believe me . . . They should stop looking at us as 'those women'. We get labelled because we've suffered violence . . . They are really shocked when they find I'm doing a degree.

The attitudes of officers can be crucial in determining how a woman is treated. Many women in our own housing study reported that they felt

judged by their interviewing officers on a wide variety of grounds –
because they were black, for example, or older, or young and pregnant, or
living unconventional lifestyles. They often felt that they were not taken
seriously. Some felt that there was a division in many officers' minds
between abused women whom they thought of as being deserving of
assistance and those whom they thought of as non-deserving. Such views
take many forms and hark back to the Poor Law which officially ceased to
exist in 1949. They take a long time to eradicate.

Potential racism and other discrimination

Many commentators and researchers have highlighted the need for housing
providers to be aware of potential racism in the delivery of their services
and to operate anti-racism policies. In her study *The Hidden Struggle*,
Amina Mama found that black women who were interviewed for the
research tended to underreport racism in their contacts with housing
authorities. Even so, it was clear that the women in the study had faced
a variety of bureaucratic obstructions, and sometimes inaction and
discrimination. Mama concludes:

> [Black women] are very often not only denied access to decent housing
> away from extremely violent men and kept in the half-life of
> homelessness for very long periods, but also subjected to the emotional
> traumas of racism, made all the more damaging because of the insidious
> ways in which it can operate over the months and even years of
> homelessness and powerlessness.

Black women in both Mama's study and our own sometimes faced
questioning in homelessness interviews which was insensitive and
ignorant of cultural issues, and in which racist attitudes were only
lightly veiled. The provision of interpreting for women who have
suffered violence and who do not speak English as their first language
can be particularly crucial due to the delicacy of the issues involved.
Interpreting services for locally spoken languages are, however, ad hoc
and piecemeal in many authorities. While a few provide comprehensive
and efficient interpretation and translation, many offer either
fragmentary services or none at all.

Women fleeing violence need access to interpreters who are women
and who have some grasp of the issues involved. As in the case of black
interviewing officers, the use of male interpreters can be particularly
inappropriate for some women, especially if they are of the same ethnic
community or heritage. Interpreters should be trained and properly paid
for their services. All too often in local authorities, the provision of
interpreting depends on the goodwill and generosity of domestic violence
service staff and council workers who are fluent in the language concerned.

It is never acceptable to use a woman's children to interpret, especially when traumatic personal issues involving abuse and violence are being discussed. While this should be obvious to all concerned, it still happens time and time again.

There are few black officers in post in many homeless persons units, homelessness sections and housing associations outside major cities, and even fewer in senior managerial or policy-making positions. Thus, the interests of black people, and perhaps of black women in particular, are often overlooked. If permanent rehousing is eventually achieved, for example, areas where accommodation is offered can be a problem. Due to the omnipresence of racism and, for some women, the presence of extended family networks, black women and women of minority ethnic heritages have to be particularly careful about areas of rehousing. An African-Caribbean woman whom we interviewed said:

> Black women's choice of area must be respected. The women know what support they will need and choose their areas accordingly . . . Black women shouldn't be put all in one area. Then you get the 'ghetto' effect and it becomes a 'no go' area for whites. Then the streets aren't cleaned as often, the bins aren't emptied. It happens . . . And women shouldn't be housed in a white racist area either. We would like to see people being housed where they want. Black people usually want to be near other black people – want to be near friends – but they might not. They want to make the choice though. Not have it pushed on to them . . .

Immigration and nationality issues should not get tangled up with housing matters, but they sometimes do. Particularly since the 1996 Act, abused women with properties in other countries may face being told that they are ineligible for any housing in the UK. For immigrant women whose immigration status may be dependent on that of their husbands, who may therefore be under threat of deportation and who will sometimes have 'no recourse to public funds', the process of seeking rehousing after leaving home due to violence can be particularly traumatic. Where immigrant women experience difficulties or threats to their status as a result of housing applications, it is vital that assistance is sought from specialist, independent advocacy and advice groups.

Lesbians, older women, very young women and disabled women, among others, can all face specific difficulties in getting housing. These problems often revolve around judgemental attitudes held by housing officers. For example, in the housing studies that we have conducted, some older women whom we interviewed felt as though they were being brushed to one side. They have felt that housing officers neither understood nor empathized with their problems. Young women also had trouble in being taken seriously as genuinely homeless due to violence. If they did not have children, like many other women without children, they faced great difficulty in being accepted for rehousing even if they had suffered quite severe sexual or physical abuse. Most of the young women whom we talked with remained homeless or moved into special projects.

Lesbians face both invisibility and a lack of concern for any difficulties they have, coupled with prejudice and discrimination. Applying as homeless therefore presents specific problems, and there is little support or help available. Some authorities have policies to treat lesbians and gay men fleeing violence exactly the same as heterosexuals, and this practice should be reinforced by the changes under the new Domestic Violence, Crime and Victims Act so that same-sex couples will be treated on the same basis as heterosexual couples, but many local authorities still do not recognize the issue. Women with disabilities have also faced difficulties and have been excluded from much housing provision. In addition, disabled women who are abused face general ignorance about the effects of violence on their lives, or about the fact that they might experience domestic violence at all. Again recent changes, under the Homelessness Act 2002 in relation to vulnerable applicants, should have begun to address this problem. However, women with disabilities who have suffered violence may have great difficulties in approaching the housing department in the first place, especially if their carer is also their abuser, and may need specialized support and help. There is also a need for councils to address mental health issues and domestic abuse. At the moment, provision for abused women with mental health special needs is woefully inadequate, as documented in the Women's Aid mental health survey published in 2004.

Some local housing authorities, as we have mentioned, do operate specific anti-discrimination policies for people with disabilities, people from minority ethnic communities, lesbians and gay men, which may also cover homelessness due to violence. These developments are to be welcomed, although they rarely go far enough. Some inter-agency projects have conducted research into the experiences of black women, lesbians, older and very young women, and disabled women in seeking rehousing. However, more research is needed. Such experiences should also be included as an integral part of all domestic violence training in housing departments and elsewhere.

Effects of the homelessness legislation

Many points could be made about the homelessness legislation, only some of which we have touched on here. A fuller consideration of the issues involved can be found in the various publications about housing available from the Women's Aid federations and others. When the 1977 Homelessness Act was passed, many in the movement against domestic violence were doubtful about how useful the legislation would be. Soon afterwards a major study of both temporary and permanent accommodation for women fleeing violence was conducted by the Women's Aid Federation of England and the Department of the Environment. This was published in 1981 as *Leaving Violent Men*. The study was also reported in Jan Pahl's widely used although now somewhat outdated book, *Private Violence and Public Policy*. The authors of the study, Val Binney, Gina Harkell and Judy Nixon, found that, 18 months after the 1977 Act came into force, fewer than half the Women's Aid groups of the time felt that the housing prospects of women in their refuges had improved. Many groups felt that the gains of the Act were only temporary and had been subsequently eroded by local authority spending cuts.

Twenty years or so later, there are still resource shortages and a severe lack of social housing, despite many new housing initiatives and the fact that some housing authorities rehouse abused women with children very quickly. Women who are homeless due to violence rely heavily on the legislation. There is no doubt that social housing provision is a desperate need for abused women and their children, and Women's Aid has continued to lobby, to run training courses and seminars, and to present evidence about this need.

The impact of the 1996 Act

Recent research has suggested that the 1996 Act, as modified, has not always had the negative consequences that were feared. Rebecca Morley, Susan Parker and Sarah-Jo Lee have recently completed research under the Violence Research Programme of the Economic and Social Research Council on the impact of changing housing policy on women experiencing domestic violence. They point out the contradictory nature of the period in which the Act was passed, including the removal of the obligation of local authorities to provide permanent accommodation to homeless people at the same time as the government was showing increased policy interest in domestic violence (see also policy reviews by one of the present authors in 2000 and 2003). At that time there were a raft of new initiatives and policies on domestic violence from the Department of the Environment and the Department of Health in 1996, the Department for the Environment, Transport and the Regions twice in 1999, the Cabinet Office/Home Office in 1999 and the Home Office in 2000. These included new improved Good Practice Guidelines on Homelessness, which are currently again under review.

The research found that most local authorities had made progress in following good practice since Mullins' and Niner's survey of housing authority practice in 1993/4 (published in 1996), although the same pattern was evident with London authorities in general the most restrictive and metropolitan boroughs outside London the most generous. As in our

1993 study, comparisons of responses from housing authorities with those from local refuge services, voluntary organizations and service users demonstrated a gap between policy and practice, with 42 per cent of refuge services saying that policy and practice differ substantially.

In some cases the new Codes of Practice had not had the impact intended, particularly in response to requiring evidence. Only 60 per cent of authorities and a minority of refuge projects (45 per cent) said that housing authorities accepted women's word on the violence without supporting evidence. (This is not a new response and is perhaps an indication of the use of evidence as a rationing device in the face of their shrinking housing stock.) The researchers found a 'culture of suspicion' among some officers, which sometimes resulted in hostile questioning. This was likely to be less so with agency backing from Women's Aid, police or solicitors, but even such support was not always effective. Women applying from refuge accommodation tended to be the most successful, underlining the importance of specialized advocacy.

There were indications in the research that figures collected by housing authorities on acceptance may be overestimates, since they did not record all approaches as applications. However, even allowing for this, the researchers concluded that the legislation had not, in itself, had a significantly negative impact on housing authorities' willingness to accept as homeless women who experience domestic violence.

All data sources in this research suggested that the impact of the Act *per se* was relatively small. Only 25 per cent of both housing authorities and projects said the response worsened following the Act. Most authorities found ways to circumvent its restrictions in order to continue providing the same service, including access to permanent accommodation. However, both surveys in the study suggested that the Act further legitimated the climate of welfare retrenchment and exclusion – for example, use of the private rented sector, insecure 'introductory tenancies', civil 'private' solutions to violence, and stock transfer. A few local domestic violence services providing refuge accommodation said that their authorities now require more proof, or that women are more likely to be allocated inappropriate accommodation, both of which create time and resource pressures for refuge organizations and stress for women. However, the worst fears that refuge services would be undermined by the Act have clearly not materialized. Moreover, some housing authorities, in particular, mentioned positive consequences of the Act, including widening the definition of violence and including specific and more generous codes of guidance to the Act. However, despite the Codes of Guidance, authorities did not tend to use the more creative possibilities available for women who were already local authority tenants, such as urgent management transfer, eviction of violent partners under a tenancy agreement or repossession under provisions of the Act itself. The generally favourable conclusions on the part of projects in the ESRC research are confirmed by the *Five Years On* survey for Women's Aid on the impact of recent legislation, where 53 per cent of refuge projects believed the 1996 Act had improved protection for women as against 31 per cent who said it had not.

However, in many of the areas under greatest housing stress, women may be turned away or may wait in temporary accommodation for several years. Temporary accommodation may be in refuge accommodation, in council or housing association projects, in bed and breakfast hotels or in privately leased accommodation. In our 1993 study and in others, the use of self-contained temporary accommodation leased from landlords and homeowners was preferred by some women who had been offered it. This continues to be the case, with many families moving on from refuge accommodation being rehoused in this type of provision for two years or more. Many councils have phased out the use of bed and breakfast, or are trying to. For women fleeing violence, such accommodation can be particularly inappropriate because of the absence of support and the lack of security in the properties, which can place women in physical danger. There may also be no facilities at all for children. However, there are some innovative women-only bed and breakfast projects and hostels in existence in some areas.

The Women's Aid federations and various housing bodies recommend that women should stay in emergency accommodation for only a short time before being transferred to self-contained temporary accommodation while they wait. In temporary accommodation of almost all types, however, and especially in the accommodation provided by private landlords under the 1996 Act, the needs of children may not be catered for adequately. Crèches, play areas and equipment, and support and assistance for children are rarely provided, and children's needs are often ignored when new temporary accommodation is designed and operated. On the other hand, some local authorities and housing associations attempt to provide good, supportive temporary accommodation in self-contained units, cluster flats and shared houses, including facilities for children.

As mentioned above, there are some, little used, provisions for women experiencing domestic violence which avoid the use of the homelessness legislation. These are detailed in a guide to protection under housing law issued by Women's Aid shortly before the publication of the 2002 homelessness legislation. Councils (and courts in relation to private tenancies other than assured shortholds) may operate policies to allow women to stay in their original homes by transfer of the tenancy, or they may offer emergency management transfers, so that women may be transferred to other properties. Housing officers on council estates can have an important role to play here, since they may be the first point of contact with the housing department when a woman council tenant wants housing assistance to deal with domestic violence. The trend towards the decentralization of housing departments into smaller local units may mean that local housing officers are more approachable, although there can also be problems of security since small neighbourhood offices may be well known to a woman's violent partner. For this reason, many decentralized housing authorities have provisions for women who have suffered domestic violence to approach different offices from their own in order to get help.

Applying for an emergency management transfer can seem the obvious solution for a woman experiencing violence, especially if the man's name is not on the rent book. With the shortage of council accommodation, however, such transfers are becoming more and more difficult to obtain in many authorities. In the study which we conducted, for example, none of the women we interviewed obtained a management transfer. Transfers can be obtained either with the same landlord (i.e. the local council) or from a local council to a housing association. Women's Aid promotes such a policy in its housing training, but transfers take quite a long time to effect. This is sometimes because the violent partner may still be living in the property and the landlord has not made any attempt to get him out, even if the tenancy is solely in the woman's name. Unfortunately, transfers are a valuable option that are not used as well as they could be. For a number of years, also, some authorities have included a clause in the tenancy agreement about domestic violence. This is usually similar to, but separate from, other clauses on racial and sexual harassment or on harassment by neighbours. They say that domestic violence is unacceptable in council properties and is an evictable offence. They have acted as a symbolic statement to all tenants and to the public that the authority will not tolerate domestic violence, but, again, may not have been used to full advantage.

Since the Housing Act 1980, council tenants have had security of tenure. There is case law establishing that one partner can end a joint tenancy, but this is rarely if ever used because local authorities fear being found guilty of maladministration. The 1996 Housing Act provides for the repossession of secure tenancies and assured tenancies with social landlords on grounds of anti-social behaviour. This specifically includes domestic violence, which is a helpful provision, but it does not cover all cases because it applies only where the couple are married or living together as husband and wife and the partner leaving is unlikely to return. However, it could be a useful back-up, especially if a woman has obtained an occupation order, and it is another way of allowing women and their children to be transferred to a new tenancy without having to go through the trauma of statutory homelessness.

Good practice in local authorities

In a generally bleak scenario of housing shortages, there are some bright spots. There has been an encouraging trend in some local authority housing departments towards rehousing women quite quickly and towards the adoption of written domestic violence policies and good practice guidelines. Some of these policies cover the council's activities as a whole, while some are limited to the housing department. The trend started in London authorities some years ago, and spread elsewhere, but the housing crisis and, in some cases, changes in political control have resulted in some of the original policies being cut back or even rescinded.

Many London boroughs have been particularly hard-hit over the years by local government spending cutbacks and 'right to buy' legislation. Due to the resultant shortage of public sector housing, many of those that operated very generous domestic violence policy and practice guidelines in the past have been forced to retract a number of their provisions. On the other hand, many local authorities in different parts of the country developed policies on domestic violence from the 1990s onwards which go beyond the minimum requirements of the law – for example, placing women in privately leased temporary rented accommodation under the 1996 Housing Act for rotating two-year stays, and rapid implementation of the provisions of the Homelessness Act 2002, which removes the two-year limit and allows homeless people high priority for permanent housing. It is important to avoid the assumption that the best – and the worst – practice is confined to London.

The adoption of domestic violence policy and practice guidelines is recommended by the Women's Aid federations and by housing bodies and research studies. Good practice guidelines contribute towards improving services, not only for women and children fleeing violence, but for all women. They standardize approaches to domestic violence cases across the authority, while still allowing for discretion and for each case to be considered on its merits. They also demonstrate to the public, to all council members and staff, and to people using council services, the commitment of the authority to opposing domestic violence as a matter of principle. Some good practice provisions have obvious financial implications, and authorities adopting such policies need to be clear about the extent of the extra resources that may be required. But many aspects of good practice do not involve additional expenditure. Even authorities facing stringent housing and funding shortages can improve their services in some ways.

In the development of domestic violence and homelessness policies, it is crucial that solid links are built with refuge services and other voluntary sector groups, with other relevant departments of the council and with the trade unions and professional associations whose members will have to put them into practice. Policy and practice guidelines are often initiated in conjunction with local inter-agency projects on domestic violence (see Chapter 8). Women's Aid and specialist projects for women fleeing violence – for example, for black women, single women or lesbians – need to be involved in drawing up such inter-agency initiated policies and guidelines. The national Women's Aid federations, which are able to take an overview of the issues concerned, also have vital expertise to offer.

The success in practice of any policy depends fundamentally on the full involvement and commitment of housing staff, who may be very hard-pressed by the current public housing shortage. Such staff need to be fully involved in the drafting and adoption of a policy, and should be offered extra training and support when the policy comes into operation. The importance of taking staff, managers, councillors and unions along with a policy cannot be overemphasized.

Domestic violence policies and good practice guidelines often cover the activities of estate managers and district housing officers as well as homelessness staff, and a sympathetic, supportive attitude adopted by these officers will encourage women to approach the housing authority for help. This usually involves such measures as using sensitive, non-intrusive interviewing techniques, adopting a believing attitude to the woman concerned, minimizing enquiries into the violence experienced and accepting a woman's statement about this as sufficient evidence. Domestic violence guidelines are also likely to operate a broad interpretation of what domestic violence covers, to involve formal or informal policy commitments to weight unified housing lists for permanent rehousing or to use other management strategies to ensure that abused women and children are not disadvantaged. There may be specific policies to refrain from putting pressure on women applying as homeless to seek protection orders where these would not be helpful, and to address the needs of black women and other women facing discrimination, such as lesbians and women with disabilities. Policies may include commitments to prioritize repairs caused by violence, to provide alarms, and to increase security in properties rented by women experiencing domestic violence from outside the home.

Domestic violence practice guidelines almost always include the provision of domestic violence training for all housing officers and managers. Interviewing women who have suffered physical, sexual or psychological abuse is a task of skill and sensitivity. Training in how to do it is of critical importance. Such training needs to include material on how to operate domestic violence policies and how to work with women homeless due to violence, and should also cover general issues of domestic violence awareness. The Women's Aid federations recommend that, even where there are officers who specialize in domestic violence work, housing department staff in general should be thoroughly trained. It is vital that Women's Aid and specialist refuge projects and other services for abused women and children are involved in the training provided. These issues are discussed further in Chapter 8. It should be noted, however, that research by ourselves and others has shown that training on its own changes very little: what is needed is a commitment by the authority concerned to take on the issue of domestic violence in an active way.

Domestic violence policies need to be monitored and reviewed regularly. They also need to be accompanied by clear public information about both the policy and the services available. How much or how little to publicize a domestic violence policy can be a matter of contention. Various housing bodies and advice centres point out that the financial and political context into which any policy of this type is introduced is critical.

Housing associations

Particularly since the Housing Act 1988, government policy has been to encourage housing associations and trusts to replace local authorities as the principal source of social rented housing. Therefore housing associations, at one time much less important than local authority housing departments, have become more and more important as providers of social housing. Government initiatives have also led to the transfer of large amounts of council stock to housing associations and trusts, known in recent years as registered social landlords (RSLs).

Some researchers have suggested that the housing associations are failing to take up the slack, that the provision of social housing has been irrevocably damaged, and that there is no longer much in the way of accountability to the public for the housing provided. Housing associations, they claim, have become increasingly like private companies. Others are more optimistic. The CORE study of domestic violence and housing associations found that housing associations provided accommodation for 54,000 women experiencing domestic violence between 1997 and 2002. About 39,000 of these were in supported housing (i.e. refuge providers) and the rest in individual accommodation.

Many in the housing association world are pleased with its management practices and with the freedom and flexibility that it can offer, as compared with bureaucratic local authorities. These officers suggest that housing associations provide a fresh way forward for social housing, open to innovation and more responsive to people's real needs than councils have ever been. But as the housing association sector gets bigger, it may well develop similar problems to local authorities, especially where managements and central or head offices are in locations far distant from housing sites.

Much of the housing association movement was set up to provide alternatives for people not traditionally eligible for council housing. In recent years, it has become increasingly large and professionalized, leaving the world of alternatives and entering the mainstream. Currently applications may be made direct to housing associations, but the applicants need also to be registered on the council waiting list because increasingly housing associations will only rehouse homeless people who are nominated for housing by the local authority. In this way, local authorities will fulfil their enabling role and housing associations their housing role.

Unfortunately, nomination to a housing association does not necessarily mean allocation of a property. Financial imperatives have become very important over the years, as a 2003 study of housing association allocation practices by Cathy Davis has shown. It has been a point of disagreement in the housing world for some time that some housing associations 'cherry pick' applicants for housing and tend not to choose homeless applicants. There are echoes of the deserving and undeserving here yet again. Yet, the changes in refuge management can work well for some women. Refuge organisations have 'nomination agreements' with their housing association landlords, and may be able to negotiate approximately two nominations per year from the refuge for housing. This has worked quite well, although there are signs that it is slowing down. It is an option that women who want rehousing from refuge accommodation are able to pursue, provided there is a nomination agreement in place, and this is something that Women's Aid favours as a path to permanent housing for some women.

A number of housing associations cater specifically to the needs of women. Some of these were set up many years ago, originally to assist women in need, especially those without children. Others have connections with the modern feminist movement and may specialize in housing for women who have suffered violence, such as Tai Havan, in Wales, Sonas in the Irish Republic and Eaves Housing for Women, which manages a number of refuge projects in London in addition to setting up the Poppy and Lilith projects, and helping women fleeing the sex industry and women who have been trafficked into prostitution.

Many refuge services are in housing association property and were established as housing association special projects. These were often, in the past, managed by the local Women's Aid group or by other organizations. In recent years, however, refuge projects run jointly by Women's Aid and housing associations have been somewhat overtaken by a new trend among many housing associations to set up their own refuge projects, independent of Women's Aid and the domestic violence movement. In addition, former Women's Aid refuges have come under direct housing association management, largely because of financial pressures, and may not necessarily be run on Women's Aid principles. This has led, in a number of cases, to the establishment of refuge services with very low staff/resident ratios, which employ housing association staff to attend mainly to the housing needs of the women and children rather than providing a fuller service. This trend has caused widespread concern in the domestic violence movement.

Another difficulty is that, if abused women and children move on from using refuge services to permanent accommodation in housing association or other RSL property, they may face the problem of high rents since associations and trusts have to borrow money on the commercial market in order to raise finance. Women fleeing violence, and others in RSL properties, increasingly find themselves trapped in the social security system because they cannot afford the rents if they get a job. On the other hand, the large housing associations and trusts may be able to offer emergency transfers to other areas, and two unrelated housing associations may also make arrangements to swap tenants in order to assist women fleeing violence.

Some housing associations, like some local housing departments, are developing domestic violence policy and practice guidelines. Such guidelines are similar to those of local authorities, although they are generally less comprehensive. Most national housing bodies now also have domestic violence good practice guidelines, but how they are operated may still be problematic, according to the experience of Women's Aid and the research by Cathy Davis to which we have already referred.

Thus, there is both good and bad news for women who are homeless due to violence. Many women fleeing violence are rehoused successfully in either council or housing association properties, and are enabled to start new lives. The Homelessness Act of 2002 will improve this situation. For others, the decrease in the availability of socially rented housing, the consequent hoops through which some councils expect abused women to jump, and the cumulative effects of government housing policies over the last 25 years can make the search for permanent housing a nightmare.

7

The caring professions: social and health services

The work of caring agencies like the social and medical services is vitally important for women fleeing violence. How they deliver their services, how easy it is to approach them, their attitudes to domestic violence – all these can affect whether women who have suffered violence make use of them or not. Often an abused woman delays seeking help, perhaps for years, because of shame about the violence that she has experienced, loyalty to or fear of her partner, and anxieties about the sort of reception she is likely to get. She may wonder, for example, if she will be believed and taken seriously, or if she will be treated in a judgemental, patronizing or pitying way. Most importantly, she may fear that the agency workers she speaks to will not be able to guarantee secrecy and that events will move out of her control. She may well have serious anxieties that her partner will find out and that she will face dangerous repercussions.

As we have discussed throughout this book, there have been substantial improvements in recent years. Even so, many researchers, activists and workers in the domestic violence field have highlighted the obstacles that women may face in seeking help from agencies. Kate Cavanagh did a piece of research in the 1980s with Rebecca and Russell Dobash on social and medical agencies, which is reported in Jan Pahl's book, *Private Violence and Public Policy*, published in 1985. In their study, these researchers found that women were generally reluctant to make contact with official caring agencies because of feelings of shame and guilt, and often because they themselves subscribed to widely held beliefs that marriage is meant to be happy, that it is the woman's job to make sure that it is, and that the domestic sphere is private. These feelings and beliefs often had the effect of making women feel like failures if they reported the violence and hence admitted to the outside world that they were experiencing problems in their personal and intimate lives. However, if the violence became more severe, with the passage of time, women in the study did seek help.

More recent studies have found the same thing. In a briefing note for the Home Office published in 2000, Audrey Mullender and one of the present authors described the long trek that abused women and their children still have to undertake from agency to agency to agency to try to get appropriate help. By 2004, however, most local authorities had strategies on domestic violence in place and were attempting to co-ordinate services to achieve a more efficient response. Many now have a commitment to try to intervene early before the problem becomes too entrenched, to hold violent men accountable for their actions and to provide a range of support services for women and children.

Even now, though, women experiencing intimate violence tend to keep quiet about it for as long as possible. Many abused women confide initially in women family members, most commonly mothers and sisters, or other relatives and friends. It is only later and after some deliberation that they might approach official agencies. In the 1980s study by Cavanagh *et al.*, women who had made the decision to get help often quested around in the face of agency unhelpfulness, trying to find effective assistance, perhaps approaching one organization after another. Once a certain point is crossed, the findings of various studies demonstrate the active and positive attempts that abused women make to change their situation, and counteract theories that stress women's helplessness and passivity, or which suggest that they enjoy the violence to which they are subjected.

Nevertheless, women may be deterred from seeking further help by the negative and unhelpful responses that they sometimes still, even now, encounter in official agencies. Such problems can be experienced particularly acutely by black women, immigrant women and women from minority ethnic communities. In her study, Amina Mama found that black women faced widespread disadvantage in their contacts with a variety of helping agencies. Lesbians may also face difficulties, as may very young and much older women who have suffered violence, or women living an unconventional lifestyle. For an abused woman in a difficult situation, getting effective and non-judgemental help can therefore depend on having someone else to represent her and to help her to put her case forward. Women in refuges are usually able to get support and help from refuge and outreach support staff, who will act as their advocates with other agencies if they wish. There is little information available, however, on what happens to women experiencing violence who approach agencies for help without the support of Women's Aid or of other domestic violence services. It seems that they fare much less well and are particularly isolated and vulnerable, especially if the agency approached responds in a negative way.

Things have improved massively recently, though, as we have constantly emphasized. Both statutory and voluntary agencies dealing with women who have experienced violence have developed good practice guidelines, resource packs and information leaflets both for the public and for workers in agencies. Bristol City Council, for example, in common with other authorities has developed a council-wide strategy through its Crime and Disorder Reduction Partnership, with policy development in all local agencies, implementation plans, action plans regularly updated, and a range of multi-agency sub-groups developing new policy, monitoring what has been achieved and reviewing what is yet to come. In the rest of this chapter, we will discuss how successful the social and medical services are in taking a role in local strategic development of this type, and in meeting the new requirements of local and central government and the demands of the women's services.

Social services

Of the agencies approached for help by women experiencing domestic violence, the local authority social services department is one of the most common. Various studies have shown that up to three-quarters of women who have experienced violence over a prolonged period have contacted social workers at least once during the violent relationship. It is therefore vital that social workers respond appropriately. Issues regarding domestic violence and social work are discussed fully in *Rethinking Domestic Violence* by Audrey Mullender, published in 1996, and in the 2000 mapping review of services across the country, called *From Good Intentions to Good Practice.*

Women approaching social services for help need to feel safe and secure in doing so, and to be treated sympathetically and with respect. Thus, the social worker's approach is crucial if a woman's trust and confidence are to be established. It is important that social workers are able both to validate and support women experiencing violence and to use their counselling skills to help women talk about what has happened. Women are very often nervous and embarrassed about what they have been through, and may feel shy in speaking to a professional about the violence, although they may wish to do so. Social workers can sometimes provide a safe and supportive environment in which women may feel that they can open up, possibly for the first time. The other side of this coin, of course, is that women should not be pressurized to talk if they do not want to. Many women complain that, having gone to see their social workers solely about a practical problem with which they needed help, the social worker 'redefined' the problem and made them talk about their personal lives.

Quite a number of women are not happy talking to social workers at all, due to their much discussed role as a kind of 'soft' arm of the law. Social workers have wide-ranging powers to intervene in people's lives. Working-class women are often strongly aware of general issues about social class and control in relationships between social services departments and their 'service users', and middle-class women are more likely to consult lawyers. Due to the pervasiveness of racism, black women may feel particularly ambivalent about approaching social workers and may not wish to involve them in their lives. The majority of social workers are still white, although more and more black women and men are now entering the profession.

Social workers themselves, of course, are not oblivious to these difficulties. Many now take domestic violence very seriously and undertake additional training about it. Various social services departments and inter-agency forums (like those in several London boroughs) have conducted local research studies leading to policy and practice development on the specific needs of women and children from minority ethnic communities: for example, South Asian women. Some black and minority ethnic women's projects have established their own counselling or advice centres (for instance, Newham Asian Women's Project in London), and black social workers have sometimes taken an active role in equalities developments within their departments and within local multi-agency work concerning domestic violence. While racism remains an issue within social services, as elsewhere, there have been some changes for the better.

However, the power that local authority social services departments have to recommend that children be removed from their parents by the courts has always acted as a strong deterrent against women, both black and white, confiding in them. In a pioneering study of the effects of domestic violence on children by NCH Action for Children in 1994, for example, three-quarters of the women interviewed said that they had not approached social services about the abuse that they were experiencing because they were afraid their children would be taken away. While such an outcome is, perhaps, less likely under the 1989 Children Act than some of these women believed, it represents a fearful prospect.

It can deter women experiencing violence from reporting to the police in the first place, since the police now usually notify social services of all cases they are called out to where there are children in the family. Social workers may follow up these notifications in a sensitive way and will almost certainly try to be helpful, but it is no joke having the social services brought into your life just because you phoned the police for help. (In the more serious cases, of course, the police will make an official referral and are recommended to do so by government guidance.)

In general, women who have not left violent relationships may lie about the violence, when questioned, rather than risk bringing their families into the social work spotlight. 'Failure to protect' children under the Children Act can lead to social work intervention and there is evidence that some women have been threatened by social workers with having their children removed from their care if they do not leave particularly violent partners.

While such situations happen fairly rarely and stem from severe concerns that social services may have about the welfare of the children involved, abused women hearing such stories are likely to feel nervous and apprehensive about seeking help, even if they are in extreme need. The intention in persuading the care system to take the impacts of domestic violence on children seriously was never for women to lose those children.

Social workers, however, are often very experienced in such matters. For example, they may have particular expertise to offer in working with very young abused women who have used the care system or with women who have a disability (although some recent studies have found that social workers sometimes have little awareness of domestic violence as an issue for disabled women). Social workers often have unique experience and expertise in working with elderly couples where the woman is experiencing abuse. In addition, domestic violence frequently comes to the attention of social services through mental health work. Violence in the home is a major source of distress and unhappiness for women. For some, this can result in contact with the psychiatric services, often mediated through social workers.

In all of these situations, one of the prime issues is security and confidentiality. This can be more complex for social workers than for other statutory and voluntary sector workers, since they are usually in contact with other members of the family as well. As a result, they may need extra support and supervision to deal with the dilemma of how to negotiate work with whole families where the wife or female partner is experiencing domestic violence. Confidentiality can be particularly important if the woman has left her partner and is in hiding. In order to protect her, it is vital that no details are allowed to slip about her whereabouts, even when, as often happens, the man is pressurizing the worker for information. Social workers can be in a particularly vulnerable position in this respect. They are far more likely than many others in the caring professions to have to deal with violent men face-to-face. Social workers need to be aware of the possible dangers, and senior social workers and line managers need to do all they can to ensure their safety.

Social work agencies are a source of information and advice. It is important that they are able to provide women who have suffered domestic violence with correct, up-to-date information and practical help, and that where necessary they can refer them on successfully, for example to Women's Aid. Most social services departments, like housing departments, display posters and other material advertising available services and making it clear that domestic violence is not acceptable. Social workers should be able to act on these and give up-to-date and accurate welfare rights, housing and legal advice about domestic violence. Some authorities and individual social workers pay particular attention to equalities issues in general and, as we discussed in Chapter 6 in relation to housing officers, the provision of sensitive interpreting and support services is also particularly important for social workers working with women whose first language is not English.

Most social work bodies now provide guidance on how to work with domestic violence and increasing numbers of social services departments have developed their own domestic violence policies, sometimes in conjunction with inter-agency forums and other organizations. Domestic violence commonly features in local strategic plans as well as community care and children's services plans and the whole range of strategic plans and partnerships that New Labour has brought into existence. Senior social services managers participate in these strategic partnerships, which may prioritize domestic violence and are sometimes able to feed into local strategic direction. Thus in recent years, since the advent of women's services, the mainstreaming of domestic violence work and changing awareness about it, social workers have tended to move away from their previous rather traditional approaches. Even so, it is still unusual for very much support from social services to be forthcoming solely to meet abused women's needs, if there is not some other factor (like the existence of children) involved. While child safety is a major issue for social workers, women's safety is not – not really.

Child protection

This is not to say that most social workers do not abhor domestic violence. They do usually, and in theory will wish to do whatever they can to assist abused women. In practice, though, what they have the time and facilities to do may be very little. Hemmed in by heavy work burdens, by statutory limitations and by endless assessment and care plan work, they may only be able to offer some advice and information, as we have mentioned, or to refer a woman to a refuge service and perhaps support her in getting there. The pressure on social services has been increasing in recent years as public and government concern about the physical and sexual abuse of children has grown. For those social workers who work directly with children and families, child protection usually dominates their work. They have a duty and a responsibility in law to protect abused children. No such duty and responsibility exists to protect abused women. Statutory commitments towards children override all else.

Social workers have come in for much criticism about child protection in the last few years. Frequently, they are severely castigated for not doing enough to stop child abuse, especially if a child dies, as in the recent tragic case of Victoria Climbié. They are often further castigated for doing too much if, as in a variety of highly publicized cases in the 1990s, they make firm interventions. In addition, child protection work is now very time-consuming and demanding, involving a great deal of paperwork and the use of lengthy, formal Children in Need and child protection procedures under the Children Act.

All of this is happening within a changing financial framework in which increasing numbers of care services have to be 'bought in' as local authority facilities decrease. Social work is once again in transition, as it has been many times before. The two major new Acts of the 1990s, the 1989 Children Act and the 1990 Community Care and National Health Service Act, have radically changed much social work practice and have now been joined by many other new pieces of legislation (such as the 2004 Children Act), regulations and guidance, including performance indicators, new assessment frameworks and an emphasis on achieving targets. Some social workers describe how the ground is shifting constantly and unnervingly beneath their feet, particularly in relation to child protection, while they juggle with people's lives.

In many ways, social work has become an impossible job, subject to fiercely conflicting demands and to expectations that are unrealizable. It is also a job for which the financial rewards are not high but the responsibility – for child welfare in particular – is enormous and rather frightening. The penalties for getting it wrong are harsh, perhaps including very public censure, not to mention private anguish. Many social workers experience high levels of stress, anxiety and fatigue. It is small wonder that the abuse of women is not high on their agendas.

In getting them to take it more seriously, however, there are two issues to consider where children are concerned. The first is the indirect effects that domestic violence may have on the lives of children witnessing it, hearing it through the bedroom wall or otherwise living with it (as we discussed in Chapter 1). These impacts can be both short and long term and include physical and emotional effects and behavioural problems. The second issue is how much domestic violence is connected to actual abuse of children in the same family.

Many studies in a variety of countries have shown that, in between one-third and two-thirds of instances, where there is domestic violence there is also child abuse and vice versa. One piece of research in the UK by Marianne Hester and colleagues with the NSPCC in the 1990s found that the two sorts of violence occurred together in about one-third of cases. However, when the staff were trained actually to ask if domestic violence was occurring, instead of omitting any questions about it as had been the case up till then, the incidence jumped to two-thirds! All the new cases had previously been overlooked, since there was no agreed way of screening for domestic violence and the mothers of the children who had been abused had not said anything about their own abuse.

The American researcher Lee Bowker and his team investigated the relationship between wife-beating and child physical abuse in a large study conducted in the 1980s, and found an even higher figure. In his study, men who abused their wives also abused their children in 70 per cent of the families where children were present. The child abuse was generally less severe than the wife abuse in the families studied. The worse the wife-beating, however, the worse the child abuse. The study involved a thousand self-selected women in the USA who had experienced domestic violence, but it suffered from not using a randomized sample and has been criticized on these grounds as perhaps leading to a falsely high result.

On a general level, it is important also to understand that the power of the abuser operates differently in cases of child abuse and cases of domestic violence. Many men who abuse their partners would never ever hurt their children. Domestic violence is usually about how men regard the women with whom they are intimate. In other words, it is about gender and power in adult relationships. Nevertheless, the two separate types of abuse occur together sufficiently frequently for it to be important for social workers to be aware that, where one type is present, the other might be too. So it is vital to be vigilant about domestic violence in cases of child abuse, and about child abuse in cases of domestic violence, and always to check both out.

Unfortunately, until the early to mid-1990s, that is exactly what did not happen. It was very often the case before then that, even where domestic violence had clearly been involved in a child abuse case, it was still overlooked and not regarded as important. The experiences of children living with domestic violence, and the possible connections between domestic violence and child abuse, were issues that escaped policy attention and the public gaze. A 1995 report to the Department of Health, produced by two researchers into child abuse, Elaine Farmer and Morag Owen, and called *Decision Making, Intervention and Outcome in Child Protection Work*, discusses what the authors call the 'missing link with domestic violence'. In an analysis of child protection cases, they found that in 59 per cent of them there was current violence in the family apart from the child abuse. One of the striking findings of Farmer and Owen's study was that the child protection work done was frequently focused not on the abusing adult but on other family members, particularly the mother. Such shifts of focus often allowed men's violence to their wives to be ignored, literally to disappear from view. This study and others have revealed how few social workers in the past have regarded domestic violence towards the child's mother as worthy of attention in child abuse cases.

From the mid-1990s, however, the impacts on children and the connection between child abuse and domestic violence have become issues that have 'found their time'. This new interest in the UK arose partly in relation to a series of child deaths at the hands of their fathers (or their mother's partners) where the existence of domestic violence was a factor identified in the subsequent public inquiries. These inquiries into the deaths of children concluded that, if the domestic violence that was being experienced by the mother had been taken seriously as a relevant issue by the authorities, the child might have been better protected and the tragedy avoided. Several research studies and the work of Women's Aid have also played their part in changing professional attitudes, uncovering the damage done to children by witnessing and being involved in domestic violence.

Thus, experience of domestic violence by children has gradually come to be recognized as an indirect form of abuse itself. As mentioned in Chapter 1, the first text on children and domestic violence in the UK was produced in 1994 by Audrey Mullender and Rebecca Morley. Also in 1994, NCH Action for Children published the research study, noted earlier in this chapter, which they had conducted on children and domestic violence, and further research has been carried out in a variety of institutions. The Women's Aid Federation of England participated in 1995 in publishing a book rooted in children's experiences of domestic violence called *It Hurts Me Too*. The NSPCC has also conducted important research on domestic violence, published in a book by Caroline McGee.

In recent years, there have been endless numbers of conferences and training courses on children and domestic abuse. New policy and practice developments, sometimes connected with inter-agency domestic violence forums and with Women's Aid, have occurred in various parts of the UK. For example, the NSPCC has now published guidelines on domestic abuse for professionals to inform its many child protection services. Other children's charities, such as Barnado's, the Children's Society and NCH Action for Children, have also developed awareness and domestic violence policies. And a variety of child protection and domestic violence guidelines have been drawn up, sometimes by local authorities, sometimes by children's sub-groups of multi-agency forums and sometimes by special inter-agency groups set up for the purpose, including perhaps the local domestic violence service, social services department and one of the children's charities.

These pioneering developments have been a bit patchy and are still by no means universal. However, they have led to the acceptance that best practice in social work consists of taking domestic violence very seriously as a child protection issue. As a result, across the country the official bodies that oversee child protection policy in local areas, the Area Child Protection Committees (ACPCs), have begun to evolve specific policies and procedures on domestic violence. These policies have been much welcomed after so much previous neglect of the issue. But there is always a danger in involving state agencies with far-reaching powers – and without much gender awareness – in work on the abuse of women. In this case, focusing attention on domestic violence has led to some examples of bureaucratic and punitive child protection responses towards the mother. On the other hand, the new awareness has begun to lead in some areas to more creative and imaginative initiatives in child abuse work in relation to domestic violence, including developing sympathetic local multi-agency domestic violence and child protection services and making connections between ACPCs and domestic violence forums. The latest edition of the government guidance on child protection and the Children Act, *Working Together to Safeguard Children* (1999) specifically recommends that these connections should be made in local areas to enable joined-up work and constructive liaison.

Importantly, in 1998 the Department of Health, with Barnardo's, the NSPCC, Women's Aid and members of our Bristol Domestic Violence Group, produced a comprehensive reader and training materials for social services on children and domestic violence, entitled *Making an Impact*. These materials, republished in 2000, provide a comprehensive guide to research, policies and practice recommendations on children and domestic violence, as we have noted earlier. The training materials have been updated in 2004 and the reader is in the process of revision. Cathy Humphreys and Audrey Mullender have also produced various pieces of helpful guidance for practitioners, and Women's Aid has published *Social Work, Domestic Violence and Child Protection: Challenging Practice*, also by Cathy Humphreys (in 2000). A new Home Office *Development Practice Report* on working with children was published in 2004.

These days, children's rights to be listened to, and to be heard, are important issues. Most children's organizations have policies that enable children to participate in that organization and the UN Convention on the Rights of the Child insists that children have the right to be consulted about issues that affect them. A project in the Economic and Social Research Council's 'Children 5:16; Growing into the Twenty First Century Research Programme', conducted by a large research team – including ourselves – published one book in 2002 for practitioners and policy-makers called *Children's Perceptions of Domestic Violence*, and another in 2003 written in the words of children, *Don't Hit Mum*. These books discuss not only the impacts of domestic violence on young people but also the amazing coping strategies that they often adopt and the useful advice and help they frequently have for other children in the same situation.

Although the age and degree of maturity of each child needs to be taken into account, the study found that children almost always know about the domestic abuse that their mothers are experiencing, have thought deeply about it and often have potential solutions to propose. But no one ever asks them about it. Including children's opinions and insights (where it is safe to do so) in possible solutions – or at least consulting them – are issues that professionals need to take on if children's voices are not to be ignored once again, as so often in the past. Children are not passive recipients of domestic violence. Rather they are 'social actors' in their own world. Their resilience and personal views and ideas can be key resources for social workers to work with.

Some agencies are trying to do just this and there are pockets of excellent practice around, while in other areas nothing much has changed. The current awareness of the impacts of domestic violence has led to some heavy-handed and inappropriate interventions or, sometimes, to crude or simplistic responses by social services against a background of lack of resources. There have been widespread cutbacks in the social and caring services that children and women experiencing domestic violence need, and there is currently a recruiting crisis in social work with many posts unfilled. There have also been increasing attacks on single parenthood. Such attacks were commonplace under the Conservative government of John Major, but were quickly taken up, in a diluted form, by the Labour government elected in May 1997. Despite initiatives like Surestart to support families in difficult circumstances, New Labour appears to regard lone mothers as part of an undesirable 'dependency culture' (and this is an element of the much-trumpeted New Deal policies for single parents).

Nevertheless, the hope of the women's services and Women's Aid is that developments which recognize both the connections between domestic violence and child abuse and also the need for a sensitive approach to the complexity of the issues may lead to further improvements in practice. The present philosophy that the protection of women can be the most effective form of child protection has begun to open up a constructive exchange between women's support services, social services and children's charities. So there is some hope to be had here.

Social work training

One of the reasons why domestic violence has so often been pushed to one side in child protection work is that, traditionally, social workers have not been trained to deal with it. Until recently, social work training often contained little material about it, and such material was frequently contradictory. Courses might have included a contribution from a local Women's Aid group positioning the violence firmly as men's responsibility. But they might also have covered the subject as part of a 'family systems' or family therapy approach which would tend to allocate responsibility for the violence more equally as part of a 'system' of family interaction.

In recent years, feminist criticisms of traditional social work practices have appeared on social work courses. Various books and articles about a feminist approach to social work have been written, and social work students now study them. There has been a growth of courses on what is sometimes called 'women-centred practice', which usually include material on domestic violence. Women's studies has become established as an academic discipline in its own right in some universities, and has given rise to a great deal of important intellectual work on women's issues, including material on male violence. Some of this material has filtered on to social work courses and to a lesser extent into health visitor training and other courses for caring professionals.

Some social workers and social work teachers have suggested that the improvements are merely a drop in the ocean of negative views about women. However, the situation is improving throughout the social work profession on women's issues, and combating discrimination of various types, at least on a superficial level, has left the margins and entered the mainstream of social work. For example, anti-discriminatory practice, which often includes material on domestic violence, was a feature of social work training under the previous diploma in social work courses. And the new undergraduate and masters' degrees in social work, which have operated since 2003/4, are usually committed to anti-oppressive practice and to combating gender disadvantage, racism and other sorts of discrimination in their work. Similarly, post-qualifying training courses now routinely feature domestic violence, and specialist in-service training on both domestic violence awareness and policies in operation in the locality is now common.

What is meant by good practice?

As we saw in Chapter 2, domestic violence activists and workers in the field have stressed empowerment as a way for abused women to rid themselves of the abuse. Empowerment is currently an important concept in social work too, although social workers often use the word somewhat differently. In an article back in 1991 in the journal *Critical Social Policy*, Audrey Mullender and David Ward suggest that 'empowerment' had come into vogue in social work circles much as a concept of 'community' had done in the 1970s. It has become something of a bandwagon term. The authors point out, however, that the word is frequently used in a misleading, generalized way so that it becomes almost meaningless, merely a synonym for 'enabling'. It gives social workers who use it an aura of moral superiority and can act to immunize them against criticism. Ward and Mullender claim that empowerment can work as a social work strategy only if linked to an analysis of oppression and action to challenge it. This is also the way in which Women's Aid attempts to use the term. As a result, there are various examples of constructive liaison and innovatory work between progressive or feminist social workers and local domestic violence services.

Some social workers take action to support refuge services having funding difficulties and to campaign for more domestic violence provision.

Many social services departments run groups for abused women or refer women to voluntary sector support groups. In these groups, women may have a chance to discuss their feelings and experiences, and to share them with others in the same situation. Groups may be therapeutic in nature or more geared to practical issues. Groups for children who have experienced domestic violence against their mothers also operate in some areas, often under the auspices of a children's charity like Barnado's. Very often, social workers work closely with local Women's Aid services, many of which have accepted social work students on placement for many years. In addition, social services departments generally participate in inter-agency initiatives on domestic violence, which aim to bring together all the concerned agencies in a locality to improve the delivery of local services on a general level (see Chapter 8).

Social services practice guidelines on domestic violence (sometimes developed in co-operation with inter-agency forums, as we have mentioned) are now in operation, and the social work agency concerned may accompany their implementation with training courses or local seminars. Some councils with a council-wide or corporate response to domestic violence produce more general guidelines and principles that apply to all departments, including social services. Such guides to good practice usually include practice procedures on the need for confidentiality, safety and security, on how to adopt a sympathetic, supportive approach, and on the provision of sensitive services. Guidelines also often contain sections on definitions and on improvements in data recording, monitoring and statistics keeping. They may have sections on why women leave, on the lengthy process that may be involved, and on the specific needs of black, minority ethnic and immigrant women, older women, women with disabilities, lesbians, young women and children. Specific guidelines for social services often include details on how to operate any policy that is in force and suggestions on empowering and validating the woman, on the importance of believing her and on enabling her to make her own choices. Importantly, guidance needs to include advice on evolving detailed safety plans with both abused women and their children.

There may also be guidelines on domestic violence and mental health issues for mental health workers and for approved social workers who have special responsibilities under the Mental Health Act 1983 for admitting people to psychiatric hospitals (soon to be overhauled by new mental health legislation). Many good practice guidelines point out the necessity for social workers to support abused women in dealing with the mental health services, which can otherwise be intimidating, and in which people sometimes find that their rights are not protected. Good practice guides may also suggest that it is important to be aware of a possible history of domestic violence where an application is being made under the Mental Health Act to admit a woman compulsorily to hospital. The social worker in this situation is obligated to consult the nearest relative, often the woman's husband or partner. While one might expect the nearest relative to have a genuine concern for the person being admitted, it is suggested that social workers should recognize the considerable power that this gives the relative or partner, especially where domestic violence is suspected. In general, women are over-represented in psychiatric hospitals, more likely than men to be assessed under the Mental Health Act, more likely to be compulsorily admitted, and more likely to be prescribed tranquillizers and anti-depressants.

Other good practice guidelines that have been adopted include the encouragement of greater awareness among social workers of the possibility of violence in the families with which they work, including of course the needs of children in domestic violence situations. For example, behavioural problems in children may be linked to domestic abuse. It is important that, in responding to such situations, the concern of the social worker is not solely for the welfare of the child, but also for the safety and well-being of the woman.

A way of assisting good practice is to have a social worker specifically responsible for domestic violence issues in the local authority concerned. This liaison officer needs to be at a senior enough level to be able to implement change and may well also have a role liaising with the local domestic violence forums and with partnership bodies in the area which have strategic responsibility. The 2000 mapping study to which we have referred throughout this book found that the appointment of a liaison officer with specific responsibilities was best practice but at that time only 40 per cent of social services departments had such workers in post.

Most good practice guides and recommendations regarding social work and domestic violence strongly advocate the provision of domestic violence training on the job. Such training often includes policy issues and practicalities as well as awareness material. Domestic violence training is discussed further in Chapter 8.

Traditional attitudes

Despite these positive recommendations and policy developments, some social workers still harbour traditional attitudes about domestic violence. Much of what social work is about has to do with families. Social services is one of the few agencies that deals directly with the intimacies and privacies of family life, and which can gain entry into people's lives at the most personal and private level, most often after things have gone wrong in some way. It is quite common for social workers to regard families in which individuals have problems as 'dysfunctional', and, in the past, this analysis has often been applied to domestic violence. The violence has been seen as a symptom of malfunction in the family as a whole, and social workers have tried various measures for improving the way that the family in question works, often involving conciliation between the parties or trying to assist the woman to be a better wife. Certainly in the past, social workers have held views that wives actually encourage or provoke abusive treatment. These types of attitude and social work intervention have led some domestic violence activists to question whether social services can play a useful role in combating violence in the home. Such attitudes, mixed up with ideas about personal dysfunction, about how women should bring up their children, and about the desirability of the two-parent nuclear family as an ideal, still have a purchase within social work despite contemporary challenges by new generations of social workers.

As we noted in Chapter 3, such assumptions are further complicated in social work by theories of 'cycles of violence' or 'inter-generational transmission of violence', which some academics and professionals use to claim an almost automatic connection between the adult use of violence and childhood experiences of abuse or witnessing abuse. It seems clear that, while this is sometimes true, it is often not. There are many examples of women and men who were abused or who witnessed abuse in childhood, but who do not enter abusive relationships as adults. There are also many examples of people who were not exposed to abuse in childhood, but who experience abuse either as the abuser or as the victim of abuse in adulthood. Nevertheless, the theory holds enormous sway. Assumptions, preconceptions and theories of these various types still underlie much of social work today, despite the developments in good practice that we have discussed.

Contact, residence and the Children Act 1989

Social workers, voluntary sector workers and CAFCASS (the agency responsible for overseeing contested childcare situations within child protection work and also after relationship breakdown) are all involved in the operation of the Children Act 1989. The Act was a far-reaching piece of legislation that changed much of previous childcare law and brought new measures into effect. It assumes that children are best brought up in families involving both parents, and that statutory intervention should be kept to a minimum. The Act introduced the formal concept of 'parental responsibility', for example, which automatically applies to mothers and to married couples. Other fathers can apply for parental responsibility, thus increasing their rights over the children.

The Act makes no mention of domestic violence. However, an amendment has been more recently introduced through the Family Law Act 1996 which can be used to exclude an abusive parent from the home, in conjunction with other measures to protect a child. This may prove useful where an abuser has harmed both the woman and the child(ren) as an alternative to professional expectations that it is the woman and children who should leave. It marks an important recognition, hitherto often neglected, that safety measures need to involve a focus on the perpetrator. Similarly, amendments introduced through the Adoption Act 2002 specified domestic violence in the checklist that the courts are obliged to consider in decision making regarding orders relating to children. The 2004 Children Act adds it as an important new category causing 'harm'.

In general, though, the Acts assume that parents are reasonable and responsible, that fathers should be substantially involved in children's lives after divorce or separation, and that even after such a separation parents will be able to arrive at amicable childcare decisions through joint negotiation. For many women who have suffered violence, however, it is not safe to be in contact with their violent ex-partner.

Research by Marianne Hester and Lorraine Radford has examined the problematic use of mediation in specific relation to domestic violence. Partly as a result of Hester and Radford's work and of research by Women's Aid, some improvements in practice have been developed. For example, the practice of interviewing both parties together has now decreased due to a recognition of the distressing effect that such meetings can have in cases of domestic violence and the disadvantaged negotiating position in which they may place abused women. The National Standards used by CAFCASS warn against joint meetings in cases involving domestic violence.

The 1989 Children Act includes provisions for 'contact orders' and 'residence orders' after separation, which replace the previous access and custody arrangements. These provisions have led on occasion to further abuse of both women and children by violent men. An in-depth, comparative research study also by Hester and Radford in 1996 has documented these difficulties. In only 7 out of 53 domestic violence cases studied was contact with fathers achieved after separation without further abuse occurring. Nevertheless, contact orders with fathers are almost always granted. In 2003, out of 55,743 cases, only 1.3 per cent (713 in all) were refused. Problems have also been experienced with residence orders, where children are sometimes ordered to remain at home with a violent father rather than accompany a fleeing mother into temporary accommodation.

The 1999 Children Act Sub-Committee Consultation Paper on contact in cases of domestic violence conceded that contact issues were often not dealt with properly in such cases. A helpful subsequent case ruled that four violent fathers should only have indirect contact. However, it does not appear that court practice has improved much since, despite the inclusion of domestic violence in the checklist that is meant to be considered in all cases involving children. It still seems that the issue of whether or not contact is safe is not always addressed thoroughly by the courts. The presumption remains that contact is almost always in the child's interest.

The government issued its report *Making Contact Safe* and tried to tackle the issue by producing Good Practice Guidelines in 2001 and by amending the law through the Adoption Act 2002. But these recommendations are seen to be having mixed effects. A Women's Aid survey of 127 refuge organizations in 2001 found that contact, some of which was unsupervised, was still being granted even to parents convicted of offences against children or whose behaviour had resulted in children being placed on the child protection register (23 cases in all). In a 2003 survey, out of 178 responses, only 10 per cent thought that practice had improved since the guidelines, 60 per cent found no improvement at all and 6 per cent thought things had actually got worse. Women's Aid reports have called on the government to set up an independent inquiry into residence and contact orders, together with a range of recommendations to improve practice.

For example, guidance should include the requirement to be mindful of the woman's safety when making orders for children who are in her care. There should also be clear guidance on how the child's wishes can be heard more safely in court proceedings and investigations. CAFCASS is now developing consultation mechanisms with children and young people to inform the organization, so this may be of help in the future.

Women's organizations have pushed for changes to the Children Act to ensure that these orders are safe for children and, in 2004, for an important (failed) amendment to the new domestic violence legislation on safe child contact after domestic violence. Instead, proposals have been put forward by the new Department for Constitutional Affairs which may increase fathers' rights and the whole issue remains contentious and the subject of lobbying and swings in policy making. Women's Aid has serious concerns about the 2005 draft Children (Contact) and Adoption Bill, which seeks to enforce contact and to introduce penalties for failing to preserve it.

A further issue under the Children Act concerns whether children experiencing domestic violence may be assessed as being 'in need' and therefore eligible for services and resources. Throughout most of the 1990s, the BBC *Children in Need* appeal funded more domestic violence children's workers' posts nationwide than social services departments did.

Social security and the Child Support Act 1991

Often one of the main contributions that social workers can make to improving life for women who have suffered domestic violence is to act as their advocates, especially when dealing with the social security system. Achieving economic independence after leaving home due to violence is one of the most important issues for women. Various researchers have provided considerable evidence that a vital factor in a woman's efforts to leave a violent relationship is her economic and employment position. Abused women often have to depend on the social security system for financial support, especially if they have children. Women in this situation are eligible for income support payments from the Benefits Agency for themselves and their children, and can obtain crisis loans to enable them to deal with the immediate trauma of leaving home, possibly with no money whatsoever. They are also eligible for housing benefit.

Many women who have left home due to violence have never claimed benefits before and may feel nervous about approaching such a formidable institution as the Benefits Agency. Domestic violence staff and social workers can offer valuable support and advocacy. They can also help to ensure that women and children get the money to which they are entitled. Having a social worker speaking on one's behalf can substantially influence what happens and improve the service available. However, the level of social security benefits was significantly lowered during the Conservative governments of 1979–97. New Deal 'Welfare to Work' schemes also have their part to play.

The Child Support Act attempts to make absent fathers financially responsible for their children. Its main aim is to cut the cost to the taxpayer of child support for the children of single parents. If the mother is on income support, she faces a reduction in her benefit if she does not reveal the name of the father. The Act is administered through the troubled Child Support Agency and was passed in 1991 despite protests against a number of its provisions from Women's Aid, refuge children's workers and many other organizations, which formed a lobbying coalition. Members of the coalition were divided as to the potential disadvantages and benefits of the legislation. All, however, agreed to a minimal position of supporting the inclusion of a 'good cause clause'. The original bill would have docked benefit from women who refused to co-operate for any reason whatsoever. The additional clause allowed for women to refuse to co-operate without loss where they had good cause to fear harm or distress to themselves or their children, for example because of domestic violence.

The Child Support Act has far-reaching ramifications in terms of making a break with a violent partner. In practice, it can sometimes mean that such a break becomes an impossibility. There is, for example, some evidence that men who have previously had no involvement with their children and their ex-partner may insist on contact if they are being forced to pay.

Developments in children's work

Within local domestic violence services themselves over the years, there has been an increasing development of sensitive ways of working with and 'alongside' children, taking children's views and needs seriously, and attempting to enable children's voices to be heard. The value of play in terms of creative expression and fulfilment, and its potential as a way of dealing with experiences of domestic violence, has been increasingly recognized, and the therapeutic value of work with children in refuge-based services has been acknowledged and developed by children's workers. In addition, they have developed innovative work practices around the empowerment of children and advocacy with and for them, as well as children's self-advocacy. Children in the Hammersmith and Fulham refuge, for example, have developed their own workbook on abuse issues and their own anti-racism policy. Children may participate in their own meetings within refuges together with children's workers, and refuge organizations have now developed both child protection policies and 'non-violence to children' policies. These policies work towards the elimination of physical punishment of children using domestic violence services and often involve very sensitive and emotionally demanding work between mothers and workers to develop alternative methods of discipline. Children's work in domestic violence services is discussed in Chapter 2. The development of preventative work in schools and youth services is examined in Chapter 9.

Health and medical services

Health visitors, nurses, doctors and health centre staff are among those groups of workers in the caring services who see abused women often, and who are most involved in responding to children who are living with the reality of domestic violence. Health visitors, for example, have special responsibilities in this regard. Practice guidance has been developed, and health visitors often attend training courses and seminars to attempt to improve how they work with abused women and children. An enduring problem for health visitors, however, as for other medical personnel, is recognizing domestic violence. Often the woman concerned does not feel able to bring up the issue, since she may have deep fears about the powers of the health visitor in relation to her children.

Nurses and midwives, and accident and emergency staff, also deal with violence on a daily basis, and training on domestic violence is now provided on recognizing and responding to domestic violence. But there is a long heritage of ignoring it and failing to take it seriously in the health service, as there is in social services.

A recent book by Emma Williamson has looked at domestic violence and health, and has uncovered and documented the poor response that has often been received from health professionals. A key piece of work in this regard comes from the United States. A team of widely respected American researchers into health issues and domestic violence, including Evan Stark, Demie Kurz and Anne Flitcraft, have developed a concept that they call 'the social construction of battering' by the American medical profession. These researchers claim that the many complicated medical and psychological factors involved in domestic violence escape the medical gaze almost completely. Due, they suggest, to both gender and class biases within medicine, the profession does not take domestic violence seriously, fails to take on board the needs of abused women and the complex symptoms that they may present, and 'labels' women who have suffered violence as problematic patients.

In one American study of medical records, 20 per cent of 'battered' women but only 4 per cent of 'non-battered' women were labelled in some pejorative or punishing way in their records – for example, as a 'neurotic female' or an 'hysteric'. Looked at the other way around, 86 per cent of all the women who were labelled in this way had suffered violence and abuse. Stark and Flitcraft suggest that the medical profession tends to disbelieve and stigmatize abused women, and to use this stigmatization as a way to avoid acknowledging the inadequacies of the medical response to domestic violence. They have called this 'not-so-benign neglect'. In recent years, however, since the renewed interest in domestic violence, there have been some improvements in this harsh picture and an increase in awareness about the inadequacies of current medical practice.

Doctors

General practitioners (GPs) are in a particularly influential and key position. Most people with physical injuries go to the doctor to get them treated: most people, that is, unless they are women who have suffered violence. Sometimes women are too embarrassed to go to see their general practitioner. Often they do not go because of fear. Research studies in the past have found that, where abused women did make visits to the doctor, these visits were often in defiance of the husband's explicit prohibition, or were allowed by him only after the woman had given assurances that she would not tell how she came by the injuries.

We have personal contact with several women who experienced violence in the home for many years, but who rarely obtained medical help due to fear of repercussions. One woman who suffered very serious abuse over a long period told us:

> Some days I could not get up. Once I was in bed for seven days. I could not get up with the swelling. I didn't go to the doctor, I couldn't. Once I did call the emergency doctor when he was out at work, but then I was too scared in case he found out. He would have killed me if he'd found I'd been to the doctor. I cancelled it. Just one time I did see the doctor in secret and she said I must go at once to the hospital. But I said no. I was too scared to go to the hospital. I even threw away the pills that she said I must take to get better in case he found them. I threw them away. I cannot forget these things until my death.

The results of failing to get medical attention can be scarring and permanent damage, and the enduring of unnecessary and unrelieved pain. Each year, many thousands of abused women in the UK suffer substantial untreated injuries.

General practitioners are also very busy. Very short appointment times mean that it is hard for a doctor to find the time to deal with such a distressing subject as domestic violence, with all its layers of complexity and personal pain. Women may then get the unspoken message that the GP does not really have time to hear what they have to say. They may already feel apologetic about taking up the doctor's time, and this can amplify feelings of worthlessness that they may be experiencing.

Doctors, however, remain a principal port of call for women experiencing domestic violence. Women who have suffered violence turn to them for help with either physical or psychological problems resulting from the violence, or are taken to casualty departments with their injuries. In very many cases, as with health visitors discussed above, women disguise the source of the injuries with the result that the incidence of domestic violence reported to doctors and to hospitals tends to be artificially low. Also, the help that a woman receives, apart from straightforward physical treatment, can still be very much the luck of the draw, depending on which health service she happens to go to. While some staff may avoid the issue in a 'conspiracy' of silence, many women doctors and health professionals are very supportive of abused women and children. They may provide counselling support, and both time and space for women to talk about their experiences, as well as up-to-date information and medical treatment. Some go out of their way to assist abused women, and organizations of women in medicine exist that may have domestic violence as one of their areas of concern.

Differences in social class and power, though, between doctor and patients are often an important factor in medical consultations, and may be compounded for women by gender differences if the doctor is a man. These differences frequently militate against women talking openly to doctors, especially about such personally embarrassing subjects as abuse. This is particularly the case when, as often happens, women do not present spectacular or specific injuries, but rather describe a range of physical and mental conditions that doctors may be tempted to brush to one side or to regard as 'not proper medicine'. Many women describe how debilitating it is, not only to have suffered abuse, but also to be fobbed off by their doctors or to be clearly regarded as a bit of a nuisance.

If the physical injuries are very severe, many doctors and health visitors take a different approach. As well as providing the required medical treatment, they may also give the woman information, possibly including telling her about the local refuge organization and other services and support groups. But it appears that very often the advice that they offer may consist of telling women that they should leave their violent partners. Doctors and other medical staff do not always appreciate how difficult such a decision may be. For an abused woman, it can mean breaking up the family, leaving the partner she may well love, taking children away from their father, and losing the support and companionship of a partner (in the good times). It can also mean admitting to the outside world that the relationship has failed, losing financial support and material possessions, and facing potentially extreme poverty, possibly becoming homeless, trying to find somewhere to go on both a temporary and permanent basis, and facing life alone as a single parent. These are not easy things. One wonders how the doctor who tells the woman to leave, and who cannot understand why she does not, would deal with such a life option.

We have known various women who have gone back several times to their doctor with injuries, and who have been told by him, or her, that they will not be seen again unless they leave their partner. Such threats can hardly be regarded as ethical. Other women who have felt unable to follow the doctor's advice to 'up and leave' may feel too guilty or embarrassed to seek medical help again if they receive fresh injuries. Popular opinion has it that it is feminists who try to break up the family and encourage women to leave their husbands or male partners. In fact, the converse is often true. Women's Aid and feminist GPs are frequently the ones who appreciate the complexity of the issue for women, who understand why they may not be able to leave, who believe in supporting the woman whatever her decision, and who do not give up on her if she keeps going back.

Whether or not women choose to leave their violent partners, it can certainly be helpful if doctors' surgeries prominently display up-to-date information about refuge-based and other services that are available, particularly telephone helplines. Doctors also need to ensure that information which they give to women during consultations is correct and not out-dated. GPs are often highly respected by their patients and the giving out of faulty information can have disastrous effects. Where several community languages are spoken, information needs to be provided in the languages concerned. However, various projects and groups concerned with the needs of black women and women from other minority ethnic communities in relation to domestic violence have noted that many GPs and health practitioners tend neither to bother with interpreters nor, when they are present, to listen to them carefully or to make good use of their services. Where complex and delicate issues of abuse are concerned, this can lead to an effective silencing of women whose first language is not English.

In her study, Mama highlighted issues of power and cultural difference between doctors and some women from black and minority ethnic communities. She also pointed out that male doctors from minority ethnic communities may be less than helpful to women from their own community seeking assistance following violence. For example, some Asian women in her study found that their GPs, who might be respected as community figures, sided with their husbands and stated that women should not try to leave violent marriages. Other women in the study were helpfully advised and assisted by their GPs, indicating that doctors can play a more positive role.

Doctors have a particularly key position in regard to providing services for older women and for women with disabilities or with mental health problems who are experiencing domestic violence. Their expertise in these areas can be of crucial importance, since they may have unique access to abused women facing these difficulties. However, doctors may have a tendency to overlook domestic violence in these situations, since they may not be expecting it. Like social workers, doctors also need to be aware of domestic abuse in their involvement with various pieces of legislation, such as compulsory admissions to psychiatric hospital under the Mental Health Act.

Routine enquiry

An issue that has received a lot of attention in recent years is routine enquiry (RE) about domestic violence. Should health professionals routinely ask about it? There is no consensus as yet, but a recent Home Office project in the Crime Reduction Programme on Violence against Women investigated it, and there have been various other research studies and systematic reviews of the evidence so far. Some studies find that it works in certain settings but not in others, where the questioning can be upsetting and disturbing to women patients.

However, if domestic violence is to be taken seriously by the health service and if data are to be kept on its true prevalence, some form of routine enquiry may be advisable. Midwives were trained to ask about it in a study conducted as part of the recent ESRC Violence Research Programme. This study found that routine enquiry was successful provided the staff were trained and supported in how to ask the questions and that they could deal with any disclosures in terms of referring women on. However, midwives tended to stop asking the questions unless supported to do so.

The North Bristol NHS Trust has pioneered training and support for midwives to conduct such enquiries, and the scheme (named the Bristol Pregnancy and Domestic Violence Programme) has recently been evaluated for the Department of Health. The outcome (published in 2004) was most positive. Participating community midwives found the training supportive and helpful, and the study came up with a raft of recommendations. Included was the recommendation that primary care trusts should engage in antenatal enquiry about domestic violence as part of their service level and commissioning agreements, should develop an inter-agency approach overall and should train and then support staff on an ongoing basis to enable them to do this work. The training offered should include modelling how to ask about domestic violence in a sensitive way. It has been shown that modelling of this type needs to be fairly comprehensive, that practitioners need to be able to respond appropriately to disclosures and to offer relevant help, and that ongoing support will be needed to make sure the practice is carried out and does not tail off after an initial period of enthusiasm.

In sum, routine enquiry remains contentious, with many health professionals suggesting that it would be too bureaucratic, upsetting and time consuming, while others suggest that comprehensive data are essential across the health service. It has been recommended by the National Institute of Clinical Excellence (NICE), and by the *Confidential Enquiry into Maternal Deaths*, and features strongly in the brief for the new national co-ordinator post for health services (see below). In the future, it looks certain that we will hear a lot more about routine enquiry into domestic violence, despite the current contention that surrounds it.

Treatment

Prescribing patterns that doctors use with women who have suffered domestic violence show that the traditional way to treat an abused woman has been to tend to her injuries – and to prescribe tranquillizers or anti-depressants. Many studies have found that abused women are very often prescribed such drugs, and staff in domestic violence services and women who have suffered violence confirm that drugs are still regarded as an appropriate treatment. Activists, researchers and providers of services in the domestic violence field have pointed out that this practice of prescribing psychotropic drugs to women experiencing domestic violence can seem like treating a woman for her husband's behaviour. The result of male violence becomes that the man gets off more or less scot-free and the woman concerned ends up taking drugs.

Women may be resistant to taking tranquillizing drugs to start with. Alternatively, they may welcome the immediate relief that they bring. Drug therapy rapidly becomes a pattern, however. Very many abused women have ended up seriously addicted to tranquillizers because of the ease with which they were prescribed in the past. These days, doctors are far more careful about prescribing Valium and similar drugs, given their proven addictive qualities. At the moment, however, anti-depressants that are meant to be non-addictive are freely prescribed. Very many domestic violence survivors are taking them, including untold numbers of women still living at home with violent partners.

While the prescribing of tranquillizers, anti-depressants and sleeping pills can assist a woman to deal with the pain and anxiety in her life, many in the field believe that such drugs can limit a woman's ability to make clear life decisions at a time of crisis or, disturbingly, to escape physically from attack. Looked at from this angle, to drug a woman so that she may be more confused and lethargic than she would otherwise have been, and then to send her home to face potential assault, is to place her in increased danger. Such a course of action could be regarded both as immoral and as an alarming example of the unequal relations between men and women.

However, doctors often have few other treatment possibilities available. Women approaching their GPs because of violence may be suicidal, anxious and frightened, or depressed, and may be experiencing a wide range of minor illnesses and types of malaise. What is the doctor to do? Drugs to treat such symptoms can play a vital part in a woman's recovery, providing the drug treatment does not become long term. Some doctors attempt to empower the woman to make her own decisions about drug treatment by giving her as much information as possible, warning her about side effects, and working closely with her to monitor how the drug affects her. Such doctors would usually attempt to build a woman's trust and confidence in herself, and would encourage her to view the drug treatment as a tool to deal with a specific situation, rather than as a panacea.

The only available alternative or complement to drug therapy may be to refer the woman for psychiatric help. More than anything else, many women are grateful for the chance to talk about their feelings and experiences. As a result, referrals to the psychiatric services or to professional counsellors may be welcomed by abused women seeking help, even though such a course of action can appear, like drug treatment, to be 'punishing' or pathologizing the woman for the violence that she

has received from a man. It is a sad fact that the psychiatric assistance offered is often imbued with traditional attitudes towards women's role in the family and blaming attitudes towards women in general.

Many women, however, have constructive therapeutic relationships with psychiatrists and counsellors, and are assisted by them to grow stronger psychologically and to deal with the violence in their lives more effectively. Workers in local domestic violence services often wish that they could provide more in-depth counselling than they may have the time or training to do, and many abused women pinpoint counselling services as one of their most important needs. More refuge-based services, outreach organizations and advice centres do provide some counselling these days, and self-help groups sometimes develop their own group counselling programmes, either formally or informally. Aware health service practitioners may make use of these options.

Nevertheless, with so few treatment options available and so little concern about domestic violence in the medical profession, doctors and hospitals often show an interest in it solely when it is the subject of a medical emergency. Overall, in the UK little co-ordinated activity exists. For example, health services rarely play much of a part in multi-agency action. One of the findings of our own 1996 study of inter-agency co-ordination was that health workers were notable by their absence from such initiatives, although health professionals in a few areas were taking an important initiating and co-ordinating role. GPs themselves were almost totally absent from multi-agency forums throughout the country at the time of the study. This situation is improving, however, with health services more likely in the 2000s to take up domestic abuse issues at a strategic level both within the NHS and within inter-agency partnerships, and to play an active part in domestic violence forums and multi-agency initiatives.

Guidelines and policies

Interest in the development of good practice is currently developing fast. Strong recommendations have been made that medical training should be improved as regards domestic violence, and regular in-service training should be held for accident and emergency staff, GPs and health visitors. Leaflets and information are often now provided for patient use, and medical staff are more likely these days to be trained to talk about domestic violence rather than ignoring the issue. Multi-agency forums sometimes participate in such work, despite the general paucity of health involvement. Protocols produced by the American Medical Association and used throughout the USA have attracted attention in the UK, and several accident and emergency departments and individual health trusts have their own guidelines in place. Multi-agency forums sometimes participate in such work. For example, the Camden and Islington Health Authority, in conjunction with the Camden Domestic Violence Forum, was a pioneer in producing comprehensive practice guidance for health service workers in 1998. Innovative schemes for primary care work have since been piloted by Camden Safety Net under the Home Office Crime Reduction Initiative.

A wide variety of health trusts have now developed comprehensive policies and guidance, including those in Bristol, Surrey and Leeds. General GP good practice guidelines have also been recently adopted in the fields of domestic violence, mental health, drugs and alcohol. Most of these guidelines cover definitions, the management of patients, the use of supportive consultation methods, the need for privacy and confidentiality, and the possibility of devising safety plans. Advice might cover the management of domestic abuse in high-risk situations, guidelines for nurses and other professionals in a variety of departments, advice on data collection and on handling disclosure, and so on.

Various research studies have been conducted (for example, on the health response, routine enquiry, the need for health policies and so on) and a national network of researchers on domestic violence and health has been established which meets regularly to share research and practice insights. A national practitioners' network named HEVAN has also been established which has evolved training, protocols and practice guidance. Co-ordinated health action has led to a variety of initiatives and improvements. Health workers now regularly attend seminars and conferences on domestic violence. Thus, things are currently on the move.

Most of the Royal Colleges and professional health associations have developed practice guidelines, including the Royal College of GPs, the Royal College of Midwives, the British Association for Accident and Emergency Medicine, the Royal College of Nursing, and the Community Practitioners and Health Visitors Association. The British Medical Association has also clearly identified domestic abuse as a healthcare issue. In 1997, the Chief Medical Officer's report named domestic violence as one of four key issues for national attention.

Importantly, in 2000, the Department of Health published a useful but rather schematic resource pack on working with domestic violence. The pack recommended that the safety of the victim be the paramount consideration and that health trusts and authorities and primary care trusts should develop policies, protocols and training on domestic violence. Women's Aid was then funded by the Department of Health to conduct a survey of health authorities, NHS Trusts and primary care trusts, looking at policies and guidelines in place across the country. As summarized in various reports, the picture nationally was a mixed one. Women's Aid coupled this work with an active campaign. Called the 'Health and Domestic Violence Campaign: a Life and Death Issue 2001–3', it worked to improve practice development and recommended that all healthcare services should have at a minimum: a commitment to the issue reflected in policies and protocols; ongoing training; monitoring, information gathering and evaluation of services; along with inter-agency co-operation to assist survivors of abuse.

Mental health also has attracted attention in terms of domestic violence, and a 2003–4 Women's Aid study and campaign assisted in this process. A new government initiative is the DH/NIMHE Victims of Violence and Abuse Prevention Programme. In fact, joining all parts of the health service together, a joint programme of work has been recently established as a result of the government's 'Safety and Justice' consultation. Building on the results of the Women's Aid study, a national co-ordinator post has been established in the Department of Health (initially from April 2004 for 12 months but since extended) to co-ordinate work across the National Health Service, including introducing routine enquiry into maternity services and primary care, further developing the role of primary care trusts and linking with specialist mental health services. Thus, health authorities and trusts are now being encouraged to increase their participation in both NHS-wide and inter-agency strategic work, and are gradually improving practice.

The voluntary sector

Many voluntary sector agencies work together with doctors, social workers, housing organizations and other service providers to assist abused women and their children. Women might be referred to these agencies by other organizations or might approach them directly themselves. They often find voluntary sector projects more friendly and welcoming than the statutory bodies. In addition to Women's Aid and women's refuge-based and advocacy services, many voluntary sector and non-statutory agencies offer valuable support, and contribute to support services to build a more comprehensive response.

Women's groups, advice agencies, community projects, partnership groupings including voluntary organizations, and even agencies such as mother and toddler groups, childminder groups and playgroups, may provide assistance and advice to women suffering violence and their children. If they do not know the answers themselves, they often know who does and can refer women on successfully. There are also many self-help groups in local communities, some of which focus specifically on violence in the home.

Children's projects and charities can offer support and help to the children of abused women. Youth and children's workers in play-schemes and youth projects often demonstrate great empathy and sensitivity in dealing with the needs of children who have been abused themselves, or who have witnessed violence. And specialist groups and organizations for black women, for minority ethnic women and for women with disabilities or special needs offer specific services that can be helpful to women and children fleeing violence. There are also voluntary sector women's projects that focus on mental health issues or on drug and alcohol dependency, all of which work as a matter of course with women who have suffered violence. The Samaritans, too, play a vital role in dealing with abused women who are suicidal.

Victim Support groups have been much encouraged by government to undertake larger amounts of work with women who have suffered violence, on the grounds that they are there to support victims of crime and that domestic violence is a crime. However, Victim Support nationally does recognize that the lead agency in domestic violence work is Women's Aid. Local Victim Support groups may offer support to abused women and children, including through witness support services, some of which can be good. Unlike Women's Aid, though, they are not specially equipped to do so, and may lack the required experience, training, expertise and understanding of the issue.

All of these agencies and groups are generally welcoming and sympathetic. Voluntary sector organizations sometimes have strong policies on domestic violence and may operate equal opportunities policies that include commitments actively to oppose discrimination. However, they are critically underfunded. If integrated and co-ordinated services are to continue to develop, the underfunding of the voluntary sector will have to be addressed in the future.

At the moment, services come and go. Amina Mama found in her study, for example, that there was a long history of black women's autonomous organizing in the UK against domestic violence, but that such organizations and services, while deeply committed, were small, massively under-resourced and understaffed. They existed on low and decreasing budgets, and frequently either went out of existence due to lack of funds or faced extreme difficulty in keeping going. Nevertheless, many voluntary sector agencies that do exist are now joining with statutory bodies to develop good practice guidelines and inter-agency work on domestic violence. These developments, together with the need for a national strategy on domestic violence, are discussed in the next chapter.

8
National policy and inter-agency co-operation

National policy

Providing services for abused women and their children, and initiating or improving policy measures that deal with domestic violence, have always been difficult tasks. One of the problems is that domestic violence spans a whole variety of agencies and national and local government departments. It refuses to fit tidily into one slot. As a result, despite improvements in recent years and the current widespread development of domestic violence policy and services and of partnership inter-agency initiatives, it can be difficult to get anybody to take it on properly.

Responsibility has always been divided. For example, in the UK, there is still no one clear funding source for the interlinking domestic violence services that women and children need. Refuge-based services have tended to get caught in a cleft stick in the past, with housing costs coming from one set of funders and care costs from another. The Supporting People programme has improved things, as discussed in Chapter 2, and currently funds both direct housing services delivered by refuge providers, and in some areas floating support and outreach projects. However, most non-housing related costs like children's services remain uncovered. Partly due to the lack of a comprehensive funding framework, the current trend for housing associations to set up refuge projects without providing adequately for social care needs, as noted in Chapter 6, looks set to continue. The same problem of lack of resourcing is experienced by all specialist domestic violence services in the voluntary sector.

The Women's Aid federations have proposed that more comprehensive 'ring-fenced' funding to encompass a wider range of support services should be made available by central and local government for distribution locally according to population and other needs. They also struggle continually for their own national funding. The network of local domestic violence services, with their national co-ordinating bodies which take up issues on a nationwide level, are the lifeblood of responses for women and

160

children experiencing domestic violence. Women's Aid occupies a unique position. However, the national offices remain underfunded and are constantly facing funding shortfalls, short-term projects and endless fund-raising.

As the national domestic violence charity, there is no way, for example, that Women's Aid can be regarded as just one service provider among several in the voluntary sector (although the contribution of other agencies must be recognized and respected). However, that is exactly what sometimes happens. This is in spite of the fact that Women's Aid federations, and the support services they co-ordinate, provide dedicated agencies that work solely on domestic violence issues – and have done for nearly 30 years. From humble beginnings in the early 1970s, Women's Aid is now widely accepted by government (sometimes jointly with the organization Refuge) as the key specialist agency dealing with domestic violence. It is therefore surprising that Victim Support is sometimes also promoted as the key agency by branches of government, although it has itself declined this role on a national level in favour of Women's Aid. Meanwhile, the services that Women's Aid provides continue to be underfunded and understaffed.

A similar problem is the promotion by government and by local strategic partnerships of 'one-stop shops'. This idea, which is being much promoted at the time of writing, is that all the services required – police, social workers, lawyers, housing officers and so on – can be accessed under one roof so that families fleeing violence only have to make one port of call. This can work excellently, as at Croydon Ambassador One-Stop where the services provided have been fronted by domestic violence survivors who meet and greet the women coming in for assistance. However, it does not help much if you are then likely to be told that the services you need are not actually funded in your area. Securing comprehensive local domestic violence services surely needs to come first. While they have a part to play, promoting one-stop shops can make it look as if agencies are actively combating domestic violence while nothing much actually changes, except that women do not have to travel so far to be told that the help they can access is very limited.

Overall, because domestic violence is a complex and widespread social problem, there is no one way of dealing with it. A range of co-ordinated services and options is required, working hand-in-hand with legal and policy measures. Legal remedies for domestic violence, for instance, can work only if they run alongside the provision of safe temporary and permanent housing, and vice versa. Positive policing, perpetrators' programmes and positive arrest and prosecution policies are effective only if backed up by the provision of adequate local refuge-based accommodation, community support and services for the women partners, and if situated within a supportive policy and practice framework.

Domestic violence affects all aspects of women's and children's lives. In this situation, it is no help at all that, as we mentioned earlier, responsibility for providing services and support falls across a range of government departments. There has been a tendency in the past for government activity on domestic violence to fall between two stools – or three, or four. These various responsibilities have yet to be effectively co-ordinated across the departments involved, although there have been many improvements recently. Currently, the work of the Home Office as lead agency and of the inter-departmental ministerial group on domestic violence, together with the all-party parliamentary group on violence against women, have led to things getting better, and the government has made much in the last five years of saying that it is now committed to a co-ordinated approach and to improving resourcing. This commitment and recent changes are discussed in the next section.

In the meantime, though, the problems of uneven or fragmented services and lack of systematic comprehensive funding continue to characterize approaches to domestic violence in the UK. Until very recently, there have been few co-ordinated or concerted government policies or strategies. As we saw in Chapter 7, the far-reaching Children Act 1989 more or less forgot the difficulties and dangers that women who have experienced violence would encounter in meeting its provisions. The provisions of the Family Law Act, Part IV, have been very helpful, but these improvements have been undermined by reductions in the availability of legal aid. Public services that women and children use are disappearing as the welfare state is reformed and liberalized. The decrease in social security benefits, in direct services run by local authorities, and crucially in the supply of council housing have had serious effects on women and children made homeless by violence. This can be demonstrated particularly starkly in the light of international commitments and initiatives on domestic violence, although these have also experienced mixed fortunes in recent years.

In Australia, for example, a National Committee on Violence Against Women was established in 1990. This committee engaged in developing a national strategy on violence against women. Despite the usual complement of setbacks and lack of implementation, the strategy was comprehensive and visionary – and way beyond anything dreamt of in the UK. It was built on the twin premises of empowering women and ending male violence. It held that condoning and excusing male violence impedes social change and reinforces the oppression of women. In October 1992, the strategy objectives adopted were as follows:

- To ensure that all women escaping violence have immediate access to police intervention and legal protection which prioritize safety for the woman, safe shelter, confidential services and the longer-term resources needed to live independently and free from violence.

- To work towards a universal intolerance of the use of violence in Australian society in general and, in particular, to achieve full acknowledgment by all Australians that violence against women is a crime, regardless of the circumstances, the background or the culture of the violent person or the victim.
- To achieve more just and equitable responses by the criminal justice system, which highlight the seriousness of the offences, and to strengthen the authority of the law in its effective and important role of influencing community attitudes and supporting social change.
- To build on the significant reforms, policy and program work of all levels of government and the community, towards improving the status of women, including the elimination of violence against all women.

Unfortunately, since the advent of the Conservative federal government, the broad 'violence against women' approach has been discontinued in favour of 'domestic violence' specifically. Some extra funding has been made available, but this has been offset by massive cutbacks in other services. Nevertheless, important advances have been made and we can learn from the Australian example.

From Canada, the news has also been mainly good. In the 1990s, Health and Welfare Canada, the lead federal agency on family violence, established a four-year, $136 million Federal Initiative on Family Violence. The aims of the initiative were to involve all Canadians within it, to mobilize community action, to improve treatment and support services, to share information and solutions, and to co-ordinate federal action on domestic violence. This included strengthening legal remedies, providing more housing for abused women and their children, and establishing services for First Nations communities. Committees involving representatives of many agencies worked with the initiative at federal, provincial and local levels. More recently, though, services have been cut back in individual provinces, such as Ontario and British Columbia.

Still, a National Clearing-House on domestic violence provides and co-ordinates policy and documentation nationally. Five family violence research centres exist across the country, set up following the Montreal Massacre in 1989 in which 14 women students were murdered. (Memorials and days of action are held about this event every year.) Canada has pioneered enhanced evidence gathering in criminal justice cases, positive charging (as oppose to merely positive arrest) policies, support for victims by civilians in police stations and domestic violence courts. Co-ordinated community interventions have been set up in many cities with one of the most respected world leaders of this type of approach flourishing in London, Ontario.

Recent developments in the UK

As we have indicated throughout this book, things are finally getting better in the UK too, although there is a long way to go. There is now considerable public and government interest in domestic violence, which has been demonstrated by the improved Home Office and police response, by wide-ranging policy development and by new legislation and government strategies. There were some advances under the previous Conservative governments (and the Conservative Party now has an active campaigning group on domestic violence). However, things have only improved substantially since the advent of the Labour government in 1997.

In 1992, the National Inter-agency Working Party report, followed by the House of Commons Home Affairs Committee Inquiry into Domestic Violence in 1993, made proposals for a national strategy to be co-ordinated among the various government departments concerned. Both reports argued for a range of measures to support abused women and children, with the full input of Women's Aid and women's services. Since then, we have had the new Acts of the 1990s, the Department of Health and Home Office circulars, and the beginnings of a government policy with the important publication of 'Living Without Fear' by the (then) Women's Unit of the Cabinet Office in 1999. This much anticipated government initiative was expected to lay out a comprehensive overall national strategy. It didn't, of course, and activist expectations were let down. What it did do was to propose a more comprehensive co-ordinated approach than had previously been the case, however, although it did little to make this a reality in terms of resources.

In 2003, as we have discussed, the government issued 'Safety and Justice', a key consultation paper proposing a broad-based approach to domestic violence organized around three major themes: first, prevention; secondly, protection and justice; and thirdly, support for victims. The paper was subjected to a wide-ranging consultation, including a consultation directly with survivors which was conducted, rather hastily due to the government's short time limit, over the summer of 2003. This consultation with survivors was published as 'Unlocking the Secret'.

'Safety and Justice' proposes a variety of measures including improvements in justice responses, recommendations for the provision of accommodation, and of outreach and advocacy support for victims, interventions with children in the education system and the contentious proposal to establish a criminal register of domestic violence offenders, about which most women's organizations have been particularly cautious and which has now been placed on the back burner. In more detail, the section on 'Prevention' is concerned with working to stop domestic violence in the first place. Together with the second section on 'Protection and Justice', it proposes such measures as increased legal protection; education on domestic violence, especially of young people; early identification of victims; the provision of information to victims; and preventing domestic violence offenders reoffending. The third section on 'Support' similarly relates to general measures to improve legal protection and the justice response. It includes proposals for improved training and awareness among agencies, extending the Family Law Act, making common assault an arrestable offence, introducing multi-agency reviews after domestic violence homicides, improving liaison between civil and criminal courts, and giving support for children. There are also proposals for improving the refuge and other support services available. To this end the government committed £9 million in April 2003 to a national capital investment programme for refuge services and the Housing Corporation committed almost £10 million.

The Domestic Violence, Crime and Victims Bill was then published. As we have discussed previously and as anticipated in 'Safety and Justice', the bill, now passed, contains major amendments to Part IV of the Family Law Act. For example, breach of a non-molestation order has become a criminal offence; cohabitees now include same-sex couples; and non-cohabiting couples are included. Changes also include a new offence of causing or abetting the death of a child or vulnerable adult, named 'familial homicide' and in force from March 2005. Common assault has become arrestable and new restraining orders are being introduced in the Protection from Harassment Act. A Code of Practice for victims, a Victim Advisory Panel and a Commissioner for Victims and Witnesses are being established.

As we discussed in Chapter 5, the Act has been something of a disappointment, although it should not be doubted that it is a step forward for national government and for the domestic violence activist movement. Some of the very good proposals in 'Safety and Justice' are absent from the Act which concentrates solely on criminal and civil justice. Major amendments which were proposed to the bill before it was passed included an expanded official definition to take into account the fact that domestic violence can affect other family members including children, and to include all forms of abuse and violence. Further proposed amendments concerned the possible inclusion in the 2002 Homelessness Act of a measure to include single women experiencing domestic violence as in priority need and measures to protect the safety of both children and women from violent fathers in child contact cases. As we discussed earlier, the latter proposals derived from concern about child contact, drawing on the 2002 Women's Aid report *Failure to Protect*. Among other amendments proposed was a development of the domestic violence concession within immigration rules and an exception to the 'no recourse to public funds' rule in cases of domestic violence. Importantly, a proposed amendment would have established a national funding framework for support and advocacy services for women experiencing domestic violence and their children. However, as we have already indicated, none of these important amendments was accepted.

Thus overall, the Act itself has serious omissions. However, it has been accompanied by a considerable funding commitment to improve the provision of refuge services, as well as the national helpline and internet service, and short-term finance for the demonstration projects in the Home Office Violence Against Women Initiative, contained in the Crime Reduction Programme. Supporting People finance is available to support women in refuge accommodation and to provide housing-related floating support, and domestic violence is now beginning to creep up the crime prevention and other strategic agendas. Thus, there have been real advances since the previous editions of this book.

Large numbers of performance indicators now exist across the board. A full national strategy on violence against women is still lacking, but the Women's National Commission Violence Against Women sub-group, Women's Aid and other women's projects are now committed to evolving a framework for one (as outlined in their 2005 document 'What a Waste'. This important work is currently in progress. The idea is that government would then be asked to develop and adopt the strategy.

So improvements are in the air. The consultation papers and the new legislation presented a golden opportunity for the UK to catch up with some other governments worldwide in terms of developing a co-ordinated and comprehensive approach to domestic violence. Arguably, the golden opportunity has been missed, but a step in the right direction has perhaps been taken.

Inter-agency work: way forward or smoke-screen?

The hope is that the new legislation will at best enable co-ordinated local action against domestic violence. Multi-agency co-ordination is the name of the game. In fact, in general, this approach has come to be seen as an appropriate officially sanctioned response to abuse of various types and to other sorts of crime prevention. Child abuse is the most obvious example, with inter-agency collaboration having an important role to play in the handling of individual cases. For domestic violence, however, the approach has been more informal. It has not had the same emphasis on individual case work, although this has been done in some areas, most formally by the innovative Cardiff Women's Safety Unit which uses joint protocols, but informally in several other places too. The tendency to use the multi-agency approach at the policy level rather than in individual work is partly because there are statutory obligations to protect children, but none to protect women: society on a general level does not take violence against women as seriously as violence against children. For inter-agency domestic abuse work, however, this has meant that there is more scope for innovation.

Multi-agency or inter-agency initiatives on domestic violence have grown in prominence in recent years. One of the first advances was the 1989 Home Office report by Lorna Smith already mentioned, which highlighted the importance of co-operation among the diverse agencies involved in order to deal effectively with the host of interrelated problems that domestic violence engenders. Subsequent Home Office guidance and other government documents clearly pointed out the relevance of inter-agency working. It was also recommended in 1986 by the UN Expert Group on Violence in the Family, in 1987 by the Brussels Council of Europe Colloquy on Violence within the Family, and in 1992 by the UN *Manual for Practitioners on Domestic Violence.* Important UK recommendations to pursue the multi-agency approach were made by the 1992 National Inter-agency Working Party Report and the 1993 Home Affairs Committee. Before these key developments, refuge-based support services had often attempted to establish inter-agency co-operation, and some were successful in doing so. In this sense, it was not a new idea at all, but one that Women's Aid had always espoused. The difference was that in the past the relevant agencies showed little interest. In recent years, however, all that seems to have changed.

Constructive liaison between women's services and local councils became somewhat easier in the late 1980s and 1990s when some authorities set up council Women's Equality Committees and/or established officer posts with special responsibility for women's issues in a variety of departments and units. As a result, some of these authorities hosted local conferences on violence against women which provided a space for the issues to be aired, and helped to build the impetus for improving local services. Inter-agency projects were set up in many cases as an outcome of such conferences.

Some domestic violence activists, who had battled with local councils for many years to try to get them to improve their service provision, were almost taken aback by these developments. The very idea of councils taking such initiatives had been inconceivable a few years earlier. Then it suddenly seemed as though at least some local authorities could not wait to take on the issue of violence against women. It was the Women's Committees and Units that made it happen in the main, with the final Labour-led Greater London Council and a few pioneering London boroughs, metropolitan and urban district councils forging the way forward. A small number of committed feminists had entered the County Halls and Council Houses and had brought women's issues into, if not the heart, then at least the margins of municipal Britain.

The changes in the police response to domestic violence have also had an effect. Inter-agency working by the police was recommended in the ground-breaking Circular 60/90, and local police forces in many areas were then instrumental in setting up multi-agency projects on domestic violence as a response to this advice and as part of crime prevention work.

The establishment of local inter-agency domestic violence forums was strongly recommended by the government in 1995 in the long-awaited inter-agency circular, 'Inter-agency Coordination to Tackle Domestic Violence', produced by the Home Office and the Welsh Office. This circular encouraged all relevant agencies to build concerted joint action as a response to violence in the home and has had a considerable impact. It is of some significance, though, that the circular gave no guidance as to how inter-agency initiatives and domestic violence forums should be resourced. The 1995 circular was consolidated by government guidance in 1999 called 'Multi-agency Guidance for Addressing Domestic Violence'. In the UK, the inter-agency approach was here to stay.

In fact, in many countries of the world, multi-agency, partnership or inter-sectoral responses to domestic violence are now being consciously pursued in both developing and industrialized nations. In various states in Australia, for example, the development of services and policy is overseen at state level by committees consisting of representatives from many agencies. Local domestic violence committees have also been established on the initiative of local communities. Their job is to develop liaison, co-operation and consultation, to make policy recommendations to state-wide domestic violence committees, and to promote community education and the recognition that domestic violence is a crime. Some of the actions and campaigns of local domestic violence committees have included the setting up of court support schemes, training and education workshops, domestic violence support groups, domestic violence phone-ins, directories of services and good practice guidelines. There are many other international examples and two of the best-known initiatives are in London, Ontario in Canada and Duluth, Minnesota in the USA. These are particularly comprehensive multi-agency initiatives. The Duluth project is discussed in Chapter 9.

Inter-agency work in practice

A major national study of multi-agency work and domestic violence was conducted in the mid-1990s by our own research team in the Violence Against Women Research Group at Bristol. This study led to the publication of a report, a practice guide, various professional papers for practitioners, a book edited jointly with Nicola Harwin, the Director of Women's Aid, and Briefing Notes for the Home Office in 2000. All of these emphasized that the prime rationale of multi-agency initiatives must be to improve service delivery for abused women and children, and to increase their safety. This may sound ridiculously elementary. However, there are many examples of statutory and voluntary agencies holding considerable numbers of joint meetings about a variety of issues and achieving no change whatsoever in the services provided. Complex systems of committees and policy development may be put into place but do nothing to improve the provision of front-line support and prevention projects.

Bearing in mind these difficulties, the overall aim of the inter-agency approach is to bring together different agencies and local authority departments in an area, specifically so that the work done against domestic violence is first consistent, second well informed and third co-ordinated. Put like this, it seems like straightforward common sense. The idea of multi-agency work is a remarkably simple one. Putting it into practice, however, is not a simple matter at all.

At best, inter-agency work can help to increase public awareness about domestic violence, to widen the choices and options available to women in both the short and the long term, to establish new domestic violence services, to influence strategic agendas locally and to provide a firm public message that domestic violence is unacceptable. To do this, multi-agency initiatives need to be clear about where they are going and what they are trying to achieve. It can take a while to work this out, and there can be some false starts. In addition, projects need to reassess as time goes on, and perhaps to change direction. The services available in local areas vary so much that each inter-agency initiative needs to be tailored specifically to the requirements of its locality. In other words, there is no single formula for a successful inter-agency initiative.

In our study, we identified over 200 domestic violence forums existing in the mid-1990s, with more being set up all the time. The first pioneers of the approach were established in Leeds, Nottinghamshire, Wolverhampton and the borough of Hammersmith and Fulham in London, often led by charismatic innovators. Now, however, most urban and a few rural areas have inter-agency domestic violence forums in place, and the fact that there is no one model for doing multi-agency work has resulted in much creativity and innovation.

This wide diversity of approaches is welcome in one sense, as agencies in different areas figure out what they need to do and set about doing it. But in another sense, it can be confusing and even immobilizing. New projects may feel overwhelmed by the volume of work that they could take on, and not know where to start. This is where the Women's Aid federations, domestic violence consultants, researchers and trainers, and already established projects can step in to offer advice and help – and they are always willing to do so if they can. Frequently, though, there is little spare time or money for this sort of liaison and co-operation.

Our national study confirmed the need for inter-agency forums to have guiding principles agreed by all members, written aims and objectives, and a clear structure. Often this involves a steering committee and active sub-groups with well-defined briefs and time-limited action plans, regularly reviewed. The types of work that such forums take on usually include intervention in local strategic partnerships, agency co-ordination, the development of good practice guidelines and domestic violence training for agencies, preventative and educational projects, and public awareness initiatives (see also Chapter 9).

Keeping domestic violence forums going is hard work, however, and nothing can happen without at least some resources and secretarial and administrative support. Meetings can then be set up relatively easily, work taken on, and information circulated. Very few of the participating agencies will have the spare labour power to provide such services on a voluntary basis, even if the tasks involved are rotated among members. If there is funding available from the local authority, from Crime and Disorder Reduction Partnerships, from the police or from other specialist grants, paid workers may be able to take on the servicing and administration, and co-ordinate the project. In fact, the employment of a domestic violence co-ordinator usually transforms local services and multi-agency initiatives. However, a finding of our 1996 study was that lack of resources is one of the major impediments to the development of multi-agency work.

Domestic violence forums are likely to start off with networking and information exchange, which can be very useful in the short term but needs to lead to something practical. They may move on to include needs assessment research in the local area, or the conducting of 'service audits' to identify gaps in provision. Directories of services are often produced, and improvements made in data collection, monitoring systems and referrals. Inter-agency initiatives may then develop further to promote the development of good practice guidelines and explicit domestic violence policies and training within local agencies.

At best, local authorities will expand their approach to domestic violence to make it a 'corporate' one. This means that awareness of domestic violence and the provision of training and services to combat it will span the whole of the authority's work, and will be taken on as a general, council-wide commitment. This sometimes includes provisions for women employees of the council itself who are experiencing domestic violence. In relation to community safety specifically, the 1998 Crime and Disorder Act has offered new opportunities for effective corporate and multi-agency work. Senior-level partnerships are tasked with developing Crime and Disorder Reduction Strategies within which government guidance states that domestic violence should be prioritized (and domestic violence survivors should be among those consulted). This prioritization should lead to at least some resource allocation and this has indeed happened in many areas. In Cheshire, for example, funding has been provided through this route to finance education programmes in schools and improved refuge co-ordination services. In general, local partnerships also contribute to domestic violence strategy across localities, and domestic violence forums are often able to feed constructively into these senior management bodies. As domestic violence forums are pulled more and more into strategic work, they have also increased their profile, liaising with Area Child Protection Committees and with senior partnership bodies. The level of seniority of participants remains an issue of difficulty, however.

In London, the Greater London Domestic Violence Project, a model of good practice in multi-agency work, assists in co-ordinating domestic violence forums in the capital. A London Domestic Violence Forum has been established to act as a meeting place for all the borough forums across the city and to work on the implementation of the Mayor's Domestic Violence Strategy for London, a pioneering and comprehensive strategy which acts as a guide for all policy development in the city. The London Domestic Violence Strategy covers the work of local authorities, the police and the criminal justice system, social and health services, women's projects and strategic partnerships and inter-agency responses. This wide-ranging work acts a catalyst for others and the Greater London Domestic Violence Project also publishes a very useful newsletter of developments nationally.

Power differences, equalities and multi-agency work

A major problem within multi-agency work results from power differences between agencies and resulting conflicts of interest. It can then be difficult to engage in constructive joint action without resorting to the 'lowest common denominator' effect, in which activity is limited by the views of the agencies that know the least and have the least commitment to domestic violence work. However, it can be better to acknowledge these differences rather than to muddy the waters by pretending to agree or by negotiating a false or fudged compromise. The involvement of the police in inter-agency work has proved particularly difficult on occasion from this point of view, as has that of the Crown Prosecution Service and health services, although constructive dialogue and joint work have taken place in many areas in recent years.

In fact, one of the most common difficulties identified in our research was the often manifested tendency of the large statutory agencies to 'take over' the work done and to adopt dominating positions, sometimes unintentionally. A multi-agency initiative that takes on these issues particularly effectively is the innovative Leeds Inter-agency Project (Women and Violence) often known as LIAP, which has managed to attract much in the way of resources and has considerable numbers of workers. This project has always had strong connections with Women's Aid, with grass-roots women's groups, and with black women's projects and organizations in the city. Its basic premise is that abusers seek to exert power and control over women in various ways. Its commitment, therefore, is to the empowerment of women to take back control over their lives, and it attempts to achieve this using a variety of types of approach. These include extensive domestic violence training, good practice initiatives and dedicated, staffed intervention projects within the criminal justice, health and education services, and around such issues as provision on domestic violence for disabled women.

The Leeds project and the other leading inter-agency projects have taken a strong line against racism, heterosexism and all other sorts of discrimination, although many others have not. However, if black women and women from ethnic minorities are not represented or are underrepresented, past experience suggests that their needs will be overlooked in any initiatives taken. It has been the experience of some black women's groups dealing with violence that they have been marginalized in domestic violence forums. This can be especially so where forums are dominated by white professionals, as is still too often the case, and particularly since the trend is towards seeking more senior representation from agencies.

In general, the needs of disabled women who have suffered violence can also be neglected in inter-agency work. It is sobering – and, for people with disabilities, distressing and infuriating – how often gatherings of workers from different agencies suddenly place disability on their agendas as soon as a disabled person attends. Analysis of past minutes often reveals that the subject has been comprehensively absent from previous discussions. Lesbians too find that their interests and needs are often overlooked or totally ignored in the work of such bodies as domestic violence forums. As a result, few inter-agency forums have seriously considered services for lesbians who have suffered violence, although some now attempt to respond to violence in same-sex relationships generally.

Equalities work needs, however, to be an integral part of the multi-agency approach, since domestic violence affects all communities. Some domestic violence forums have adopted equalities policies and an equalities agenda, including developing training and relevant practice guidelines; providing culturally sensitive translations; producing literature in large print; setting up projects for specific communities; and combating discrimination within the forum itself.

Multi-agency forums are rarely accountable in any way to domestic violence survivors. In fact, in the national study that we conducted, very few of the abused women interviewed had heard of their domestic violence forum, even in passing. While details of agency policy and practice may not need to be easily visible to women using the services provided, it is still a matter of concern that their voices appear so often to be absent. A study by the Violence Against Women Research Group, conducted jointly with the Centre for the Study of Safety and Well-being at the University of Warwick, and funded by the Economic and Social Research Council's Violence Research Programme in the early 2000s, identified both the difficulties and sensitivities involved and also highlighted some creative solutions to this dilemma being tried out around the UK.

In some areas, the involvement of domestic violence survivors is being mediated through Women's Aid and specialist domestic violence projects. In a few others, advisory or monitoring groups of survivors or domestic violence survivors' forums have been set up to oversee inter-agency work. These groups offer support as well as fulfilling an advisory function, and usually work alongside the wider forum since it is rarely successful to invite domestic violence service users to the forum meetings themselves. Particularly creative work in this way has been done by the Westminster Domestic Violence Forum and the Phoenix Group of survivors and also by Voice for Change in Liverpool. Other methods include women's focus groups, public meetings with survivors, community art and theatre, direct campaigns and internet consultation. Women's Aid with the Hansard Society has conducted an innovative consultation with women over the internet which was published in 2000 as *Womenspeak*. Guidance on these various methods of survivor consultation is available in a Women's Aid guidebook called *Professionals by Experience* and a general book called *Is Anyone Listening?: Accountability and Women Survivors of Violence*, both also available from the research team.

None of this participation and equality work is possible without funding. The involvement of service users automatically in all policy development fits in with current government commitments to user participation but is impossible unless it is resourced. Financing inter-agency work remains a problem overall, although the recent Home Office Crime Reduction Programme Violence Against Women Initiative funded a set of innovative multi-service interventions. Most general inter-agency projects – even the relatively well-resourced ones such as the Leeds initiative – have funding in the short to medium term only. Other inter-agency groups have extremely insecure funding and may have quite a limited survival time; few projects have paid workers in post.

It could be that, in general, multi-agency work on domestic violence will have a short life. Nevertheless, the UK government currently continues to favour inter-agency approaches. Some domestic violence activists have suggested that this is because such approaches do not cost much money, but make it look as though both central and local government are doing something. And the money which is provided may be spent on costly meetings of professionals, conferences and so on, rather than on improving services. This difficulty is improving slightly in that domestic violence is often now the subject of strategic partnership work (which should, in theory at least, lead to improved provision) and multi-agency service developments. Thus, at best, inter-agency initiatives can be a creative development – but at worst, they can be a smoke-screen and face-saver to disguise both lack of action and lack of grass-roots women's services and other resources.

Women's support services and the multi-agency approach

The relationship between inter-agency work and women's support and advocacy services is a complex and sometimes contradictory one. What underlies it is the overall relationship between the refuge movement and women's domestic violence services on the one hand, and both local and central government on the other. Refuge providers now work more closely with such authorities than they ever thought they would. The same is true in many areas for women's groups collaborating with the police (especially with police domestic violence units).

However, there are sometimes problems of Women's Aid and other women's support projects being marginalized or pushed to one side within inter-agency forums, and of a pro-women analysis being diluted beyond recognition. The women's service concerned might then find itself giving credibility by its presence to the multi-agency work, even while disagreeing with it. On the other hand, some domestic violence organizations work round the clock to keep inter-agency projects going and take a powerful role within them.

The important thing is that there are independent services which meet the needs of women who have suffered violence and their children, and Women's Aid continues to be the key agency in this respect. It is also important that inter-agency initiatives remember that much of their expertise comes from the experiences, views and knowledge of domestic violence survivors and women active at the grass-roots level, who do not always themselves have the opportunity to express this knowledge and experience publicly. Multi-agency work owes a debt to all these 'invisible' women. Services have been transformed on a more general level by professionals who are themselves survivors of violence and we have argued in various places, including the publications mentioned above, that it is important now in the 2000s to acknowledge and celebrate their usually unsung contributions.

Women's Aid and the network of local domestic violence services as a whole have welcomed inter-agency work, applaud its intentions and the improved services that it can engender, and have become more and more involved in it over the years. But local authorities may not appreciate the dynamic working processes that are necessary to meet the needs of women and children, and refuge providers involved with never-ending crisis work may not have the time to develop very extensive inter-agency liaisons. Various concrete strategies can be adopted to keep local women's domestic violence services centre-stage. For example, the women's support service may take the chair of the inter-agency forum (while sometimes being relieved of accompanying administrative duties), or may occupy a reserved place on the management or steering body. It is vital that Women's Aid, the domestic violence network and women who have suffered violence have a key role in the further development of inter-agency work, and are included in all planning and implementation procedures – or, at the very least, are fully consulted. Without the contribution of this network and movement over the last 30 years, inter-agency initiatives would not exist. The initiatives are valuable in themselves, and they may lead to vastly improved service provision in the future. But they are only part of the picture.

How effective is inter-agency work?

Our own research and other studies demonstrate that it is very hard to judge whether multi-agency work really makes things any better for women and children who have suffered violence. If workers are given training in domestic violence awareness and operate codes of good practice, does anything change? Do women survivors of violence notice a difference? Workers in the field think and hope that the answer is yes, if the development is viewed from an overall perspective. In some local areas, domestic violence staff and women escaping domestic violence have indeed reported improvements in services and in the responses that they get from other agencies. The outcomes of some other projects have been measured in terms of their ability to reduce repeat victimization of women or to decrease attrition. Small improvements can usually be seen.

In general terms, women who have suffered violence may initially notice little change, but this may not mean that nothing is in fact changing. The multi-agency aim, admittedly gradual, is to improve partnership strategic direction in the locality, to co-ordinate local responses better, to provide more services, to improve provision through the adoption of good practice guidelines, and to provide a more comprehensive and co-ordinated overall response.

One of the most obvious dangers is that inter-agency work can become a talking shop. Attending a domestic violence forum can be a time for professionals who are deeply involved in domestic violence work to get together and chat to their friends. What they talk about will almost always be related to improving agency practice and may well result in the provision of enhanced services and in the undertaking of fresh innovations. However, an abused woman who is on the streets and trying to find her way to a run-down, underfunded refuge that is already full to overflowing may have little patience with this approach.

Domestic violence training

Domestic violence training is of key importance in developing good practice in service provision. It is now becoming widely accepted that officers in all agencies, including the police force, local authorities, health services and the voluntary sector, need to be trained in how to work with women and children who have experienced domestic violence. This realization has been a long time coming. In general, domestic violence training has been absent in the past from the agendas of statutory and voluntary agencies. Women's Aid and domestic violence services throughout the UK have been initiating and running occasional training sessions on an ad hoc basis for years, but there was never much of an interest in them until recently. Now training seems to be the order of the day. Once again, some workers in the domestic violence field have expressed a degree of scepticism. It is perfectly possible, they suggest, for officers to go on training courses but then to continue their work exactly as they did before. Also training often only reaches front-line staff, not the people who actually make the policy decisions.

Inter-agency projects have been at the forefront of instigating the new training schemes, and now generally make it a priority to provide training for workers in member agencies. Codes of good practice almost always contain commitments to provide domestic violence training. The provision of training for all statutory and voluntary sector officers has been recommended by all the relevant professional bodies and research studies, and is now widely practised, although courses are invariably very short.

Domestic violence awareness training needs to go hand in hand with training on the implementation and delivery of any domestic violence policies and strategies that are in place, so that workers are trained in what they have to do more than what they are meant to think. The most effective training also covers wider issues about how services are delivered within the framework of domestic violence work in general.

It is important that an awareness of equality issues (for example, for disabled or black and minority ethnic women) runs through domestic violence training as an integral part of it, rather than being tacked on almost as an afterthought – as happens far too often in the provision of general training services. Integrating an analysis of discrimination and disadvantage into the very fabric of the course structure and design leads to a richer type of training that is more real and truthful.

Information on domestic violence training is available from the Women's Aid federations, which maintain an overview of the issue. They can advise on what is available and they also produce relevant publications and leaflets. Domestic violence training consultants and research groups can also help. Some inter-agency projects and local authorities produce their own training packs for sale, and training is often offered on a 'training the trainers' basis. An important point is that training needs to be informed at the very least (if not delivered, with pay) by domestic violence services. As for inter-agency work as a whole, it would be a tragedy if domestic violence training became detached from Women's Aid and from local specialist provision. Another potential problem is that one-off short training courses in agencies might achieve little change. Rather, training needs to be provided in a rolling programme, perhaps on an annual basis with follow-up sessions. A systematic commitment is required from the management of the agency involved. The next stumbling block can be that, once the management has taken this lesson to heart, it may be tempted to regard training as a panacea – and to implement training initiatives without accompanying policy and practice developments. Without the services, however, even the best training programme in the world will have little effect. At best, it may result in service providers saying 'no' in a more respectful and humane way. Women survivors of violence are likely to appreciate this courtesy – being treated with dignity can be empowering in itself. But more should not be claimed on behalf of training than it can deliver. The provision of concrete resources and services must always be primary.

One final point should be noted. There have been differing views within and between refuge and activist organizations in the past both about providing training for the police and about engaging in inter-agency co-operation with them. Their role as social controllers of political protest and the public exposure of oppressive policing in black, Irish and other communities have led on occasion to calls by black groups, the left and others for non-cooperation with the police. However, the police role in combating domestic violence is one of the most essential, and their handling of violence cases is of key significance to abused women and children because of the traumatic and crucial point at which they are asked to intervene on women's behalf. In addition, the police have not been previously noted for pro-women sympathies, so the new police policies are demanding changes in long-established police practices and attitudes. For all these reasons, domestic violence training can be even more vital for the police than for other agencies. Further, a constitutional objective of the Women's Aid federations is to educate other bodies, which of course includes the police. Some local Women's Aid organizations have been delivering training to local police forces since the 1970s, and police training is now well established. Thus, the Women's Aid federations, refuge and outreach organizations, professional domestic violence trainers and inter-agency forums, including the Greater London Domestic Violence Project (which conducts extensive national training with the police, as does Women's Aid itself), all now engage in police training on local, national and international levels. And police services across the board demand and fund such training. Things have changed.

9

Men's programmes, public education and campaigning

Programmes for violent men

Political campaigns against domestic violence and for the empowerment of women have a vital role to play in transforming both individual men's attitudes and behaviour, and society in general. As we have emphasized throughout this book, it is only because of the political movement of women against violence that domestic violence is such a public issue today. Women working for and with women have revolutionized the way in which we think about violence in the home and the services available for women survivors. But what about the men?

Activists and domestic violence workers giving publicity talks are asked this question so often it can become tiresome. 'What are you doing to stop the men being violent?' 'Can't you work with the men as well?' 'Nothing will change unless you do something about the men, will it?' Public concerns like these are understandable, and locate the problem accurately. It is indeed the men who have to stop being violent. But domestic violence workers can find these questions frustrating when they are working so hard to provide services for women and children, especially in situations of resource shortage. Nevertheless, in the 2000s, many Women's Aid organizations and local domestic violence services are working closely with programmes for perpetrators to ensure a co-ordinated response, while suggesting that the responsibility for dealing with men's violence lies not with the women's movement, but with society in general – and men in particular. The understanding usually is that women domestic violence activists in the field can influence and advise the men's services (and many projects for violent men do employ women workers).

Despite adhering to this broad position, there is some doubt and scepticism in the network of domestic violence services as to whether men's programmes, especially the more therapeutic ones, can work. When we discussed the issue with a friend who has established a new life after fleeing domestic violence, she said after a long and serious pause:

> I'm sorry but I don't think it can work. I wish it could but I don't think it will, ever. Once a batterer, always a batterer. You're not going to get them to change just like that. Maybe a few of them, but not many. They don't really want to change, do they?

In our many years working in and with domestic violence organizations, not many of the male partners of women living there would have entered a programme for violent men willingly, or at least with an open mind. Most of them would have regarded such a programme with derision.

While many individual men, and some groups of men, may be lacking in self-esteem and may themselves feel powerless, the phenomenon of male violence as a whole is actually about men exerting power and control over women. And male power and control over women, even in the twenty-first century, is still institutionalized in various forms throughout society. Although cut across by social class and other factors, the weight of centuries of male-dominated society remains behind men. To try to challenge by a few small programmes this great mass of tradition, history, economics, culture and social organization, which backs up and bolsters aggressive or violent male behaviour, can seem a hopeless task.

From this point of view, structural transformation of society is what we need, brought about through political, economic and social movements for change. And, as a result, women who have suffered violence, or who are activists in the field, are often sceptical about perpetrators' programmes. Women's fingers have been burnt too many times. They may point out that, for any other crime of violence, men are put into prison, not sent on a therapy programme and allowed to go on living with the very person whom they attacked.

Others argue that it is nevertheless worth a try. Men's programmes, they say, seem to be here to stay, and domestic violence activists are better off exerting some influence over them than being excluded and possibly regretting it later. There are now quite a variety of programmes available for violent men. In North America, in particular, these programmes have thrived, but they have been set up in various other countries throughout the world as well. In the UK they are growing in number (through the probation service Pathfinder Programme which we discuss later, for example), and more are planned. We will undoubtedly hear and see more of them in the future. Most of the men's projects owe some debt, however, to the North American originators.

Rebecca and Russell Dobash devote a whole section of their book *Women, Violence and Social Change* to what they call the 'therapeutic society', particularly in the United States. They explain how the North American approach has a tendency to regard many social and economic problems as faulty traits in people's personalities that require therapy to be put right – after which everything will be fine. The burgeoning psychological and therapeutic professions in the States, treating ever-increasing numbers of people, have become a significant part of the American economy. New York City, for instance, now has more psychoanalysts than any single European country. The Dobashes describe how these professions could be seen to feed into American culture and history, which have always encouraged individual solutions and individualism, and have often discouraged social movements.

Some of the current men's programmes can be understood in this context. David Adams, an expert on American men's programmes and a co-founder of one of the original pro-feminist ones, EMERGE, in Boston, has provided a useful analysis of the major models of treatment programmes for men. The five models that he suggests have been quite widely used and adapted (for example, in Australia), and are discussed below.

Adams discusses a general issue that underlies all perpetrators' programmes. Although things have improved since his original analysis in the late 1980s, he and others highlight how, in many of the therapeutic programmes (in the past at least), the violent battering behaviour has often been identified not as a main treatment issue, but as a symptom of some other underlying problem. Men in the programmes can then get the message that non-violence is negotiable – and that their own violence is undesirable, but understandable. Some approaches may actually collude with the violent man in avoiding the issue of his violence. The specific programmes that Adams discusses use group and individual therapy. They are far more firmly established in the United States and Canada, but they exist in the UK as well – albeit in less high-powered therapeutic packages.

Men's programmes in North America

In recent years, pro-feminist abusers' programmes based on the Duluth model (see below) have become quite common in North America and elsewhere. However, the other models identified by Adams still have influence. The first type in his classification is the 'insight model', a traditional approach to understanding violence. The idea is that the man is violent because he is frustrated or depressed, has poor impulse control or some other psychological problem. If he could become more aware of how he has been affected by past experience, more insightful into his own problems, then he could learn to respond less violently to his current situation. Part and parcel of this approach is the idea that men who are violent have a very fragile sense of self, that they are trying to live up to an impossible, 'macho', masculine ideal, and that they take it out on their partners when they cannot do so. Feminist criticisms of these programmes do not dispute the value of insight therapy as a tool for personal change or the frequent fragility of ego and self-confidence. Many women and men have used therapeutic or counselling approaches to understand their lives and their behaviour. But critics are extremely doubtful about the fact that challenging violence is not a central feature of the programme – and in fact the abuse may still be going on while the man is attending the sessions.

Women's activists are also critical of the use of a purely psychological explanation of abuse which ignores the wider social and political factors. For example, the insight model usually overlooks the way that violence may be instrumental to men in terms of dominating a relationship and may play into wider understandings in society about it being acceptable for men to control things. This model of treatment makes out that it is a matter of individual failure for the man concerned and his impaired intra-psychic processes. It usually places considerable emphasis on increasing self-esteem. The insight model can also lead to situations in which men may in fact learn to identify their use of violence as part of a power dynamic, but continue to use it anyway, or learn to use other means to the same end. Gaining insight does not necessarily mean making changes. Feminists additionally criticize the model for the way in which clients are therapeutically bolstered up and validated at all times due to their supposed fragile sense of themselves. The approach is as unthreatening and non-challenging as possible.

Adams' second model is the 'ventilation model'. It is about people's need to 'get rid of' their anger rather than suppressing it. This idea can be detected in a lot of counselling methods that have developed since the 1960s. It refers to the concept of ventilating one's angry feelings in a safe, non-physical way. Activists dealing with violence against women would not dispute that bottling up anger is bad for people. But there tends to be, in this model, a belief that showing anger verbally will make physical violence less likely. Research tends to show just the opposite – that domestic violence often escalates from the solely verbal to the physical. Verbal violence and aggression can in itself be extremely distressing and part of a pattern of abuse.

The third model is the 'interaction model', in which couples are seen together and joint therapy takes place. This model derives from the family systems school of thought in social work and family therapy that we mentioned in Chapter 3 and Chapter 7. A difficulty with it can be that it tends to equalize responsibility for the violence between the woman and the man, so that both may be held to be to blame for the interactive cycle that leads to abuse. The differences in power between them in cases of abuse are often not acknowledged, and women may be frightened and disadvantaged in joint negotiating and therapy sessions. Family therapy has many benefits but is not always helpful in cases of domestic violence. Very many therapists recognize the problems and try to build up the abused woman's strength and ability to challenge her partner safely.

However, a problem with this model, if practised uncritically, is the identification of who is to be held responsible if difficulties are encountered or if it goes wrong.

Some women, of course, may wish to engage in 'conjoint' therapy of this type. There can be value in it – which of us could not do with a bit of counselling help with our intimate relationships? And many family therapists now adopt a strong position against domestic violence and have incorporated feminist critiques into their practice. Mediators and organizations like Relate, for example, will often see the woman separately in private to assist her. But it is vital for women to be aware of the dangers. One of the most pernicious aspects of the interactive approach is that the man's violence may be regarded as a highly regrettable but understandable response to provocative or difficult behaviour by the woman. Of course, both women and men do often behave in provocative or difficult ways, but that does not mean that violence in response is acceptable. Adams points out that the issue of who is responsible for the violence is often clouded in this approach. And the therapy itself can be dangerous for women partners. Abused women may expose themselves to further violence by expressing previously disguised dissatisfactions during family therapy sessions.

The fourth type of model identified by Adams is rather grandiosely called the 'cognitive behavioural and psycho-educational model'. This approach does make the violence the prime focus of counselling. The men participate in groups. The idea is that violence is learned behaviour, and can therefore be unlearned. Skills of stress reduction, relaxation and non-aggressive assertion are taught. And men are encouraged to observe and learn about their behaviour, so that they can find out what their triggers are – what sets them off and when the point of no return is passed. They are encouraged to learn to take 'time out' to interrupt the build-up of potentially violent anger by literally walking out of the situation temporarily. Members of the group learn about each other's rigid anger responses and can challenge each other and work out alternative ways of responding.

In this way, the men learn useful anger management techniques. They learn how to control their anger, how to communicate and generally how to cope with life better, so that they do not get angry in the first place. However, an American monitoring programme of apparently reformed violent men found they merely switched, after the programme, from expressing anger to other psychological means to get what they wanted from their partners. In addition, anger control can let the community off the hook yet again by making out that domestic violence is an individual problem of men who cannot cope adequately with life and with angering situations.

Edward Gondolf and David Russell, leading American researchers on men's programmes, have critiqued 'anger control treatment programs for batterers'. They pointed out that anger control may imply that the victim provoked the anger and so precipitated the abuse, and that it can be seen as a 'quick fix' but might actually endanger women in the long run. In other words, the man has anger control treatment and then everyone thinks things are better, but in reality nothing has changed.

While all this is often true, the best of the programmes using anger management approaches do address controlling behaviour by men and include an analysis of power between men and women. Without this analysis, it is difficult for anger control programmes to explain why so many men who cannot cope with anger, and need to develop new skills to do so, attack only their partners and not other people. *With it*, though, and at their best, assertion practice, anger control techniques and other education programmes are linked to a call for stronger legal remedies against domestic violence and for a society-wide condemnation of it.

Even such a schematic and inevitably somewhat caricatured account as this shows that there is some useful material in each of these four models of therapeutic intervention. They are often used in combination. Men's programmes may take some bits from one approach and some from another. What they all clearly need, however, from an activist point of view, is an analysis of the violence that takes gender politics into account.

The fifth type of programme identified by Adams does just this. Often called the 'pro-feminist approach', it consists of men's programmes that work closely alongside the women's movement against male violence. These programmes understand violence against women as one form of controlling behaviour that helps to maintain the imbalance of power and dominance by men over women. They recognize the need for participants to learn how to take care of others, to be educated in non-violence and to develop communication and assertion skills. But they hang these methods on a core structure of principles and politics that is committed to challenging male controlling behaviour and ending male dominance and violence.

These programmes have become more skilled over time. While each one varies in its approach, they have developed some common features that are a standard part of their philosophy and practice. They tend, for example, to use group methods of counselling. And their first priority is always the safety of women partners. Men participants are expected to make 'safety plans' to minimize the possibility of continued violence. The safety plans must be strictly adhered to and are usually monitored. Separate contact with the woman should be made through the refuge or shelter movement or through an autonomous but connected sister project.

Throughout the programme, the man's violence is centre-stage. Other underlying or contributing problems that he might have will be addressed, but will not be allowed to dislodge his violent and controlling behaviour from its position as the primary focus of attention. Most pro-feminist programmes confront as a priority two important and very common defences consciously or subconsciously used by violent men. The first is denial, either of the violence or of responsibility for it – the 'it wasn't my fault' approach. The second is minimizing the extent of the violence or its impact on women recipients. Thus one of the primary identified tasks of the programme is to get participants to take full responsibility for their own behaviour. And this means doing so in a real and deep way, rather than making excuses, refusing to face it, or blaming someone else (usually their women partners) as abusive men often do. The taking of personal responsibility by perpetrators for their own actions is of key importance in the programme. It includes not only the violence but also all the other forms of controlling behaviour that men might later substitute for it, but which they may be reluctant to acknowledge or recognize.

Men undertaking perpetrators' programmes are often expected to keep anger diaries and 'control logs' in which they must detail their controlling and angry behaviour for consideration by the group. They may also keep a written checklist of their violent and controlling behaviour traits, and learn how each of these may be damaging to their partners. This can be achieved through the use of videos, role-play, and group and individual exercises. Later in the programme, attitudes, expectations and feelings are also examined, especially in the light of the way men often devalue or undervalue their women partners and women in general. Issues of power and control between men and women are continually confronted. Pro-feminist programmes see violence, much as the feminist women's services do, as one part of a long continuum of male controlling behaviour.

One of the first and best-known of the American pro-feminist men's programmes was EMERGE, mentioned earlier. Formed in Boston in 1977 at the request of the local shelter movement, EMERGE was then a model of good practice for men's programmes, and, even though it has perhaps been overtaken in some ways by more recent projects, it attempts to maintain itself in this position. This pioneering project has always regarded it as a priority to campaign for funding for women's projects and for shelters, and the majority of pro-feminist projects have followed suit. They attempt to ensure that resources are not diverted from women's organizations, recognizing that men's projects can create a lot of publicity and can sometimes attract money, while shelters in the same area may remain starved of funding. Guidelines for funding were developed jointly between EMERGE and local women's organizations in 1980 as follows:

> No program for men who batter should be funded without the existence of shelters or safe home projects for battered women in the immediate community . . . (The availability of refuge for battered women when the abuser is in treatment is critical for reasons of safety of the women and children and of the efficacy of treatment for the abuser.)
> Treatment programs for men who abuse must work cooperatively with

shelters or safe home projects in their area. Programs for abusers must share the same philosophical understandings of the reasons for violence against women and must work in concert with the shelter movement to end violence against women.

Where the amount of funding in a community, foundation, or corporation is limited and insufficient to sustain both the shelter and abusers' program, the financial resources should be directed to shelter programs until they achieve financial stability.

Although arrangements may not work out quite as these guidelines suggest and many abusers' programmes have not embraced such standpoints, they are still thought by many to be good practice. These types of project take a political approach. All of their work revolves around issues of power and control, both between men and women, and between men. Some of them were formed as a result of initiatives by committedly anti-sexist men who had been influenced by the Women's Liberation movement, and who often had a history as political organizers in the vibrant and extraordinarily widespread movements of the 1960s and early 1970s in North America. These gave rise to women's and gay liberation, and later to something that is sometimes called the men's or anti-sexist movement.

This 'men's movement' differs massively from some 1990s/2000s organizations that use the same name, but have a very conservative, right-wing and anti-women agenda. It started out at the opposite end of the political spectrum, with a commitment to anti-sexist organizing and struggle. One branch of it gradually developed towards New Age philosophy and eventually gave rise to the non-political American men's groups that

we know today, such as the 'movement' run by Robert Bly that has attracted so much publicity. The other branch of the men's group spectrum stayed more political and connected to women's struggles.

It is these latter men's organizations of the political type that have been involved in national organizing work in the United States to end violence against women. National and local conferences have been held on men and masculinity for many years, and men's groups have launched various national and local initiatives, including country-wide groups and newsletters. A national networking organization of mainly white men, now called the National Organization for Men Against Sexism, has been in existence for 20 years. It takes what it calls a pro-feminist, gay-affirmative and anti-racist stance and has developed task groups to focus on specific issues – ending male violence, child custody, fathering, gay rights, homophobia, male/female relationships and so on.

In Canada also, men's groups dedicated to opposing violence exist in every city. In many, they have established men's forums to work on violence issues in a co-ordinated way and well over a hundred dedicated perpetrators' intervention programmes exist across the various provinces. The Men's Network for Change is a coast-to-coast pro-feminist Canadian network, also committed to supporting lesbian, gay and anti-racist issues (and comparable to a similar European network of pro-feminist men's groups). Some of these mainly North American groups and organizations have been facilitated by academic studies of masculinity and by the more pro-feminist end of men's studies as an academic discipline. They take a wide political view and often campaign actively for greater legal protection and service provision for abused women.

Various examples exist of men's projects that take this view. For example, the men's programme affiliated to the Marin Abused Women's Service in Marin County, California, has campaigned for many years and runs hundreds of re-education classes for violent men every year. The long-established RAVEN (Rape And Violence End Now), set up in St Louis in 1977, has a similarly long pedigree, and very many newer batterers' projects have been set up in recent years. Some of these pro-feminist programmes now attempt to take on diversity and racism, and to examine issues for Latino, African-American or Native American men. In this work, they are currently forging a new way forward. They include specific initiatives for African American, Native American and other men. Examples are Sacred Circle and various First Nations programmes which provide funding to strengthen the justice systems of the tribal governments and to provide batterers' programmes dealing with violent crimes against First Nations Indian women.

Programmes have also been set up in other countries and have attempted to be sensitive to cultural issues. For example, the Hamilton Abuse Intervention Pilot Project in Hamilton, New Zealand, provides a model programme working with both Maori and non-Maori women and men, and incorporating Maori issues into the abusers' programmes that it provides as one part of its community response.

How effective are the American programmes?

The effectiveness of even the best programmes has yet to be fully demonstrated, although increasing numbers of research studies show rather limited and unstable reductions in violence. On this evidence, however, at least 30 states in the USA have adopted quite rigid standards for abusers' programmes. What we do not yet know is whether the programmes result in sustained and permanent patterns of non-violent behaviour, and whether they make meaningful contributions to wider social change.

A consideration of these North American programmes is presented by a Canadian therapist, Ron Thorne-Finch, in a wide-ranging book, *Ending the Silence: The Origins and Treatment of Male Violence Against Women*, originally published in 1992. He points out that growing numbers of men are criticizing male violence and working towards sweeping changes in our ideas about masculinity and about what being a man means. Various men's groups have called this trend negotiating the transition for men from 'power-over' to 'power-with'. However, as Thorne-Finch suggests, the overall percentage of men involved in these activities is still small, and they are split in their approaches to male violence, and in their relationship to wider political struggles about issues of class, wealth, race and so on. The potential for great things is there, but will it be realized?

Many women in the shelter movement say 'no'. The Pennsylvania Coalition Against Domestic Violence undertook the ambitious task of studying pro-feminist services for batterers and published their findings in a still useful 1988 publication, *Safety for Women: Monitoring Batterers' Programs*, by Barbara Hart. Hart suggests that most activists believe counselling and education for violent men work in the short term only, and that what is needed is a strong and consistent community intolerance of domestic violence. She contends that

> Programs for men could be no more than a dangerous charade which holds out false hope to battered women. Many activists have concluded that work with batterers is an inappropriate diversion from the more critical tasks of enabling battered women and children to escape violence and establish safe lives.

As a result of this study and various others, the following expanded guidelines have been evolved. The first is that services for women must have primacy. No programme for men should be initiated unless the women's programme is successfully funded. Second, women advocates for women who have suffered violence should participate in the design and implementation of the programme. Third, the primary goal should be to end violence against women and to focus on confronting male violence. It is vital that men make a formal contract to be non-violent as part of the programme, and that there are adverse consequences for non-compliance. Fourth, all programmes must be evaluated.

The initial belief in the North American batterers' projects was that men should participate in the programmes voluntarily, so that they would be motivated to change. However, the current trend in the USA is that programmes should have the force of law and of community intolerance of violence behind them. Programmes should not be seen as an easy way out – a soft option. Rather they should be established as one part of a strong legal and community response. Under the influence of women's movement services, this viewpoint has grown in prominence and has led to a growth of court-ordered programmes in which violent men must participate as mandated by the courts.

Many quite high-powered evaluations have been conducted in more recent years in North America, where the carrying out of such an evaluation is usually a condition of grant aid. There has been an attempt to make these evaluations more rigorous and replicable than they were at first. Ed Gondolf, for example, has conducted long-term studies in several different places in the States. One multi-site study extended over 7 years with nearly a thousand perpetrators taking part. He suggests that there is some limited success in reducing male violence for men who complete the programmes offered, but the drop-out rate is always very high, which could place female partners at further risk. Gondolf and others have called for more expanded evaluation work as part of a broadly based community response to male violence. Court-ordered programmes in Duluth and Minneapolis, together with others in San Francisco, Atlanta, Denver, San Diego, Seattle and Quincy, Massachusetts, have taken the lead in pioneering this approach and in initiating positive arrest, and prosecution policies in the criminal justice system as part of a broad, multi-faceted and co-ordinated response. In this way, the perpetrators' programme forms just one part of the jigsaw.

The Duluth Domestic Abuse Intervention Project

Perhaps the best-known project, and certainly one of the most highly thought of in feminist circles, is the comprehensive and highly developed Domestic Abuse Intervention Project (DAIP) in Duluth, Minnesota. An enormous number of men's programmes make use of the Duluth model, although the context of its operation should be remembered as a factor in its success. Ellen Pence, who has written widely about the project, very often preludes any discussion by emphasizing the previously favourable political climate that originally nurtured it, due to the long tradition of grass-roots activism in Minnesota.

The Duluth project has always sought to influence the criminal justice system and the social services involved with domestic violence. It incorporates men's programmes into a wide-ranging co-ordinated community-based strategy that also involves women's services and policy and practice initiatives throughout the locality, including the adoption of agency guidelines and strong positive arrest policies co-ordinated with the response of the courts. The DAIP now monitors and tracks the progress of all individual cases going through the system and co-ordinates the intervention of law enforcement, criminal justice, human services and battered women's shelter and advocacy programmes. Further policy changes have been implemented throughout the caring services and related justice projects as a result. The monitoring role of the DAIP aims to prevent community collusion with abusers, about which Ellen Pence wrote a useful paper back in 1988, *Batterers' Programs: Shifting from Community Collusion to Community Confrontation*.

A book about the co-ordinated community response, edited by Ellen Pence and Melanie Shepard, was published in 1999. This book describes in detail the methods used in Duluth, including the conducting of institutional audits to assess how well agencies are doing in implementing good practice. A useful chapter on bringing anti-racism into men's programmes and establishing programmes for African-American, Latino and First Nations men was contributed by Fernando Mederos. (A shorter description of the Duluth approach by Ellen Pence and Martha MacMahon is contained in the book on multi-agency approaches edited by Nicola Harwin and ourselves in 1999.)

In implementing the Duluth programme, workers attempt to put feminist ideas into action. At each step, practice is matched against theory, and input is obtained from women who have suffered domestic violence themselves. The grass-roots approach is one of empowerment of women, and this strategy is then expected, indeed made, to pervade all the services and programmes provided. The involvement of women survivors of violence and of the shelter movement is seen to be vital. Women are nurtured, supported and encouraged throughout their use of the justice system and the courts, and advocacy work with women is also undertaken, whether or not they are using shelters. Women advocates establish empowering educational groups for women that meet in various neighbourhoods to discuss in a secure and non-threatening environment such topics as the dynamics of 'battering'. Support for women, both through the programme and in the community, is seen to be an essential part of the project. Without it, the positive arrest policies and men's programmes cannot work effectively and women may be placed in even more danger.

The courts require that abusers participate in a substantial counselling and educational programme co-ordinated by the DAIP. In the first part of the programme, the groups focus on stopping the violence, with an emphasis on anger management training and on confronting men's minimizing and denying behaviour towards their violent acts. The men then enter a second phase of the programme run by community activists trained by the DAIP. They are encouraged to stay in the programme after the court mandate is completed.

The underlying assumptions are that men who batter use a range of abusive tactics. Physical violence is rarely used to the exclusion of other methods. The DAIP has developed a chart showing how the different types of abuse relate to each other. It was elaborated in extensive consultation with women survivors of violence and takes the form of a wheel known as the 'power and control wheel'. It is widely used by the project itself and by others in many countries of the world. A second wheel diagram, the 'equality wheel', similarly widely used across the world, is used towards the end of the men's programme to assist them in developing more equal, honest and non-controlling ways of relating.

The Duluth project has been replicated in over twenty other Minnesota communities, although the organizers are well aware that each community is different and needs to develop its own approach. The Duluth model, however, has acted as a source of inspiration and of good working ideas for many agencies and for women's movement services in various countries. A closely connected project is the Domestic Abuse Project established in Minneapolis in 1979, providing a similar multi-systems intervention project.

Men's projects in the UK

Men's projects are less developed in the UK as compared with the situation in the United States. While they will undoubtedly develop further in coming years, it is encouraging that, to date anyway, the most traditional, therapeutic American programmes have not taken strong root, since British society is so much less 'therapized'. However, many of the positively regarded pro-feminist approaches and the complex debates in the States have made their way to the UK.

The most committed pro-feminist UK men's programmes have formed a national network, which produces directories, nationally available publications and training initiatives. This National Practitioners Network is now known as Respect and its mission is to promote adequate provision of programmes for men and associated support services for women. Respect issues comprehensive good practice guidance and minimum standards of practice, and offers support to pro-feminist projects. The good practice guidelines were redrafted in 2004 and provide comprehensive materials on the aims and principles that should govern men's programmes. Respect is now piloting a helpline for perpetrators. New projects can join Respect and there are national and local conferences and meetings. Currently, in 2004, Jill Radford and others at Teesside University are conducting a feasibility study for Respect regarding the accreditation of perpetrators' programmes and associated women's projects.

One of the ongoing discussions (as previously in North America) is the debate between projects that believe in voluntary self-referral by men and those that believe in court-ordered programmes. Men attending voluntary programmes might be more motivated to learn and change, whereas men who are court-mandated often have such a long history of violence behind them, before they reach the stage of being ordered by the court to attend a programme, that they may be hardened in their ways. However, court-ordered programmes give domestic violence greater weight and seriousness as a criminal and legal issue. In the UK, a few projects of both types exist. The self-referral ones are often one-off projects run by committed men. The court-mandated ones tend to be run by probation services or to be part of a broader criminal justice approach to domestic violence, and both are sometimes connected into a more multi-layered community response.

A few projects accept both voluntary and court-mandated referrals, in a flexible approach that is regarded favourably by many due to the commitment and motivation that voluntarily participating men may show. One of the best-known UK projects is the Hammersmith Domestic Violence Intervention Project in London which offers a well-honed programme to both voluntary and court-mandated men, and has taken a pioneering role. The project provides both a perpetrators' programme and a women's support service, both of which have gone through various phases of evolution. It also currently offers comprehensive 5-day training programmes to both statutory and voluntary agencies on working with perpetrators and with women who have experienced abuse.

Voluntary men's groups include the Men's Centre in London, publicized through the work of Adam Jukes, Ahimsa in Plymouth, the London Everyman Centre and MOVE. There have been various MOVE groups over the years that have come and gone, and have sometimes been connected to the co-counselling movement. MOVE groups have not usually offered support to the women partners of violent men, in common with the London Everyman Centre, which has resulted in some anxiety for Women's Aid and other women's groups.

If men are mandated by the criminal justice system to attend abusers' programmes, on the other hand, there are various different issues to consider. One is the lack of real motivation to participate that men may display if they are forced to attend and are denied any agency in the decision to do so.

A second debate among men's projects connected to the justice system is about diversion schemes. A few programmes have developed in such a way that men are 'diverted' either from imprisonment or from prosecution in the first place. Most men's projects, however, following the Duluth approach, uphold the idea that programmes must be part of a strong legal and criminal justice approach, and that they should themselves campaign for a strengthening of the law. Thus, they advocate a strong justice response, within which perpetrators' programmes form just one strand. Years of experience of diversion programmes in North America, often through the American family court system, have shown that they do not work well in cases of domestic violence, and their use is not now favoured in the UK. This is not to say, however, that exposure to a tough and degrading prison regime is any more successful. So how can this problem be surmounted?

Over several years in the 1990s, Lothian Regional Council pioneered an innovative programme which re-educated violent men without allowing them to bypass the criminal justice system. The men were placed on probation and ordered by the court to participate actively in the programme. In this way, treatment was offered, but domestic violence was not decriminalized. In the last few years, there has been a substantial growth in the popularity of this type of approach, and many probation services in the UK have now set up programmes for domestic violence perpetrators, in which men who are on probation attend a group (although not all are mandated by the courts to do so).

Another pioneer of perpetrators' programmes in the UK was the CHANGE project in Central Region, Scotland, which began in 1990. CHANGE developed a system involving extensive liaison with Scottish Women's Aid, which offered support to the women partners. The project offered a very structured and challenging group work programme run by a male and a female facilitator working together. While CHANGE is no longer functioning in the same way and now provides other services, its previous contribution cannot be over-emphasized. Both CHANGE and the Lothian project have been formally evaluated by Rebecca and Russell Dobash. Their well-regarded evaluation found that, in marked contrast to domestic violence offenders treated in other ways, only 33 per cent of men participating in the programmes committed another violent act against their partners during the 12-month follow-up. On the other hand, this is still one-third and translates into quite a large number of violent incidents. Encouragingly though, coercive and other forms of controlling behaviour were also reduced. The study, published by the Home Office and the Scottish Office in 1996, suggested that criminal justice programmes like Lothian and CHANGE, which make use of cognitive-behavioural principles and take a committed anti-violence position, can make a positive contribution to reducing domestic violence, but it noted that more research is needed to confirm these findings. The evaluation also came down firmly in favour of court-mandated men's programmes as part of a strong criminal justice response.

The main argument against perpetrators' programmes of this type is that men guilty of violent offences stay in the community, possibly still with their partners, which could be seen as a kind of 'soft' option. The argument is that violent men must learn by facing serious criminal sentencing that the law will not allow them to get away with domestic violence, that society will not stand for it. Even at their worst, however, the present legal penalties are fairly mild. It is rare either for men to be sent to prison for domestic violence or for any prison sentence imposed to be longer than a few days or weeks. Even probation is a more serious sentence than men often get. It is not usually the case that attending a men's programme while on probation allows the man to escape a more severe penalty. Some domestic violence workers argue, however, that the existence of men's programmes will militate against legal changes which could result in violent men being dealt with more seriously in the future.

Abused women themselves often want the violence to stop; however, they may not want their partner to get a criminal record or to go to prison. The possibility that this could happen may deter a woman from reporting the violence at all. She may fear that, if her partner does serve a sentence, she will experience violent repercussions when he comes out, or she may still love him. She may wish to avoid a harshly punitive response, and may prefer the possibility of a community-based option. Such considerations can be particularly relevant for black women. A woman whose partner or ex-partner is African-Caribbean, for example, may be very wary of exposing him to possible prison sentences due to the unfair and racist treatment that he might receive at the hands of the criminal justice and prison system. Thus overall, while some domestic violence activists and survivors may feel very opposed to perpetrators' programmes, many abused women currently appear ready to give them a chance.

Another important evaluation of a perpetrators' programme was completed in 1997 by Liz Kelly, Sheila Burton and Linda Regan at the Child and Woman Abuse Studies Unit in the University of North London. The project evaluated was the Hammersmith Domestic Violence Intervention Project (DVIP), discussed earlier. Like other British pro-feminist projects, the DVIP insists that men take full responsibility for their violence and uses both re-enactments (where men re-enact real incidents in which they have been violent for dissection by the group) and carefully structured time-outs (as a practical technique at home for avoiding a potentially violent situation building up). Since the evaluation, the project has continued to thrive at the forefront of UK perpetrators' programmes. It was one of the pioneers of the setting up of a 'sister project' to support women partners. The sister project approach, in which men's programmes are expected to make women's safety their priority and to provide an accompanying women's project to support the partners of the men in the programme, is now regarded as essential good practice and is strongly recommended by Respect. The evaluation of the DVIP particularly emphasized the value of sensitive pro-active work with women partners, in which the initiative for instigating contact and interaction with the women lies with the project, not with the woman herself.

The study found that some perpetrators undoubtedly do change their behaviour and their values if they complete the programme offered. The drawback is that an enormous proportion of participants drop out along the way. This very high attrition rate has been noted by the great majority of men's programmes. Thus, while the evaluation had positive things to say about accompanying support work with women partners, the authors say in their final section: 'Our conclusions will not offer succour to any of the players/positions in current debates about working with violent men.'

They also have a word of warning about the trend among probation services to run their own perpetrators' programmes with little or no input from local women's services. These programmes may be set up at the expense of independent or 'partnership' projects in the voluntary sector. The issue here is that the independent projects (which may be associated with an inter-agency forum) often work in conjunction with women's and refuge-based services, and can offer a more critical, informed and 'political' practice.

Thus we can see that the field of abusers' programmes is actually a minefield. However, a useful account of the current situation is offered in the Home Office Briefing Note by Audrey Mullender and Sheila Burton published in 2000, and in the mapping study of domestic violence provision noted previously, funded by the Joseph Rowntree Foundation and conducted by a collaboration of researchers and children's charities, led by Cathy Humphreys at the University of Warwick. Both these accounts emphasize the importance of setting up women's projects to accompany perpetrators' programmes. They also highlight the importance of including victims' views in all evaluations that are carried out, on the grounds that the only people who really know if violent men have decreased their violence are the women themselves. A further source of anxiety is how well violent men can parent their children (as we have discussed elsewhere in relation to contact orders). A recent study by Lynne Harne of the Violence Against Women Research Group came to the conclusion that the parenting abilities of male perpetrators of domestic violence might well be compromised (and are often actually lacking) and that this is a key area which needs to be appropriately assessed in terms of contact with children.

Overall then, best practice in British men's groups currently includes the following principles:

- ensuring the safety of the women and children involved as a first priority
- liaison with and some form of involvement in or accountability to women's domestic violence services
- the instituting of some form of 'sister' support initiative, working with women partners
- the use of a programme based on ideas about gender and power in relationships between men and women
- the insistence that men take responsibility for their violence, that collusion with violent men is avoided and that participants are violence-free
- the importance of including the views of victims in any evaluation of a programme or of its success

These principles form part of a broad pro-feminist response. Respect and many activists in the field point out that such a response is not an alternative to other types of men's programme and cannot be understood as 'one system among many'. Rather it is a philosophy and practical approach that should inform and underlie *all* men's programmes, whatever individual method and intervention strategy they may use.

Using the Duluth model to varying extents, there was a variety of successful projects in the Home Office Crime Reduction Programme on Violence against Women of the early 2000s, which included programmes for perpetrators. Pathfinder and other funding has also been made available to try to develop good practice in terms of using the probation route.

Importantly, the probation service has now pioneered a Pathfinder Accreditation Programme for perpetrators' programmes, which was set up by the Home Office with pilot sites in London and West Yorkshire. In several probation areas in each site, pilot programmes have been run since 2002, based loosely on the Duluth project (although not officially approved by it), to hold offenders accountable while working with the victims. Men in the programmes are required to attend at least 48 hours of sessions over 6 to 8 months. The programme run by London Probation has now been expanded to 12 boroughs, with more expansion to come, and has won a London mayoral prize for pioneering work on domestic violence. Overall, the Pathfinder Programme has been independently evaluated and is leading to nationally accredited programmes and accredited criteria of good practice. The National Probation Service intends to role out this accredited programme (IDAP) across the country in 2004–5 and at least 20 additional probation services are already running programmes, although often dogged by lack of resources.

So practice is getting better in some areas. Some of the concerns of Women's Aid and the network of domestic violence services in the past have been addressed by the establishing of a joint and clear framework of good practice, as set up, for example, by Respect. However, concerns continue, especially over the need for parallel programmes for women, which is sometimes overlooked, particularly if funding is scarce.

The sources of contention and difficulty in work with violent men remain many. The most important issue of all, however, is the increasingly widespread understanding that men's programmes (like positive policing, positive arrest and prosecution policies) will not – indeed, cannot – work effectively on their own. In the end, it is possible for them to achieve their aims and their vision only if they form just one part of a wider multi-faceted community and agency response to domestic violence, which includes adequate protection, support and services for abused women and their children, a powerful domestic violence movement, a strong criminal justice response and a culture of community intolerance of violence against women. This is what they have built in Duluth.

Safer City partnerships now integrate perpetrators' programmes into such a wider support and justice strategy across some probation areas – in London, for example – and a recent evaluation of the Camberwell programme, which is part of a broad Safer Southwark Initiative, found that of 107 men completing the programme, only 6 appear to have reoffended. The first programmes in the UK that are specifically replicating the Duluth model are having some success, in particular the Standing Together Against Domestic Violence project in the Hammersmith and Fulham area of London. Standing Together tracks cases through the criminal justice system, provides advocacy and support for women, assists victims using the courts and co-ordinates responses on a partnership basis. It has been outstandingly successful, reducing repeat offences by 14 per cent in its first 2-year evaluation and increasing convictions by 54 per cent. Standing Together has also conducted sensitive and imaginative consultations with domestic violence survivors and users of services. Thus, innovation and creativity are certainly present. We have yet to see where they will lead in the long term.

Schools, community development and public awareness campaigns

If we widen our understanding of male violence against women still further, we need to confront the fact that we live in a society in which cultural representations of violence are commonplace. For pleasure, people often choose to sit passively watching episodes of repeated and sometimes extreme violence, perhaps in violent sport or on television. Violent books are massively popular, and violent crime is on the increase. But the violence is not randomly distributed. Generally speaking, violent behaviour is associated with men, not women. Society and mass media culture in western societies are full of images of men being aggressive, angry and violent, and of women being passive and often scantily clad. To confirm this view it is enough to glance at any edition of the *Sun,* to trawl through the TV channels on a Saturday night, to go into a video store, or to look at the films of the moment that are the biggest box office successes. Often these films consist principally of violent episodes strung together one after the other. They are seen by millions, and particularly by teenagers. Even in the case of comedies and romances, it is hard to find a super-popular film that does not include at least one scene in which the principal male characters are engaging in quite severe violence. It is also rare to find such a film in which the relationships between men and women are truly equal, and in which women characters are not dominated or devalued in some way by the men.

Even though many men are not themselves violent, popular culture encourages us all to see aggression and violence as appropriate male behaviour. Men in the media who are emotional, gentle and reluctant to engage in violence are frequently presented as figures of derision, contempt and ridicule. Toyshops are rigidly segregated by gender, and the boys' section looks like a war and weapons storehouse. It is chilling to see a 2-year-old boy running around with a plastic machine gun pretending to murder everybody; or to see larger boys huddled together over computer screens for hours, zapping and destroying enemies.

People trying to bring up boys in this culture in an anti-sexist, non-violent way face a tough job. They have to pit themselves against the might of television, against the enormous advertising industry aimed at children, and against playground pressure from young peers. As a consequence of all this, they tend to be subjected to unremitting demands from their male offspring to provide toys and games that glorify male violence. Very often the best that they can achieve is a damage limitation exercise. It becomes a question of strategic giving-in – on violent cartoons for pre-schoolers, on forts and soldiers, on computer games, on aggressive sports, on bombers and guns.

In many households, boys are allowed to engage in fantasy violence and to play with war toys on the grounds that such play releases aggression rather than adding to it, and that, in any case, fantasy does not usually lead to the real thing. Others still encourage boys to be 'macho' and aggressive as a matter of course. Fathers and sons may engage in violent play and in activities that repress emotions of tenderness and softness. Playground games and organized activities for boys are frequently rough and unforgiving. Boys are often brought up to be tough, to hide and repress their feelings, and only in the most traumatic circumstances to display vulnerability or fear or, worst of all, to cry.

If bringing up boys to be non-violent and to be able to express their feelings is a monumental task, so too is the project of bringing up boys to respect women and to learn how to engage in equal, mutually supportive adult relationships. Much work in education and psychology has shown at just what a young age boys learn to devalue their mothers and other women and girls, and to believe that girls are less important, less instrumental in the world, than boys. It operates in reverse for girls. Everything from Barbie to teen romance to clothes and make-up teaches them to be compliant, emotionally nurturing and expressive, non-violent and sexually alluring to men.

It is beyond the scope of this book to investigate these vast subjects. This brief anecdotal account can only indicate what a huge task it is to attempt to change popular culture. None of us can escape it. In our lives, it is both a mirror and a cause of why we behave as we do, although it is not without contradictions. This applies as much to male violence as to anything else. There are sanctions against it and public outcry about its prevalence. Veiled, however, behind popular culture about male violence lies the reality of unequal economic and social relations between men and women, within an economic system and culture that values qualities of toughness, profit and competition, and downgrades values of collectivism, sharing and tenderness.

If domestic violence is finally to end, the vast project of transforming these social and economic relations and of challenging male domination throughout society and culture must be embraced. Raising boys to be non-violent is one small part of it. And of course in some places efforts are being made to do just that. Most playgroups, nursery schools and primary schools operate policies of non-violence and of teaching children to relate to each other in equal, respectful ways. Secondary schools also condemn violence. Some run courses on domestic violence and on how to develop caring adult relationships. On the other hand, genuine discussions about sexual feelings, responses and ways of engaging in equal, mutually satisfying sexual relationships are apparently seen as controversial, and are rarely held in schools.

Some children's TV programmes are consciously pro-women and anti-violence, and there are plenty of children's books and games that combat violence and present men as capable of being gentle and retiring, and women as being strong and powerful. Some organizations specialize in selling books that try to break down cultural stereotyping of male and female roles, and notions of power and control by men over women. Such books and games might also attempt to counter racism and other sorts of discrimination. So it is not all a pro-violence monolith by any means.

Activists have long argued for the development of education, community services and parenting patterns that work against the stereotyping of gender roles between women and men, and which attempt to minimize dominating and violent behaviour in boys and submissive behaviour in girls. To this end, Women's Aid staff including child support workers give talks in schools and colleges, and work closely when they can with teachers and educators.

An important development over the last few years has been the introduction of information about domestic violence into the curricula of schools. Several inter-agency projects (discussed in Chapter 8) have instigated initiatives in the education system and among youth workers (for example, in Keighley, Yorkshire). A pioneer of this approach was provided by the *STOP Domestic Violence Pack* produced in the 1990s in the London Borough of Islington. More recent packs and programmes include the *Respect Pack* originally produced in Hackney (and no relation to the perpetrators' programme network), a comprehensive pack produced in Glasgow and the ongoing work of the Leeds Inter-agency Project on education initiatives. The recent Home Office Crime Reduction Programme on Violence against Women included several projects which ran education programmes in schools (for example, in Thurrock, Southampton, Bridgend, Camden and Yorkshire) and found that participation in these projects had a positive effect on pupils' knowledge of domestic violence and on their attitudes towards it. Womankind Worldwide has also produced reports and programmes.

The Westminster Domestic Violence Forum in London has put in place an innovative education programme in schools originally designed by Thangam Debbonaire. The programme has been a success in Westminster schools and is currently being evaluated and rolled out across the capital. All of these schools packs are accompanied by training for teachers and often for youth and community workers. Attempts are increasingly being made to mount interventions of this type within the formal school curriculum, so that domestic violence makes it into the standard classroom, rather than being an optional extra dealt with occasionally by progressive or feminist teachers, or touched on in passing during A-level social science courses but in no others. The idea now is to integrate the work into the personal, health, social and citizenship education curriculum.

Most of the programmes that exist provide activities, exercises and lesson plans for children, together with supporting materials, guidance on child protection issues and on how to handle disclosure of abuse, teacher training, and background information for schools and for pastoral support services. There are now attempts to introduce such educational materials in both secondary and primary schools and anxieties that domestic violence is not a suitable subject for very young children are being overcome by the production of age-sensitive materials. The Cheshire Domestic Abuse Partnership, for example, has produced a story-telling production for primary school children which has been viewed by many thousands of children and hundreds of teachers.

Some of this material draws on models of non-violent resolution of conflict. On a general level, the field of conflict resolution originated in the business world, but has now filtered through to schools in some places. For example, various schools in the UK now operate conflict mediation programmes, sometimes operated by pupils themselves after special training and with support and help from adults. In the United States, progressive programmes on limiting boys' violence and on conflict resolution are currently being practised in many schools. In the teeth of considerable adversity, for example, hundreds of grade school teachers from 50 New York City schools were trained in the 1980s and 1990s in ways of resolving conflict non-violently. Myriam Miedzian, in *Boys Will Be Boys: Breaking the Links Between Masculinity and Violence*, explains how teachers and students learned that 'handling conflict well is a skill like riding a bike or using a computer'. Such an explanation is necessary because the ability to resolve conflicts in a mutually supportive and non-violent way has never been thought of as something one learns in schools. Until recently it was not thought of as something one learns at all.

At a broader level, domestic violence projects, various local education authorities and now the government itself have recommended education programmes to be put in place in schools, so we will see more of such programmes in the future. There have also been wide-ranging recommendations that programmes of public education to raise awareness about domestic violence and to engage in community development should be further developed as a key element in the prevention of domestic violence, and should also be part of the government's present three-pronged emphasis on providing protection, prevention and support for victims. The theory is that community education will lead to a greater public intolerance of domestic violence. What is visualized is something similar to the part of the Duluth programme that concentrates on community involvement, and which aims to convert acceptance or apathy regarding domestic violence to a public attitude of abhorrence of abusers.

Public education campaigns against domestic violence are beginning to be initiated in many countries: for example, Papua New Guinea, Israel, Malaysia, Uganda and Brazil. In Canada, a campaign of public information and awareness has been going on for many years now and, in most Canadian provinces, television advertising critical of domestic violence is accompanied by billboard advertisements, posters and radio announcements, and the provision of free public helplines, financed through the various levels of government. In Zimbabwe, publicity campaigns have been held on a recurring basis. With the slogan, 'It's your mother, your daughter, your sister', women have produced plays, demonstrations, television and radio programmes, and a variety of public and community events that have drawn connections between gender violence and current political issues in the country. White ribbon public awareness-raising campaigns have been developed in a variety of countries with the participation of domestic violence activists and often of anti-violence, pro-feminist men. In post-apartheid South Africa, for example, an innovative white ribbon campaign with accompanying public awareness-raising events has been conducted, co-ordinated in the Gauteng area by NISAA Institute for Woman Development in Lenasia, Johannesburg. Some of this work has fed into the international '16 Days of Activism' campaigns which are held annually in many countries (now co-ordinated through the US Centre for Women's Global Leadership) and the International Day of Action to Eliminate Violence Against Women, held each year on 25 November and celebrated throughout the world.

Public education work has been well developed in Australia, where the emphasis has been on public and community awareness, putting forward the position that domestic violence will stop only when men stop being violent, when the community as a whole stops condoning it, and when, in the words of the Australian National Committee on Violence Against Women, 'everyone, everywhere [becomes] intolerant of violence against women and upholds the belief that no woman deserves violence'. Public awareness work has been geared towards protection and community safety for women, and towards the development of collective community responsibility for elevating the status of women and building a society in which violence against women is not tolerated.

In the UK, Women's Aid has co-ordinated a variety of national campaigns, working with local and national media. Both television and radio in the UK have conducted public information campaigns and there have been numerous poster and leaflet awareness-raising efforts. For example in 2003, the BBC carried out a wide-ranging publicity campaign on domestic violence called *Hitting Home*, which ran across all BBC TV and radio channels and was accompanied by a range of support materials. In one week, domestic violence featured on programmes as wide ranging as *Woman's Hour, Neighbours, Casualty, Panorama* and *Newsround* on children's television.

Many inter-agency forums and women's domestic violence organizations have conducted their own public awareness-raising programmes. Local police forces, social services and Crime and Disorder Reduction Programmes have also run awareness-raising campaigns, and the Home Office has co-ordinated a campaign called 'Breaking the Chain' with leaflets, adverts, posters and other publicity materials. Importantly, over the last decade we have seen the growth of Zero Tolerance campaigns, deriving from the original ground-breaking campaign run by Edinburgh District Council Women's Committee. The materials used involve the use of a series of moving posters in which the letter 'Z' gradually becomes understood as a symbol of 'zero tolerance of male violence'. This innovatory campaign covers all forms of violence against women, including sexual violence. It is usually accompanied by public events, community programmes, schools interventions and local conferences, and can span several years if funding is available. However, although many local authorities have taken up the idea with some enthusiasm, they have tended to run very short versions over a matter of weeks, which are clearly of doubtful long-term value. The campaign has been evaluated in a few areas and has come out of the evaluations very positively. For example, improved awareness of domestic violence and public approval were strongly noted in the evaluation of the Edinburgh campaign.

A drawback of the public education programmes carried out so far is that there is rarely enough funding for adequate community development work with abused women and children to accompany the campaign. And an active campaign can increase the demand for services in an area so much that local refuge-based services and other domestic violence organizations can no longer cope. On the other hand, the presence of a public education campaign can increase the likelihood of funding being made available for services. The implementation of awareness-raising work has been patchy around the country, and often depends on whether there are active local women's groups and a committed local authority in the area. One problem with all the public awareness-raising work that has been conducted so far is that it is sporadic and short-term. Funding for co-ordinated ongoing campaigns has not been forthcoming so that, as for much domestic violence work, the results have been variable and uneven depending on area. The need remains for a sustained and longer-term national publicity campaign to spread the message that domestic violence is unacceptable.

Campaigning and lobbying

Community education, education programmes in schools, inter-agency partnership strategies and national publicity campaigns are a far cry from the situation back in the early 1970s, when none of these things had even been mooted. Sometimes we forget all that has happened in between. We continually need to remind ourselves and each other that the current response to domestic violence, both nationally and internationally, has gone far beyond the imaginings of activists 30 years ago and is a product of the social movement of women for liberation from degradation and violation by men. These days, though, such memories can get lost in the daily grind of pushing for new policies and wider domestic violence partnership strategies, trying to implement good practice guidelines, attending endless meetings and struggling to keep threatened services open or to initiate new ones.

Throughout this book, we have emphasized the role and importance of Women's Aid and the rest of the domestic violence network. We have also noted the contradictions that the movement has had to face in its dealings with the local and national state. Political activity against male violence and the establishment of widespread feminist services for women survivors in the last 30 years gave rise to something new. In some ways, women's activism and the movement against domestic violence was able to learn from other experiences and social movements. Largely, however, it found itself having to make up the rules itself, being new in its own historical context, often going against the grain, having to create something out of nothing with very few guidelines or models around of how to go about it.

An example is the way that the pioneering commitment of the network of Women's Aid and the network of domestic violence services to empowerment and collectivity has been continually subjected over the years to outside forces pulling it the other way. Domestic violence workers and activists live under these conflicting forces all the time. They often feel as though they are being wrenched first one way and then the other by their own determination to work in a new and experimental way, and by the demands of government, of funders and of other statutory and voluntary agencies. Trying to work in a new and equal way is constantly undermined, for example, by pervasive notions of the need for authority and hierarchy from officialdom and funding bodies. Add to this the problems of underfunding, overwork and exhaustion which almost always characterize independent women's domestic violence work, and then add the painful nature of work with survivors of abuse, of endless exposure to the effects of male violence and brutality towards women. It is hardly surprising that activists sometimes feel overwhelmed and that the burn-out rate is high.

One of the dilemmas of the domestic violence movement has always been between, on the one hand, staying true to its ideals and, on the other, trying to provide the best possible services for women and children – and facing possible co-option in the search for funding to provide these services. Co-option means giving up on the 'new' and being sucked back into traditional ways of doing things. It means being forced to compromise strongly held beliefs and visions of how things could be different. Back in the 1980s, the American activist Susan Schechter wrote an inspirational book, *Women and Male Violence: The Visions and Struggles of the Battered Women's Movement.* She made an impassioned case for retaining the political vision of liberation and social transformation. In the UK, the movement has retained a substantial degree of independence and political autonomy. But the increasing number of professionals in the domestic violence field, the incorporation of domestic violence into high-powered strategic agendas and its mainstream position, as well as being achievements, raise clear cause for concern for activists looking towards the future.

Nevertheless, the movement against domestic violence and the network of women's services keep on going, as mainstreaming happens, and maintain their zeal and commitment to feminist ways of organizing and to improving services for abused women and children. The national Women's Aid federations continue their vital role in monitoring legislation and policy, and in lobbying, influencing and putting pressure on government. They also participate in, and on occasion initiate, direct campaigning work on behalf of women who have suffered violence and their children.

Over the years, there have been a variety of campaigns about domestic violence. Southall Black Sisters (SBS), the dedicated and long-serving campaigning group based in the Asian community in Southall, London, have always been committed to working against male violence towards women. Founded in 1979, they have campaigned both against racism and on behalf of women and girls ever since. In recent years they have taken an important role in the Women Against Fundamentalism movement. Southall Black Sisters have been deeply involved in political work about domestic violence on many levels, from one-off actions publicizing individual cases to national campaigns about policy issues.

Women Against Violence Against Women (WAVAW) was a political organization working against male violence up to the mid-1980s. It organized political actions, meetings and conferences, and had local groups in towns and cities all over the country. Actions and campaigns have also been organized by women's groups running services for rape and incest survivors. While rape crisis centres have faced funding and other difficulties in the 1990s, and many have disappeared, including the redoubtable and long-standing London Rape Crisis Centre and the Rape Crisis Federation itself, a campaigning group called the Campaign to End Rape is now in action and a more recent national campaign, the Truth About Rape Campaign, was established in 2002. All of these groups have organized actions about male violence but have concentrated mainly on rape and pornography issues.

There have been many small and localized campaigns. Some Women's Aid groups, for example, have mounted local actions on behalf of women murdered by their husbands. Due to their position as both a local and a national political organization, some of the most publicized of these campaigns have been conducted by Southall Black Sisters. In conjunction with Brent Asian Women's Refuge back in 1985, for example, a series of national actions and demonstrations was held after the tragic murder of Balwant Kaur inside refuge premises. These widespread actions involved many Women's Aid groups. Since then, there have been other similar, although smaller, campaigns on behalf of individual women in a variety of towns and cities, involving a range of political actions.

The feminist organization, Justice for Women, has campaigned since the early 1990s about women subjected to male violence. A small group that is not linked to service provision, it specifically campaigns against the life sentences imposed on abused women who kill their husbands after enduring domestic violence, perhaps for many years. The campaign has pointed out how men who kill their wives have often in the past received lighter sentences than women who kill their husbands. Further, women who kill their husbands are very often convicted of murder rather than manslaughter, and murder carries a mandatory life sentence.

Action on behalf of abused women who kill was spearheaded in the 1990s by the Kiranjit Ahluwalia campaign primarily co-ordinated by Southall Black Sisters, initially with the involvement of Crawley Women's Aid, and supported by Justice for Women and many Women's Aid groups. Kiranjit Ahluwalia killed her husband after enduring ten years of beatings, rapes and burnings. When she was imprisoned for life in 1989, her case attracted widespread press and public interest. Women campaigned on her behalf up and down the country, and a large number of campaigning groups became involved. Kiranjit Ahluwalia was finally released amid jubilation in the summer of 1992 when her case came to appeal – a triumph for the many organizations involved. She has since written a book about her experiences.

Justice for Women, Southall Black Sisters and other organizations have also supported active local campaigns on behalf of many other women, and they continue to do so. These women include Amelia Rossiter, Janet Gardner, Sara Thornton, Carol Peters, Elizabeth Line, June Scotland, Pamela Sainsbury and many others. One young woman, Emma Humphreys, was released from prison after a campaign in her support, but later died. Since her death in 1998, a memorial programme was put into place with an annual Emma Humphreys prize.

In many of these cases the campaigns have been successful and women have been released on appeal or have received suspended sentences. The high-profile campaign on behalf of Sara Thornton in the 1990s elicited support from a variety of political parties and organizations. Local and national demonstrations, petitions, pickets, vigils outside prisons and the Home Office, representations and lobbies finally led to her release. More recent and current campaigns include those for Jane Andrews, Joanne Cole, Rose Swann and a campaign, co-ordinated by Southall Black Sisters, on behalf of Zoora Shah, currently serving a life sentence.

Women's Aid, Rights of Women, Justice for Women, Southall Black Sisters and other women's organizations continue the fight. The successes of campaigns on behalf of some women have run alongside other cases in which women have continued to receive punitive convictions and sentences. As yet, the law shows little consistency. Together with Rights of Women and other organizations, Justice for Women has been calling for some years for a reform of the law. They claim that the defence of provocation, which can reduce a charge from murder to manslaughter, works unfairly against women (see Chapter 5). Rights of Women and

Justice for Women have recommended over many years that a new partial defence of 'self-preservation' on the grounds of prolonged abuse and intimidation should be introduced. Various submissions along these lines are currently being considered in relation to the 2004 Law Commission consultation paper on partial defences to murder, particularly a suggested new partial defence known as 'pre-emptive use of force in self-defence', which would be broadly similar in intent.

Whether or not these initiatives to change the law will be successful remains to be seen. However, the successes of the individual campaigns to reduce harsh sentences imposed on abused women who kill have been very important for women who have suffered domestic violence, and for activists in the movement.

In general, many national demonstrations against violence against women have been held over the years, and local vigils, lobbies and demonstrations have been organized in different areas. Political actions have also been held in response to specific pieces of legislation and, in the last few years, successful actions and campaigns against domestic violence in general have been organized by many different groups around the UK. It is heartening to see the issue on the political and public agenda.

Now, in the 2000s, there is constant lobbying and policy work going on. There are national and local actions. And there are new and innovative services appearing almost weekly, domestic violence policies and practice guides, co-ordinated inter-agency initiatives, projects and strategic partnerships, men's programmes against violence, and international agreements and actions. Current activity against domestic violence is increasingly mainstreamed, powerful and creative, and is linked in various obvious and not so obvious ways into the international movement of women against inequality and injustice. Worldwide, there is a vast network of women's grass-roots projects, services, safe houses, activities, policies and legislation on behalf of abused women. Thirty years ago, there was almost nothing.

It is a considerable achievement. Throughout this book, we have continually reiterated the importance of acknowledging and recognizing that achievement. The most important time to remember it can be when the going gets tough, when mistakes are made, when everyone involved is tired, and when the whole enterprise feels like banging your head persistently against a brick wall. Despite the recent favourable government policies and actions, with funding still inadequate or insecure, there is no room for complacency. The vital recognition of all that has been achieved, of how fundamental and comprehensive the changes are, must be balanced against an awareness of how much more there is to be done. There is a need for more funding, more community services for abused women and their children, more women's refuge-based, support and advocacy services, including specialist projects for specific groups of women, better remedies in both criminal and civil law, further improved policing, better housing provision, more inter-agency co-ordination and more political campaigns.

It is of crucial importance that, in all future developments, the Women's Aid network and the rest of the movement against domestic violence stays centre-stage and does not become marginalized if, or as, violence in the home becomes more and more unacceptable to society, and opposition to it continues to occupy the mainstream. Most important of all is to preserve and to be guided by the enduring and passionate vision among domestic violence activists of a world where women can live abuse-free lives and where male violence against women is finally a thing of the past.

Further information and useful addresses

Women experiencing domestic violence and their children can obtain advice, support and help from their local Women's Aid group, which usually has a public telephone number in the telephone directory. Refuges outside Women's Aid may be listed by name in the *Phone Book*, or can sometimes be found under 'Social services' in the *Yellow Pages*. In some areas, specialist projects for women suffering domestic violence are available: for example, for black, immigrant or ethnic minority women, lesbians, very young women, and women who have suffered sexual abuse or have special needs.

Doctors' surgeries, council offices and community centres often display information about local refuges and available services, and in some local authorities helpful leaflets and booklets containing information on where to go for help are freely available. Women can also get help from the local police station, social services office, citizens' advice bureau, Samaritans, housing department office and other agencies.

In an emergency, the police or the social services (including the emergency social services team out of office hours) should enable a woman to get to a place of safety. The Women's Aid Federation of England, in partnership with Refuge, runs a national 24-hour helpline (with a minicom system) for women threatened by or experiencing violence, and refuges work together to refer women and children to a safe location. All the Women's Aid federations can also offer assistance. The addresses and contact numbers are as follows:

National 24 Hour Helpline (Women's Aid and Refuge), tel.: 0808 2000 247 (with minicom)

Women's Aid, the National Women's Aid Federation of England, PO Box 391, Bristol BS99 7WS; tel.: 0117 944 4411; email: info@womensaid.org.uk; website: www.womensaid.org.uk

Scottish Women's Aid, 2nd Floor, 132 Rose Street, Edinburgh, EH2 3JD;

tel.: 0131 226 6606; email: info@scottishwomensaid.org.uk; website: www.scottishwomensaid.org.uk

Welsh Women's Aid:
Helpline: 0808 80 10 80
Aberystwyth: 4 Pound Place, Aberystwyth SY23 1LX; tel.: 01970 612748
Cardiff: 38–48 Crwys Road, Cardiff CF2 4NN; tel.: 01222 390874
Rhyl: 26 Wellington Road, Rhyl LL18 1BN; tel.: 01745 334767;
email: team@welshwomensaid-cardiff.freeserve.co.uk;
website: www.welshwomensaid.org.uk

Northern Ireland Helpline, tel.: 01232 331818 (24 hours)

Northern Ireland Women's Aid, 129 University Street, Belfast BT7 1HP;
tel.: 028 9024 9041; email: info@niwaf.org.uk;
website: www.niwaf.org.uk

Information about local policies on domestic violence, on inter-agency work and on services available can be obtained from local Women's Aid groups and other refuges, and, where these exist, from local authority Women's Equality Committees and Units, from police Domestic Violence Family Protection or Community Safety Units, from inter-agency projects on domestic violence and from specialist projects and organizations, such as those for black women and women from different ethnic heritages. Imkaan, a national 'second-tier' charity, provides support and capacity building to Asian women's refuges, including policy and legal advice, research and training:

Imkaan, 76 Brewer Street, London, W1; tel.: 020 74349945; email: admin@imkaan.org.uk; website: www.imkaan.org.uk

Bibliography

Abrahams, C. (1994) *The Hidden Victims*, NCH Action for Children.

Abrahams, H. (2004) 'A long hard road to go by: a study of support work carried out in women's refuges', PhD thesis, University of Bristol.

Adams, D. (1988) 'Treatment models of men who batter: a pro-feminist analysis', in K. Yllo and M. Bograd (eds), *Feminist Perspectives on Wife Abuse*, Sage.

Atkins, S. and Hoggett, B. (1984) *Women and the Law*, Blackwell.

Barron, J. (1990) *Not Worth the Paper? The Effectiveness of Legal Protection for Women and Children Experiencing Domestic Violence*, Women's Aid Federation of England.

Barron, J. (2001) *Health and Domestic Violence*, Women's Aid.

Barron, J. (2002) *Five Years On: A Review of Legal Protection from Domestic Violence*, Women's Aid Federation of England.

Barron, J. (2004) *Health and Domestic Violence Two Years On: Survey 2002–3*, Women's Aid.

Barron, J. (2004) *The Struggle to Survive: Domestic Violence and Mental Health*, Women's Aid.

Beasley, C. (1999) *What is Feminism?* Sage.

Binney, V., Harkell, G. and Nixon, J. (1981) *Leaving Violent Men*, Women's Aid Federation of England.

Binney, V., Harkell, G. and Nixon, J. (1985) 'Refuges and housing for battered women', in J. Pahl (ed.), *Private Violence and Public Policy*, Routledge.

Blaffer-Hrdy, S. (1999) *Mother Nature: A History of Mothers, Infants and Natural Selection*, Pantheon.

Bossy, J. and Coleman, S. (2000) *Womenspeak: Findings from the Parliamentary Domestic Violence Internet Consultation*, Women's Aid Federation of England.

Bourlet, A. (1990) *Police Intervention in Marital Violence*, Open University Press.

Bowker, L., Arbitell, M. and McFerron, R. (1988) 'On the relationship between wife beating and child abuse', in K. Yllo and M. Bograd (eds), *Feminist Perspectives on Wife Abuse*, Sage.

Burton, S., Regan, L. and Kelly, L. (1998) *Supporting Women and Challenging Men*, The Policy Press.

Bush, T. and Hood-Williams, J. (1995) *Domestic Violence on a London Housing Estate*, Research Bulletin no. 37, Home Office.

Children Act (1989) HMSO.

Children and Adoption Act (2002) The Stationery Office.

Children (Scotland) Act (1995) HMSO.

Children's Subcommittee of the London Co-ordinating Committee to End Women Abuse, London, Ontario (1994) 'Make a difference: how to respond to child witnesses of women abuse', in A. Mullender and R. Morley (eds), *Children Living with Domestic Violence: Putting Men's Abuse of Women on the Child Care Agenda*, Whiting & Birch.

Cobbe, F. P. (1878) 'Wife torture in England', *Contemporary Review*, April, pp. 55–87.

Conflict Tactics Scale II, Family Violence Laboratory, University of New Hampshire.

Cretney, A. and Davis, G. (1996) 'Prosecuting "domestic" assault', *Criminal Law Review*, March, pp. 162–74.

Crime and Disorder Act (1998) HMSO.

Crown Prosecution Service (November 2001) *Guidance on Prosecuting Cases of Domestic Violence*, CPS.

Davies, M. (1994) *Asking the Law Question*, The Law Book Company.

Davies, M. (1994) *Women and Violence: Realities and Responses Worldwide*, Zed Books.

Davis, C. (2003) *Housing Associations: Rehousing Women Leaving Domestic Violence: New Challenges and Good Practice*, The Policy Press.

Debbonaire, T. (2002) *Domestic Violence Prevention Pack for Schools*, Westminster Domestic Violence Forum.

Department of Health (1995) *Domestic Violence and Social Care*, HMSO.

Department of Health (2000) *A Resource Manual for Health Care Professionals*, DoH.

Dobash, R. E. and Dobash, R. (1980) *Violence Against Wives*, Open Books.

Dobash, R. E. and Dobash, R. (eds) (1998) *Rethinking Violence against Women*, Sage.

Dobash, R. E. and Dobash, R. (1992) *Women, Violence and Social Change*, Routledge.

Dobash, R. E., Dobash, R. and Cavanagh, K. (1985) 'The contact between battered women and social and medical agencies', in J. Pahl (ed.), *Private Violence and Public Policy*, Routledge.

Dobash, R. E., Dobash, R., Cavanagh, K. and Lewis, R. (1996) *Re-education Programmes for Violent Men: An Evaluation*, Scottish Office.

Domestic Violence, Crime and Victims Act (2004) The Stationery Office.

Draft Children (Contact) and Adoption Bill, CM6462, Department for Education and Skills and The Stationery Office

Edwards, S. (1989) *Policing Domestic Violence*, Sage.

Edwards, S. (2001) 'Domestic violence and harassment: an assessment of the civil remedies', in J. Taylor-Browne (ed.), *What Works in Reducing Domestic Violence?*, Whiting & Birch.

Edwards, S. (2001) 'New directions in prosecution', in J. Taylor-Browne (ed.), *What Works in Reducing Domestic Violence?*, Whiting & Birch.

Eekelaar, J. M. and Katz, S. N. (1978) *Family Violence: An International, Interdisciplinary Study*, Butterworth.

Ellis, B. (1994) *Disabled Women's Project Report*, Greater London Association of Disabled People.

Family Law Act (1996), Part IV, HMSO.

Farmer, E. and Owen, M. (1995) *Decision Making, Intervention and Outcome in Child Protection Work*, report to the Department of Health.

Fawcett, B., Featherstone, B., Fook, J. and Rossiter, A. (eds) (2000) *Practice and Research in Social Work*, Routledge.

Gayford, J. J. (1976) 'Ten types of battered wives', *Welfare Officer*, vol. 1, no. 5, p. 9.

Gelles, R. and Loseke, D. (eds) (1993) *Current Controversies on Family Violence*, Sage.

Glass, D. (1995) *All My Fault. Why Women Don't Leave Abusive Men*, Virago.

Gondolf, E. (1997) 'Expanding batterer program evaluation', in G. Kaufman Kantor and K. Jasinski (eds), *Out of the Darkness: Contemporary Perspectives on Family Violence*, Sage.

Gondolf, E. (1998) *Multi-site Evaluations of Batterer Intervention Systems*, www.minicava.umn.edu/arts/asp.

Gordon, L. (1988) *Heroes of Their Own Lives*, Viking.

Grace, S. (1995) *Policing Domestic Violence in the 1990s*, Home Office Research Study no. 139, HMSO.

Grace, S. (1998) 'Policing domestic violence and inter-agency work', in N. Harwin, E. Malos and G. Hague (eds), *Domestic Violence and Multi-agency Working: New Opportunities, Old Challenges?*, Whiting & Birch.

Graham, D., Rawlings, E. and Rimini, N. (1988) 'Survivors of terror: battered women, hostages and the Stockholm syndrome', in K. Yllo and M. Bograd (eds), *Feminist Perspectives on Wife Abuse*, Sage.

Greater London Domestic Violence Project (April 2004) *Domestic Violence, Crime and Victims Bill*, GLDVP.

Hague, G. (1997) 'Smoke screen or leap forward? Inter-agency initiatives as a response to domestic violence', *Critical Social Policy*, vol. 17, no. 4, pp. 93–109.

Hague, G. (2001) 'Multi-agency fora', in J. Taylor Browne (ed.), *What Works in Reducing Domestic Violence?*, London: Whiting & Birch.

Hague, G., and Malos, E. (1996) *Tackling Domestic Violence: A Guide to Developing Multi-agency Initiatives*, The Policy Press.

Hague, G. and Mullender, A. (2000) 'Unsung innovation: the history of work with children in UK domestic violence refuges', in J. Hanmer and C. Itzin with S. Quaid and D. Wigglesworth (eds), *Home Truths about Domestic Violence*, Routledge.

Hague, G. and Mullender, A. (2002) *Professionals by Experience: A Guide to Service User Participation and Consultation for Domestic Violence Services*, Women's Aid.

Hague, G., and Wilson, C. (1996) *The Silenced Pain*, The Policy Press.

Hague, G., Kelly, L. and Mullender, A. (2001) *Challenging Violence Against Women: The Canadian Experience,* The Policy Press

Hague, G., Kelly, L., Malos, E., Mullender, A. and Debbonnaire, T. (1996) *Children, Domestic Violence and Refuges: A Study of Needs and Responses*, Women's Aid Federation of England.

Hague, G., Malos, E., and Dear, W. (1996) *Multi-agency Work and Domestic Violence*, The Policy Press.

Hague, G., Mullender, A. and Aris, R. (2002) *Is Anyone Listening? Accountability and Women Survivors of Domestic Violence*, Routledge.

Hall, A. (1992) 'Abuse in lesbian relationships', *Trouble and Strife*, vol. 23, spring, pp. 38–40.

Hanmer, J. and Griffiths, S. (2000) *Domestic Violence . . . What Works? Policing Domestic Violence*, Home Office Briefing Note, London: Home Office.

Hanmer, J. and Griffiths, S. (2001) 'Effective policing', in J. Taylor-Browne (ed.),

What Works in Reducing Domestic Violence: A Comprehensive Guide for Professionals, London: Whiting & Birch.

Hanmer, J. and Maynard, M. (eds) (1987) *Women, Violence and Social Control*, Macmillan.

Hanmer, J. and Saunders, S. (1984) *Well-founded Fear: A Community Study of Violence to Women*, Hutchinson.

Hanmer, J., Radford, J. and Stanko, E. (1989) *Women, Policing and Male Violence*, Routledge.

Harne, L. (2004) 'Violence, power and the meanings of fatherhood in issues of child contact', PhD thesis, School for Policy Studies, University of Bristol.

Harne, L. (2004) 'Researching violent fathers', in T. Skinner, M. Hester and E. Malos (eds), *Researching Gender Violence: Feminist Methodology in Action*, Willan Publishing.

Hart, B. (1988) *Safety for Women: Monitoring Batterers' Programs*, Pennsylvania Coalition Against Domestic Violence.

Harwin, N., Malos, E. and Hague, G. (1998) *Domestic Violence and Multi-agency Working: New Opportunities, Old Challenges?*, Whiting & Birch.

Hearn, J. (1998) *The Violences of Men*, Sage.

Hester, M., and Radford, L. (1997) *Domestic Violence and Child Contact Arrangements in England and Denmark*, The Policy Press.

Hester, M. and Westmarland, N. (2004) *Tackling Street Prostitution: Towards a Holistic Approach*, Home Office Research Study no. 279, Home Office, RDS.

Hester, M., Hanmer, J., Coulson, S., Morahan, M. and Razak, A. (2003) *Domestic Violence: Making It Through the Criminal Justice System*, University of Sunderland Northern Rock Foundation, www.nr_foundation.org.uk.

Hester, M., Pearson, C. and Harwin, N. (2000; 2nd edn forthcoming 2005) *Making an Impact: A Reader*, London: Jessica Kingsley.

Hester, M., Pearson, C. and Radford, L. (1997) *Domestic Violence: A National Survey of Court Welfare and Voluntary Sector Mediation Practice*, The Policy Press.

HMCPSI/HMIC (2004) *Violence At Home: A Joint Thematic Inspection of the Investigation and Prosecution of Cases Involving Domestic Violence*, Home Office.

Hoff, L. (1990) *Battered Women as Survivors*, Routledge.

Holder, R., Kelly, L. and Singh, T. (1994) *Suffering in Silence: Children and Young People Who Witness Domestic Violence*, Hammersmith and Fulham Domestic Violence Forum.

Homelessness Act (2002) The Stationery Office.

Home Office (1990) *Circular 60/90*, HMSO.

Home Office (1995) *Inter-agency Circular: Inter-agency Co-ordination to Tackle Domestic Violence*.

Home Office (1999) *Multi-Agency Guidance for Addressing Domestic Violence*, Home Office.

Home Office (2000) *HOC19/2000: Domestic Violence: Revised Circular to the Police*, Home Office.

Home Office (2003) *Safety and Justice: The Government's Proposals on Domestic Violence*, Home Office Consultation Paper Cm 5847, Home Office.

Homer, M., Leonard, A. and Taylor, P. (1984) *Public Violence, Private Shame*, Cleveland Refuge and Aid for Women and Children.

House of Commons Home Affairs Committee (1993) *Inquiry into Domestic Violence*, HMSO.

Housing Act (1996) HMSO.

Housing Regulations 1997/8.

Humphreys, C. (2000) *Social Work, Domestic Violence and Child Protection*, The Policy Press.

Humphreys, C. and Kaye, M. (1997) 'Third party applications for protection orders: opportunities, ambiguities and traps', *Journal of Social Welfare and Family Law*, vol. 19, no. 4, pp. 403–21.

Humphreys, C. and Mullender, A. (2002) *Children and Domestic Violence*, Dartington Department of Health Unit.

Humphreys, C. and Thiara, R. (2002) *Routes to Safety*, Women's Aid Federation of England.

Humphreys, C., Hester, M., Hague, G., Mullender, A., Abrahams, H. and Lowe, P. (2004) *From Good Intentions to Good Practice*, The Policy Press.

Jaffe, P., Wolfe, D. and Kaye, S. (1990) *Children of Battered Women*, Sage.

James-Hanman, D. (1994) *Domestic Violence: Help, Advice and Information for Disabled Women*, London: London Borough of Hounslow.

Johnson, H. (1996) *Dangerous Domains: Violence Against Women in Canada*, Toronto: Nelson.

Kelly, L. (1988) *Surviving Sexual Violence*, Polity Press.

Kelly, L. (1994) 'The interconnectedness of domestic violence and child abuse: challenges for research, policy and practice', in A. Mullender and R. Morley (eds), *Children Living with Domestic Violence: Putting Men's Abuse of Women on the Child Care Agenda*, Whiting & Birch.

Kelly, L. and Humphreys, C. (2000) 'Outreach and advocacy approaches in reducing domestic violence', in *Reducing Domestic Violence: What Works?*, Briefing Notes, Home Office, Policing and Reducing Crime Unit.

Kelly, L. and Lovett, J. (2005) *What a Waste: The Case for an Integrated Violence against Women Strategy*, Women's National Commission and London Metropolitan University.

Kelly, L. and Radford, J. (1990–1) 'Nothing really happened: the invalidation of women's experiences of sexual violence', *Critical Social Policy*, winter, pp. 39–53.

Kennedy, H. (1992) *Eve was Framed: Women and British Justice*, Chatto and Windus.

Kirkwood, C. (1993) *Leaving Abusive Partners*, Sage.

Kurz, D. and Stark, E. (1988) 'Not-so-benign neglect: the medical response to battering', in K. Yllo and M. Bograd (eds), *Feminist Perspectives on Wife Abuse*, Sage.

Law Commission (1992) *Family Law: Domestic Violence and Occupation of the Family Home*, report no. 207, HMSO.

London Borough of Islington Women's Equality Unit (1992) *A Good Practice Guide: Working with Those who have Experienced Domestic Violence*.

London Strategic Policy Unit (1988) *Police Responses to Domestic Violence*, Police Monitoring and Research Group Briefing no. 1, LSPU.

Lord Chancellor's Department (1997) *Domestic Violence: The New Law – A Guide to Part IV of the Family Law Act, 1996*, Family Policy Division.

Lundgren, E. (1998) 'The hand that strikes and comforts', in R. E. Dobash and R. Dobash (eds), *Rethinking Violence Against Women*, Sage.

McCarry, M. (2004) 'The connection between masculinity and domestic violence: what young people think', PhD thesis, School for Policy Studies, University of Bristol.

McCarry, M. (2004) 'Issues of ethics when conducting social research with young people', in T. Skinner, M. Hester and E. Malos (eds), *Researching Gender Violence: Feminist Methodology in Action*, Willan Publishing.

McGee, C. (2000) *Childhood Experiences of Domestic Violence*, Jessica Kingsley.

McGregor, H. and Hopkins, A. (1992) *Working for Change: The Movement Against Domestic Violence*, Allen & Unwin.

McKenry, P., Julian, T. and Gavazzi, S., (1995) 'Towards a biopsychosocial model of domestic violence', *Journal of Marriage and the Family*, vol. 57, no. 2, pp. 307–20.

Malos, E. (2000) 'Supping with the devil? Multi-agency initiatives on domestic violence', in J. Radford, M. Friedberg and L. Harne (eds), *Women, Violence and Strategies for Action*, Open University Press.

Malos, E. (2003) 'Domestic violence, research and social policy in Britain', in M. Izuhara (ed.), *Social Policy in Britain and Japan*, The Policy Press.

Malos, E. and Hague, G. (1993) *Domestic Violence and Housing*, Women's Aid Federation of England and University of Bristol.

Malos, E. and Hague, G. (1998) 'Facing both ways at once? The effect of the Housing Act 1996 on legislation and policy for women and children escaping domestic violence', in D. Cowan (ed.), *Housing, Participation and Exclusion*, Dartmouth Publishing.

Mama, A. (1996) *The Hidden Struggle: Statutory and Voluntary Sector Responses to Violence Against Black Women in the Home* (2nd edn), Whiting & Birch.

Maynard, M. (1985) 'The response of social workers to domestic violence', in J. Pahl (ed.), *Private Violence and Public Policy*, Routledge.

Metropolitan Police (1987) *Force Orders*.

Metropolitan Police Service (2003) *Findings from the Multi-agency Domestic Violence Murder Reviews in London*, Metropolitan Police Service.

Miedzian, M. (1992) *Boys Will Be Boys: Breaking the Links Between Masculinity and Violence*, Virago.

Mooney, J. (1994) *The Hidden Figure: Domestic Violence in North London*, London Borough of Islington, Police and Crime Prevention Unit.

Morley, R. and Mullender, A. (1994) *Preventing Domestic Violence to Women*, Police Research Group Paper no. 48, Home Office.

Muir, J. and Ross, M. (1993) *Housing the Poorer Sex*, London Housing Unit.

Mullender, A. (1996) *Rethinking Domestic Violence*, Routledge.

Mullender, A. and Burton, S. (2001) 'Dealing with perpetrators', in J. Taylor-Browne (ed.), *Reducing Domestic Violence: What Works?*, Whiting & Birch.

Mullender, A. and Hague, G. (2001) 'Women survivors' views', in J. Taylor-Browne (ed.), *Reducing Domestic Violence: What Works?*, Whiting & Birch.

Mullender, A. and Morley, R. (1994) *Children Living with Domestic Violence*, Whiting & Birch.

Mullender, A., Hague, G., Imam, U., Kelly, L., Malos, E. and Regan, L. (2002) *Children's Perspectives on Domestic Violence*, London: Sage.

Mullender, A., Hague, G., Imam, U., Kelly, L., Malos, E. and Regan, L. (2003) *Don't Hit Mum*, Young Voice.

National Inter-agency Working Party Report (1992) *Domestic Violence*, Victim Support.

Nazroo, J. (1995) 'Uncovering gender differences in the use of marital violence: the effect of methodology', *Sociology*, vol. 29, no. 3, pp. 475–94.

New South Wales Women's Co-ordination Unit (1991) *Programs for Perpetrators of Domestic Violence*.

NiCarthy, G. (1990) *Getting Free: A Handbook for Women in Abusive Situations*, Journeyman (available from Women's Aid).

Pagelow, M. D. (1981) *Women-Battering*, Sage.

Pagelow, M. D. (1984) *Family Violence*, Praeger.

Pahl, J. (1985) *Private Violence and Public Policy*, Routledge.

Pahl, J. (1989) *Money and Marriage*, Macmillan.

Park, Y., Fedler, J. and Dango, Z. (2000) *Reclaiming Women's Spaces: New Perspectives on Violence Against Women and Sheltering in South Africa*, Nisaa.

Parliamentary Select Committee on Violence in Marriage (1975) *Report from the Select Committee on Violence in Marriage*, HMSO.

Peled, E., Jaffe, P. G. and Edleson, J. L. (eds) (1995) *Ending the Cycle of Violence: Community Responses to Children of Battered Women*, Sage.

Pence, E. (1988) *Batterers' Programs: Shifting from Community Collusion to Community Confrontation*, Domestic Abuse Intervention Project, Duluth.

Pence, E. and Paymar, M. (1990) *Power and Control: Tactics of Men who Batter – An Educational Curriculum*, Domestic Abuse Intervention Project, Duluth.

Pence, E. and Shepard, M. (eds) (forthcoming) *The Coordinated Community Response: The Duluth Experience*, Sage.

Pizzey, E. and Shapiro, J. (1982) *Prone to Violence*, Hamlyn.

Pleck, E. (1987) *Domestic Tyranny: The Making of Social Policy Against Family Violence from Colonial Times to the Present*, Oxford University Press.

Protection from Harassment Act (1997) HMSO.

Radford, J. and Russell, D. (1992) *Femicide: The Politics of Woman Killing*, Open University Press.

Rai, D. and Thiara, R. (1997) *Re-defining Spaces: The Needs of Black Women and Children in Refuge Support Services and Black Workers in Women's Aid*, Women's Aid Federation of England.

Respect (2004) *Statement of Minimum Principles and Minimum Standards of Practice for Domestic Violence Perpetrator Programmes and Associated Women's Services*, www.respect.uk.net.

Russell, D. (1982) *Rape and Marriage*, Macmillan.

Saunders, D. (1988) 'Wife abuse, husband abuse or mutual combat', in K. Yllo and M. Bograd (eds), *Feminist Perspectives on Wife Abuse*, Sage.

Saunders, H. (2003) *Whatever Happened to Safety and Justice for Children?*, Women's Aid Federation of England.

Saunders, H. (2001) *Making Contact Worse? Report of A National Survey of Refuge Services into the Enforcement of Contact Orders*, Women's Aid Federation of England.

Schechter, S. (1982) *Women and Male Violence: The Visions and Struggles of the Battered Women's Movement*, Pluto.

Scottish Women's Aid (1998) *Young People Say*, Scottish Women's Aid.

Sen, P., Humphreys, C. and Kelly, L. (2003) *Violence Against Women in the UK: CEDAW Thematic Shadow Report*, Womankind Worldwide.

Sherman, L. and Berk, R. (1984) 'The specific deterrent effects of arrest for domestic violence', *American Sociological Review*, vol. 49, no. 2, pp. 261–72.

Siddiqui, Hannana (2000) 'Black women's activism: coming of age?', *Feminist Review*, no. 64, spring, pp. 83–96.

Smith, L. (1989) *Domestic Violence: An Overview of the Literature*, Home Office Research Studies, no. 107, HMSO.

Southall Black Sisters (1989) *Against the Grain: A Celebration of Survival and Struggle*.

Southall Black Sisters (April 2004) *Domestic Violence Immigration and No Recourse to Public Funds: A Briefing to Amend the Domestic Violence, Crime and Victims Bill*, www.womensaid.org.uk/policy&consultations/DVBill.

Standing Together (2003) *Heard and Not Judged: Consultation with Survivors of Domestic Violence in the London Borough of Hammersmith and Fulham 2002–3*, Standing Together and Home Office.

Stanko, B. (ed.) (2003) *The Meanings of Violence*, London: Routledge.

Stanko, E. (1985) *Intimate Intrusions: Women's Experience of Male Violence*, Routledge.

Stanko, E., Crisp, D., Hale, C. and Lucraft, H. (1998) *Counting the Costs: Estimating the Impact of Domestic Violence in the London Borough of Hackney*, Crime Concern.

Stark, E. and Flitcraft, A. (1996) *Women at Risk: Domestic Violence and Women's Health*, Sage.

Stark, E., Flitcraft, A. and Frazier, W. (1979) 'Medicine and patriarchal violence: the social construction of a "private" event', *International Journal of Health Studies*, vol. 9, pp. 461–93.

Steinmetz, S. (1977) *The Cycle of Violence*, Praeger.

Steinmetz, S. (1978) 'The battered husband syndrome', *Victimology*, vol. 2, pp. 499–509.

Straus, M. (1990) 'The Conflict Tactics Scale', in M. Straus and R. Gelles (eds), *Physical Violence in American Families*, Transaction.

Straus, M. and Gelles, R. (1990) *Physical Violence in American Families*, Transaction.

Straus, M., Gelles, R. and Steinmetz, S. (1980) *Behind Closed Doors: Violence in the American Family*, Anchor.

Taylor-Browne, J. (ed.) (2001) *Reducing Domestic Violence: What Works?*, London: Whiting & Birch.

Thapar-Bjorkert, S. and Reverter-Banon, S. (2001) 'An appropriate capital-isation? Questioning social capital', London School of Economics, Gender Research Institute Research Paper Series, no. 1.

Thiara, Ravi, K. (2002) 'Domestic violence and women from black and minority communities, *Fempower*, no. 6, March.

Thorne-Finch, R. (1992) *Ending the Silence: The Origins and Treatment of Male Violence Against Women*, University of Toronto Press.

Trinder, L. (2000) 'Reading the texts' in B. Fawcett, B. Featherstone, J. Fook and A. Rossiter (eds), *Practice and Research in Social Work*, Routledge.

United Nations (1986) *Report of the Expert Group Meeting on Violence in the Family*, UN.

United Nations (1995) *Beijing Declaration and Platform of Global Action, Adopted by the Fourth World Conference on Women*, UN.

Walby, S. and Allen, J. (2004) *Domestic Violence, Sexual Assault and Stalking: Findings from the British Crime Survey*, Home Office Research Study no. 276, Home Office.

Walker, L. (1984) *The Battered Woman Syndrome*, Springer.

Welsh Women's Aid (1988) *Report of the International Women's Aid Conference*.

Williamson, E. (2000) *Domestic Violence and Health: The Response of the Medical profession*, The Policy Press.

Wilson, E. (1983) *What's to be Done about Violence Against Women?*, Penguin.

Wilson, M. and Daly, M. (1998) 'Lethal and non-lethal violence against wives', in R. E. Dobash and R. Dobash (eds), *Rethinking Violence Against Women*, Sage.

Women's Aid, *Briefings on Children and Domestic Violence*, www.womensaid. org.uk/policy&consultations/briefings/children.

Women's Aid (2004) *Response to the Law Commission Consultation Paper 173: Partial Defences to Murder*, February, www.womensaid.org.uk/ policy&consultations.

Women's Aid Federation of England, *Briefings on Housing*, www.womensaid. org.uk/briefings/housing.

Women's Aid Federation of England (1988) *Breaking Through: Women Surviving Male Violence*.

Women's Aid Federation of England (1992) *A Woman's Aid Approach to Working with Children: An Information Pack for Women Working with Children in Refuges*.

Women's Aid Federation of England (1992) *Written Evidence to the House of Commons Home Affairs Committee Inquiry into Domestic Violence*.

Women's Aid Federation of England (2002) *Safe and Sound: A Resource Manual for Working with Children who have Experienced Domestic Violence*.

Women's Aid Federation of England (2003) *Children's Welcome Pack*.

Women's Aid Federation of England (2004) *Briefing: Domestic Violence: Crime and Victims Bill*, April.

Women's Aid Federation of England (2004) *Domestic Violence, Crime and Victims Bill*, www.womensaid.org.uk/policy&consultations/DVBill, 12 January.

Women's National Commission (2003) *Unlocking the Secret: Women Open the Door on Domestic Violence: Findings from Consultations with Survivors*, DTI/ WNC (www.DTI.gov.uk).

Women's Unit, Cabinet Office (1999) *Living Without Fear*, Cabinet Office.

Yllo, K. and Bograd, M. (eds) (1988) *Feminist Perspectives on Wife Abuse*, Sage.

Index

ISSUES IN SOCIAL POLICY

The approach of the Issues in Social Policy series is both academically rigorous and accessible to the general reader. The authors are well known and active in their fields.

Nudes, Prudes and Attitudes: Pornography and censorship
Avedon Carol

Shortlisted for the Women in Publishing Pandora Award

> **'a stimulating read'** *New Humanist*
>
> **'a provocative and challenging book'** *Gay and Lesbian Humanist*
>
> **'an important statement on the modern feminist stand against the horrors of censorship'** *Desire*
>
> **'sets out clear and reasoned responses to all the arguments commonly trotted out against pornography'** *SKIN TWO*
>
> **'What impresses me most about the book is the combination of personal experience, contemporary cultural commentary and historical analysis ... If you only read one book about the crippling dispute among feminists over pornography and censorship, make *Nudes, Prudes and Attitudes* that book.'**
> Dr William Thompson, *New Times*

Pornography and censorship have carved a divide in the feminist movement and beyond. On one side is an improbable alliance of pro-censorship feminists – most famously Catharine MacKinnon and Andrea Dworkin – and the moral right. On the other are civil libertarians of various shades and anti-censorship feminists.

Nudes, Prudes and Attitudes is the only UK-based single-author account of the pornography debate from a feminist perspective. It argues strongly that the movement for sexual censorship gives enormous and dangerous powers to the state, promotes the very repression that is implicated in causing sexual violence, and derails feminist discussion of sexuality and related vital issues.

Avedon Carol is a feminist, an activist and a member of Feminists Against Censorship. She is co-editor of *Bad Girls and Dirty Pictures: The challenge to reclaim feminism.*

x + 213 pages, illustrated
Published 1994
Paperback   £11.95   ISBN 1 873797 13 3
Hardback   £25.00   ISBN 1 873797 14 1

Drugs: Losing the war
Colin Cripps

Few social welfare problems have become so pressing in recent years as drug abuse. The spread of ecstasy-taking among the young and the arrival of crack as an international threat have all but overwhelmed the efforts of drugs workers and governments to resist them.

Drugs: Losing the war explains the appeal of cocaine, ecstasy, heroin and cannabis in modern society, and describes their effects on both the user and the wider community. It offers an insight into the closed world of young people's drug use and advocates the provision of an integrated drugs service for young people.

This book does not attempt to be a definitive guide to illegal drugs, although it examines the major drugs in some depth. Neither does it seek to be a comprehensive history or social policy review, a practitioner's guide or pharmacology. Instead it seeks to ask the right questions and to explore the interaction between all these elements that makes the drugs issue such a complex, involved and seemingly intractable one.

The book raises the dilemmas we all need to face in our society. It explodes the myths of the 'drugs war' – those held by both the left and the right, the libertarians and the authoritarians – and argues that a new pragmatism is urgently needed which will challenge those who seek 'quick fix' solutions.

Colin Cripps is the Assistant Director of the Newham Drugs Advice Project in London, and has first-hand experience of fighting drug abuse among the young in an inner-city environment.

vii + 163 pages, illustrated
Published 1997
Paperback   £10.95   ISBN 1 873797 20 6
Hardback   £25.00   ISBN 1 873797 21 4

Genetic Politics: From eugenics to genome
Anne Kerr and Tom Shakespeare

Shortlisted for the *Sociology of Health and Illness Journal* 2003 book prize for outstanding contribution to medical sociology

> 'a thought-provoking book, laden with information and detailed historical records' *Times Higher Education Supplement*
>
> '[an] important new book . . . I would thoroughly recommend it for use in a wide range of educational settings, including the sociology of science and technology, medical sociology and disability studies.' *Medical Sociology News*
>
> 'a very welcome and timely analysis of "the new genetics" from a disability rights perspective . . . an important text, offering a well-argued and reasoned analysis of current genetic policy' *Disability and Society*
>
> 'a superb, historically rooted narrative . . . highly readable' *Health, Risk and Society*

Genetic Politics explores the history of eugenics and the rise of contemporary genomics, identifying continuities and changes between the past and the present. Anne Kerr and Tom Shakespeare reject the two extreme positions that human genetics are either fatally corrupted by, or utterly immune from, eugenic influence. They argue that today's forms of genetic screening are far from equivalent to the eugenics of the past, but eugenics cannot simply be dismissed as bad science, or the product of totalitarian regimes, for its values and practices continue to shape genetics today.

Triumphalist accounts of scientific progress and the merits of individual choice mask how genetic technologies can undermine people's freedom, by intensifying genetic determinism and discrimination, individualizing responsibility for health and welfare, and stoking intolerance of diversity. Regulation is largely ineffectual at limiting these dangers because it is often guided by the goals of perfect health and commercial profit. The authors argue that we need to listen to the people directly affected by the new genetics technologies, especially disabled people and women, and to challenge the values and practices that shape genetics.

Anne Kerr is a lecturer in sociology at the University of York with specialist interests in genetics and gender. **Tom Shakespeare** is Director of Outreach at the Policy, Ethics and Life Sciences Research Institute, Newcastle, and has written widely on disability and genetics.

vii + 211 pages, illustrated
Published in 2002

Paperback	£12.95	$24.95	ISBN 1 873797 25 7
Hardback	£25.00	$49.95	ISBN 1 873797 26 5

Antibody Politic: AIDS and society
Tamsin Wilton

'This useful book explains what HIV infection is, how you can get it and how not to. It might also help you to decide what you think should be done about it.' *Guardian*

'an invaluable guide ... a must for students from a variety of disciplines' *AIDSLINK*

'particularly interesting to those who are looking for a feminist perspective on the AIDS epidemic' American Library Association

'a recommended book ... deserves a place in all academic and medical libraries' *AIDS Book Review Journal*

'an accessible yet sophisticated analysis ... an extremely valuable resource' Lesley Doyal, Professor of Health Studies, University of the West of England

The global AIDS epidemic that appeared in the 1980s brought with it a social epidemic: the fear, hatred, bigotry, denial and repression with which the peoples of the world have reacted. The way we, as a society, respond to AIDS is an acid test of our values, our humanity and our social policy.

This book discusses the issues raised by AIDS for every member of society. It outlines concisely the history of the epidemic and summarizes the basic medical information on HIV and AIDS. It then considers AIDS in relation to the gay community, to women and to minority ethnic groups, and analyses its policy implications. From an account of community responses to the epidemic, and of the problematic relationship between the state and voluntary sectors, the book moves to a construction of the probable future and recommendations for personal and political action.

Tamsin Wilton lectures in health studies and women's studies at the University of the West of England, Bristol. Her publications include *AIDS: Setting a feminist agenda* and *En/Gendering AIDS*.

xii + 164 pages, illustrated
Published 1992
Paperback   £9.95   ISBN 1 873797 04 4
Hardback   £25.00   ISBN 1 873797 05 2

For more information on books published by New Clarion Press:
New Clarion Press, 5 Church Row, Gretton, Cheltenham GL54 5HG
tel./fax 01242 620623; www.newclarionpress.co.uk